Humanizing School Counseling for Multilingual Learners

This book highlights the necessary support and collaboration needed to help multilingual learners succeed and how to address opportunity gaps in schools and beyond.

School counselors need to have a working knowledge about the diverse needs of all students to effectively support the academic, career, and social development of those students. Chapters offer recommendations across multiple aspects of school counseling, including integration of multi-tiered systems of support (MTSS) concepts and American School Counselor Association (ASCA) National Model domains. Practical hands-on activity suggestions, case studies, and vignettes are integrated throughout the text that allow readers to envision these concepts in real-world practice.

Focused on humanizing approaches in school counseling for multilingual learners, this book is an essential read for both preservice and practicing school counselors as they integrate these concepts into their work with students.

Luciana C. de Oliveira, Ph.D., is a Professor in the Department of Teaching and Learning in the School of Education at Virginia Commonwealth University.

Carrie A. Wachter Morris, Ph.D., is a Professor in the Department of Counseling and Educational Development at the University of North Carolina, Greensboro.

Humanizing School Counseling for Multilingual Learners

Equity, Collaboration, and Transformation

Edited by Luciana C. de Oliveira and Carrie A. Wachter Morris

Routledge
Taylor & Francis Group
NEW YORK AND LONDON

Designed cover image: Getty Images

First published 2027
by Routledge
605 Third Avenue, New York, NY 10158

and by Routledge
4 Park Square, Milton Park, Abingdon, Oxon, OX14 4RN

Routledge is an imprint of the Taylor & Francis Group, an informa business

ISBN: 978-1-041-19310-4 (hbk)
ISBN: 978-1-041-19309-8 (pbk)
ISBN: 978-1-003-71112-4 (ebk)

DOI: 10.4324/9781003711124

Typeset in Times New Roman
by KnowledgeWorks Global Ltd.

Contents

About the Editors

Luciana C. de Oliveira, Ph.D., is a professor in the Department of Teaching and Learning in the School of Education at Virginia Commonwealth University. Her research focuses on issues related to teaching multilingual learners at the K-12 level. She has authored or edited 35 books and has several and has over 200 publications in various outlets. Dr. de Oliveira has over 30 years of teaching experience in the field of TESOL. She is the recipient of the 2026 TESOL International Association's James E. Alatis Award for Service to TESOL, which recognizes exemplary service to TESOL, and the 2025 Leadership through Research Award by Second Language Research Special Interest Group of the American Educational Research Association (AERA). She served as President (2018–2019) and was a member of the Board of Directors (2013–2016) of TESOL International Association. She was the first Latina to ever serve as President of TESOL.

Carrie A. Wachter Morris, Ph.D., is a professor and school counseling coordinator in the Department of Counseling and Educational Development at UNC Greensboro. Her research focuses on issues related to school counseling practice, and the preparation of school counselors and counselor educators, including pedagogy, innovation, and crisis and trauma. A former K12 teacher, Dr. Wachter Morris, has over 20 years of experience as a counselor educator. She is the author or editor of 4 books and has published over 40 peer-reviewed publications. She is the past-president of the Indiana School Counselor Association and the Association for Assessment and Research in Counseling.

About the Contributors

Bruno Andrade, Ph.D. candidate at the Federal University of Rio de Janeiro, is an English teacher at international schools in Brazil. As a diversity-equity-inclusion (DEI) practitioner, he focuses his studies on DEI; bilingualism; queer studies; and raciolinguistics. He has presented and published on bilingual education and queer studies.

Katherine Barko-Alva is an Associate Professor and Program Director of ESL/Bilingual Education at William & Mary, School of Education. She also serves as co-director for WMSURE (W&M Scholars Undergraduate Research Experience). She serves on the executive board for the Virginia Dual Language Educators Network (VADLEN). She has been awarded the Virginia Latino Advisory Board Latinx Leadership Award in Education and the Janet Brown Strafer Award at William & Mary, School of Education, recognizing her efforts in promoting equitable and inclusive learning spaces. Her research explores the role of language, equity, and agency in ESL/Dual Language contexts. Email: kbarkoalva@wm.edu

Melissa Boyanton holds an MS degree in school psychology and is currently pursuing an education specialist (EdS) degree in school psychology at Florida International University. She is a learning specialist and behavior interventionist for children and adolescents with intellectual and behavioral disabilities. Her professional interests include advocating for underrepresented student populations, increasing visibility of barriers to education and student outcomes for rural students, and analyzing the Native Hawaiian academic achievement gap.

Priscila J.B.M. Costa, Ph.D., is a Multilingual Learner Program Specialist at the Richland School District Two in Columbia, SC. Originally from Brazil, she has taught English as a foreign or second language in various settings in her home country and in the United States since 2007. Her research focuses on intercultural awareness, teacher education, and the affordances of multimodal literacies (with a socio-semiotic approach) applied to second-language academic writing.

Alexis Dowdell is a Doctoral Student in the Counselor Education and Supervision Program in the Department of Special Education, Rehabilitation, and Counseling at Auburn University. She began her career as an elementary school counselor where she developed a deep passion for helping students excel academically and develop key socioemotional skills. Her research interests center around access to mental health services for underrepresented student populations in school systems at various levels.

Drew S. Fagan is a Clinical Professor of Applied Linguistics and Language Education and Coordinator of TESOL In-service Programs at the University of Maryland. He works closely with the Maryland Legislature and State Department of Education to enact change in laws, certification policies, and accountability standards to be equitable for multilingual learners. He was the Maryland TESOL Association 2022–2023 President, the 2023 Teacher of the Year for the TESOL International Association and National Geographic Learning, and currently serves as a member of the Board of Directors (2025–2028) of TESOL International Association.

Norma Feriz-Gordon, MsEd, is a College and Career Success Coach with NYC Public Schools, leveraging over 20 years of leadership in nonprofit and educational settings. As a licensed Bilingual School Counselor, she has helped students secure millions in financial aid and enhance postsecondary planning. Norma holds advanced certifications in School Building and District Leadership and contributes as a reviewer and writer for Bestcolleges.com. A dedicated advocate for equitable education, she also teaches at her alma mater, NYU, and has previously taught at St. John's University and Hunter College.

Victoria Giles-Vázquez (she/her/ella) is a doctoral student in the Department of Counseling and Educational Development (CED) program at the University of North Carolina – Greensboro (UNCG). She is a licensed professional counselor who is dually licensed in Colorado and North Carolina and owns her private practice, Calma Counseling and Wellness LLC. She loves working with individuals and families across the lifespan and focuses on implementing culturally relevant skills for the LGBTQ+ and Latin/e communities.

Shelby Gonzales is an Assistant Professor in Counselor Education at The Ohio State University. As a previous school counselor in North and South Carolina, she has worked with K-12 students with a diverse spectrum of needs. Her research focus includes facilitating role understanding and interdisciplinary collaboration between pre-service and practicing school professionals. Dr. Gonzales joined The Ohio State University in August 2025 following her appointment at Boise State University (Aug 2022 to May 2025).

Isabel Haller-Gryc has over two decades of experience working with multilingual learners, having served as a teacher, instructional coach, and administrator. As a MLL Curriculum Coordinator, Dr. Haller-Gryc leads district-wide efforts to enhance instruction and support MLL students from kindergarten through 12th grade. A major focus of her work is supporting the high school co-teaching model and collaborating closely with the P-CEP MLL assistant principal at the high school level.

Socorro G. Herrera is a Professor in the Department of Curriculum and Instruction, College of Education at Kansas State University and the Executive Director of the Center for Intercultural and Multilingual Advocacy (CIMA). As an international keynote speaker, district consultant, and trainer of trainers, she has collaborated with families, teachers, and administrators in charting new paths for the success of culturally and linguistically diverse students. Dr. Herrera has authored six textbooks and numerous articles for publication in journals such as *Bilingual Research Journal, Journal of Research in Education, Journal of Latinos and Education,* and *International Journal of Multicultural Education.*

Chelsea Hilliard is a Visiting Clinical Assistant Professor at Loyola University Maryland. Before this position, she was a high school counselor in WJCC schools for four years supporting her school's multilingual learners. She completed her Ph.D. in Counselor Education and Supervision at Old Dominion University where her research focus was on school counselors supporting multilingual learners. She is both a licensed professional school counselor (LPSC) and a licensed professional counselor (LPC) in Virginia.

Jihee Im is a Ph.D. student in the Language, Literacy, and Technology program at Washington State University. She has a B.S. in TESOL and a minor in Linguistics from SUNY Oswego, and a master's degree from Arizona State University in TESOL. She taught MLLs for 5 years in New York and South Korea, and is interested in researching more about the trauma-informed instructions for pre-service teachers whose students are mainly marginalized group of students.

Leonissa V. Johnson is an Associate Professor at Clark Atlanta University in the Department of Counselor Education. She began her career as a school counselor and is passionate about students receiving the support required for success at all academic levels. Her research investigates the experiences of school counselors and counselors-in-training as they identify needs, build relationships with, and develop interventions for multilingual learners. Additionally, she examines the experiences of diverse students in behavioral health training programs.

Angel Lett holds an M.Ed in Counselor Education/School Counseling and Guidance Services and is currently pursuing a Ph.D. With six years of experience as a School Counselor, she transitioned into school administration and has been serving as an Assistant Principal for the past eight years. Currently, Angel oversees both the Multilingual Learner (ML) and Counseling departments, where she focuses on student advocacy, academic achievement, and fostering inclusive learning environments that support diverse student needs.

Brittani Level is a Doctoral Student in the Department of Counseling and Educational Development (CED) program at UNC Greensboro. She received her Bachelor's degree in Health & Exercise Science and Master's degree in Counseling from Wake Forest University. She has served as a school counselor in K-12 schools prior to returning to complete her doctoral degree. She is passionate about seeing students thrive in and out of the classroom. Her research interests include the practice of school counseling and pedagogical and andragogical methodologies.

Eugenie Mainake is a Ph.D. student in the Language, Literacy, and Technology program at Washington State University, Pullman, USA. He is a Fulbright alumnus from Indonesia and earned an MA in TESOL from Southern Illinois University, Carbondale. His current research focuses on the intersection between students' psychological states and their task engagement. His work centers around CALL, digital literacy, and teacher education.

Emily Martinez holds a bachelor's degree in Early Childhood Development and Education and is currently pursuing a master's degree in Counselor Education at Florida International University. Emily's professional interests include school counseling, child development, community music therapy, and school-based play therapy.

Jessica Diaz McKechnie is an Associate Clinical Professor of School Counseling, Director of Field Experience, and Coordinator of the Supporting Immigrant Students for School Counselors Certificate Program at the University of Maryland. Jessica grew up in Prince George's County, MD and continues to work within the Latinx and disabled community to promote equitable access to education.

Andy V. Pham, Ph.D., is a Professor of school psychology at Florida International University. His research interests include examining how neurocognitive and sociocultural factors affect academic and mental health outcomes of children, adolescents, and diverse populations. He aims to reduce disparities in mental health and education using culturally responsive practices and interdisciplinary collaboration.

Zachary Pietrantoni, Ph.D., is an Assistant Professor of Counselor Education at Florida International University. His research interests include school counselor development, interdisciplinary collaboration, and multicultural competency training. He was a K-6 school counselor before entering academia.

Ryan W. Pontier, Ph.D., is an Associate Professor of Bilingual Education and TESOL at Florida International University. A former 2nd and 3rd grade dual language teacher in Texas and Florida, his current research interests center on dismantling a monolingual mindset in education and include teacher education, teachers' language ideologies, and approaches to supporting bilingual students.

Lisa Porter is an Associate Professor of Sociology at James Madison University where she teaches courses on the sociology of education and nonprofit organization. Her Ph.D. is in Cultural Studies. She began her teaching as an SDAIE high school content teacher in migrant education in Southern California before transitioning to adult education as an ESL teacher serving immigrant and refugee families in Massachusetts. She has taught in multiple countries with students of all ages prior to settling in Virginia. Currently, she co-chairs the Many Voices of Harrisonburg, a community-based collaborative dedicated to enhancing intercultural relations. Her scholarly work within the sociology of education focuses on equitable relationships between families, schools and communities. Email: porte2ll@jmu.edu

Lucy Purgason is an Associate Professor and School Counseling Internship and Placement Coordinator at Oregon State University-Cascades. A former elementary and high school counselor, she has supported newcomer immigrant and refugee students and her research centers on recognizing and integrating the cultural strengths of students and their families. She is co-director of a Department of Education grant-funded program aimed to increase the number and diversity of qualified school counselors in high-needs, rural K-12 schools.

Tom Salsbury is an Associate Professor in the College of Education at Washington State University. He conducts research in second language acquisition and teaches graduate and undergraduate courses in the elementary and secondary teacher preparation programs and the Language, Literacy and Technology graduate program. Prior to coming to WSU, he taught English for 18 years in Mexico City, Indiana, Spain, and Taiwan.

Qi Shi is a Professor in School Counseling and the Director of the Center for Equity, Leadership, and Social Justice in Education (CELSJE) at Loyola University Maryland. Her research interests include school counselors' role in personal, social, and academic development of underrepresented student populations in K-12 schools, broadening participation for immigrant youth and English Language Learners in STEM disciplines and careers, and school counseling profession's development in international contexts. Dr. Shi is serving as the Editor for the *Journal of School-Based Counseling Policy and Evaluation* (JSCPE), the official journal of the International Society for Policy Research and Evaluation in School-Based Counseling (ISPRESC).

Andy Szeto, Ed.D., is a former school leader with New York City Public Schools, specializing in supporting overage and under-credited students. He supervised counselors and advocate counselors in that role. Currently, he supports academic policy work and serves as an adjunct assistant professor in educational leadership and teacher education at various NYC metropolitan area colleges.

Malti Tuttle is an Associate Professor and School Counseling Program Coordinator at Auburn University. Her research science aligns with social justice issues, school counseling advocacy, school counselor collaboration, English Learners, and Animal Assisted Therapy/Interventions. Additionally, she is the Project Director for a $2.8 million grant which funds the School Counseling Integrated Program (SCIP). It is funded by the US Department of Education. The goal of SCIP is to prepare school counseling master's students to collaborate with school nurses and ESOL teachers to increase mental health services in rural Alabama schools.

Jennifer Scaturo Watkinson is a Professor in School Counseling at Loyola University Maryland. Watkinson led the school counseling program at Loyola for 9 years and published articles associated with school counselor preparation, specifically focusing on working with ML student populations. Watkinson also provides training on leadership strategies within school counseling, both nationally and locally, and recently received her certification as a Board Certified Coach. Watkinson is a licensed professional counselor and school counselor in Md. Watkinson is on the review board for Counseling Scholarship and Practice in Educational Communities and is a reviewer for the *Professional School Counseling Journal*.

Chapter 1

Equitable, Collaborative, and Transformative Approaches to Humanizing School Counseling for Multilingual Learners

Luciana C. de Oliveira and
Carrie A. Wachter Morris

Demographics Shifts and the Changing Face of U.S. Education

The landscape of K-12 education in the United States is undergoing a profound and permanent transformation. As of 2024, multilingual learners (MLs) represent one of the fastest-growing student populations in the United States, with the number of English Learners (ELs) rising from 4.5 million in 2010 to over 5.3 million by 2021, now accounting for roughly 10% of the total student body (National Center for Education Statistics [NCES], 2024). This demographic shift is no longer confined to traditional gateway states like California, Texas, and New York. Recent data reveals a "sustained demographic transformation" across the South, Midwest, and Northeast, with states like Louisiana and Delaware experiencing growth rates exceeding 130% over the last decade (Migration Policy Institute [MPI], 2024; NCES, 2024).

This population is as diverse as it is expansive, encompassing over 400 languages. To serve these students effectively, the profession must adopt an inclusive definition of ML that moves beyond labels. This includes Emergent Bilinguals and Dual-Language Learners who are actively adding languages to their repertoire, as well as Former ELs who, while reclassified, continue to use their home languages as vital cognitive and social resources. Despite this growth, access to school counselors has not kept pace, particularly in high-growth districts. This gap necessitates a shift from reactive approaches to proactive, humanizing counseling models that leverage the existing linguistic resources of these established communities.

The Intersection of a Humanizing Framework and School Counseling

In response to these shifts, this volume advocates for the integration of humanizing approaches into the school counseling profession. Grounded in the work of Freire (1970), a humanizing framework rejects deficit-based mindsets that view

DOI: 10.4324/9781003711124-1

a student's home language as a barrier to be overcome (Viesca & Commins, 2026). Instead, it centers the complete selves of MLs, ensuring that their identities, lived experiences, and heritage languages are recognized as essential assets for academic and personal growth.

Humanizing school counseling is defined by a commitment to:

- Affirming full identities: Intentionally celebrating a student's linguistic and cultural background as a source of strength and focusing on MLs' full identities, acknowledging the intersection of race, gender, languages, socioeconomic status, and backgrounds.
- Fostering critical consciousness: Positioning students as active meaning-makers rather than passive recipients of standardized education.
- Utilizing asset-based lenses: Utilizing a culture of curiosity to bridge social differences and dismantle institutional barriers and seeing MLs' experiences as a source of strength and resilience, aspects that MLs can draw from in schools and beyond.
- Embracing linguistic resources: Utilizing MLs' wealth of linguistic and cultural resources that need to be recognized as strengths, including their languaging practices and viewing language as an active, fluid process, and highlighting how MLs use every tool they have to participate in various situations.
- Amplifying opportunities: Using MLs' linguistic brilliance for capacity building.
- Cultivating active inquiry: Using open-ended questions to learn about MLs' experiences and backgrounds; this practice models how MLs can be curious about one another, reducing bias and conflict in the broader school culture.

By merging the shared goals of a humanizing framework and school counseling, school counselors become architects of inclusive spaces where MLs are seen, held, and empowered to navigate the complexities of their educational journeys.

Redefining School Counseling for Multilingual Excellence

As the population of MLs in K-12 settings continues to grow, the role of school counselors is evolving from a traditional generalist to a specialized advocate and systemic change agent (de Oliveira & Wachter Morris, 2015). The following chapters collectively argue that supporting MLs requires more than just linguistic translation; it demands a fundamental shift toward humanizing, equitable, and interdisciplinary practices. By moving away from deficit-based mindsets and monolingual norms, these chapters provide a roadmap for school counselors to dismantle systemic barriers and foster environments where linguistically diverse students can thrive.

Core Pillars as Foundation

Three core pillars emerge as the foundation for this transformation: reflexive advocacy, relational connections, and systemic collaboration.

Reflexive Advocacy and Identity

School counselors' own internal work is critical to effective practice. Cultural competence is not a static credential but an ongoing process of cultural self-reflection and knowledge of self.

- Cultural mapping: Counselors are encouraged to use mapping tools to understand their own cultural dimensions, ensuring they approach MLs with an awareness of their own biases.
- Combatting microaggressions: Advocacy involves the active identification and mitigation of microaggressions—the subtle, everyday exclusions that impede the socioemotional well-being and academic growth of MLs.
- Challenging neutrality: Moving beyond the neutrality often expected in institutional settings, counselors must recognize how linguistic and racial hierarchies shape which student voices are legitimized and whose emotions are heard.

Relational Connections and Belonging

These chapters highlight the necessity of emotional infrastructure. This is built through what is termed "Authentic Cariño" and radical kinship, centering the lived biographies of students and their families.

- Humanizing approaches: Rather than viewing students through the lens of standardized test scores, humanizing practices prioritize the individual contexts of immigrant and multilingual families.
- Belonging in various contexts: The work explores how belonging is negotiated across borders, challenging social-emotional learning (SEL) frameworks and advocating for culturally pluralistic mental health support.

Systemic and Interdisciplinary Collaboration

The complexity of supporting MLs exceeds the capacity of any single department. A recurring theme across these chapters is the move toward integrated systems of support.

- Collaborative models: From multi-campus coordination to partnerships with school nurses, English to Speakers of Other Languages (ESOL) teachers, and community agencies, the focus is on breaking down departmental silos.

- Interdisciplinary teams: By combining the expertise of school psychologists, school counselors, and administrators, schools can implement Multi-Tiered Systems of Supports (MTSS) that utilize translanguaging pedagogy and accurate, non-biased assessment data.
- Technological and structural innovation: As schools look toward the future, the responsible integration of artificial intelligence (AI) offers new ways to bridge communication gaps in postsecondary guidance, provided it is balanced with human oversight and ethical guardrails.

Tools for Sustained Equity

To move these concepts from theory to practice, this collection provides tangible resources for school counseling practitioners and counselor educators. This includes needs assessment tools for evaluating program strengths, professional development frameworks for in-service professional learning, and post-master's certificate models designed to equip counselors with specialized skills in immigrant-based school counseling. Reflection questions were added in every chapter to ensure praxis for the readers who are using the text. Practical, hands-on activity suggestions, case studies, and vignettes are integrated throughout the text to allow readers to picture integration of concepts into their current or future practice. Together, these chapters offer a comprehensive vision for a justice-oriented counseling profession, one that affirms linguistic identities, centers equity, and ensures that every ML has a positive path to success.

Overview of Chapters

Chapter 2 by Carrie A. Wachter Morris and Luciana C. de Oliveira, positions school counselors as central figures in the academic, career, and personal development of all students, with a specialized focus on achieving equity for MLs. The authors argue that counselors must move beyond reactive support by developing comprehensive, proactive programs designed to dismantle systemic barriers to enrollment and access. By highlighting humanizing approaches to school counseling, the chapter defines specific roles for practitioners, emphasizing the necessity of strategic collaboration with partners to close achievement and opportunity gaps both within the school environment and the broader community.

In Chapter 3, Shelby Gonzales and Priscila J.B.M. Costa explore the essential role of cultural self-reflection in preparing school counselors to meet their ethical responsibility toward MLs in K-12 settings. By introducing key cultural dimensions as lenses for self-examination, the authors emphasize the need for counselors to advance their multicultural advocacy, awareness, and competencies across academic, career, and social-emotional domains. The chapter addresses a critical gap in existing literature, which frequently overlooks the K-12 context in favor of higher education, by offering a culturally responsive framework and mapping tools specifically tailored to the complexities of MLs and their families. Ultimately, it advocates for the intentional cultivation of culturally competent practices, providing practitioners with the reflective strategies necessary to support the unique developmental needs of linguistically diverse students.

Chapter 4 by Victoria Giles-Vázquez and Brittani Level, examines the pivotal role school counselors play in identifying and addressing microaggressions that target MLs. Because these subtle forms of discrimination can severely hinder a student's socioemotional well-being and academic trajectory, the authors draw on ASCA's cultural competence standards to outline necessary intervention skills. The chapter provides practical microintervention strategies and a case vignette, equipping counselors with the tools to dismantle identity-related barriers and foster truly inclusive school environments.

In Chapter 5, Bruno Andrade investigates how MLs experience emotional well-being and institutional recognition within the complex linguistic and racial landscape of international schools. By challenging the "universal" nature of Global North SEL frameworks, the author uses a qualitative study in international schools in São Paulo, Brazil, to highlight the emotional infrastructure necessary for equity. The findings reveal how counselors can enact micro-resistances against linguistic hierarchies to ensure that racialized and multilingual students are authentically seen and supported.

Chapter 6 by Socorro G. Herrera, Lisa Porter, and Katherine Barko-Alva, centers the family biography as the heart of effective support for MLs, advocating for a model rooted in radical kinship and deep contextual understanding. Through field-based narratives, the authors illustrate how counselors, students, and families navigate the tensions between personal heritage and the increasing standardization of the educational system. The text offers strategies that prioritize the unique socio-political contexts of ML families to foster more authentic, relational counseling practices.

Chapter 7 by Malti Tuttle, Lucy Purgason, Leonissa Johnson, and Alexis Dowdell, explores how school counselors can build and maintain strategic partnerships with a wide range of stakeholders, including school leaders, ESOL teachers, school nurses, and community agencies, to support the holistic success of MLs. By providing practical steps and illustrative examples, the authors demonstrate how intentional collaboration ensures that multilingual students gain equitable access to educational, health, and post-secondary resources.

In Chapter 8, Isabel Haller-Gryc and Angel Lett showcase an innovative leadership model from a large educational complex in Michigan, emphasizing systematic coordination across departments and campuses. The authors detail how strategic administrative oversight, professional learning communities, and standardized data protocols can move student advocacy beyond individual expertise. This integrated system allows for more consistent support and flexible resource allocation for linguistically diverse populations.

Chapter 9 by Zachary Pietrantoni, Andy Pham, Ryan Pontier, Melissa Boyanton, and Emily Martinez, analyzes the systemic barriers and "monolingual expectations" that often obscure the strengths of MLs and lead to inappropriate educational placements. The authors advocate for an interdisciplinary approach that utilizes translanguaging pedagogy and culturally responsive MTSS. By aligning the work of counselors and school psychologists, the chapter offers recommendations for affirming linguistic identities and dismantling institutional deficits.

In Chapter 10, Drew S. Fagan and Jessica Diaz McKechnie detail the development of a specialized post-master's certificate program designed to bridge the gap between growing ML populations and the limited professional development available to in-service educators. The authors provide a roadmap for creating such a program, covering everything from curriculum design to administrative logistics, while offering lessons learned from early cohorts on the value of interdisciplinary training in meeting the needs of immigrant students.

Chapter 11, by Tom Salsbury, Jihee Im, and Eugenie Mainake, introduces a practical 30-item assessment tool designed to help stakeholders evaluate the strengths and priorities of their counseling services for MLs. Based on multi-year research in middle schools, the tool focuses on five key areas: connections, data usage, cultural awareness, social justice leadership, and workplace satisfaction. It provides a structured framework for schools to discuss their current performance, resource availability, and goals for improvement.

Chapter 12 by Norma Feriz-Gordon and Andy Szeto, explores the dual nature of AI in reshaping postsecondary pathways for MLs. While identifying how AI can either bridge or widen equity gaps, the authors provide a case study on the ethical implementation of these tools. The chapter emphasizes that while AI can enhance translation and data use, it must be balanced with human oversight and cultural responsiveness to maintain the professional judgment central to the counselor's role.

In Chapter 13, Chelsea Hilliard, Jennifer Scaturo Watkinson, and Qi Shi address the critical gap in targeted preparation for school counselors working with MLs within a MTSS framework. Recognizing that many practitioners lack the specialized training necessary to meet the complex cultural and linguistic needs of this population, the authors outline a comprehensive professional development framework grounded in social justice and multicultural principles. The chapter introduces three interconnected training pathways, Knowledge of Self, Prevention and Intervention, and Collaboration, and offers actionable recommendations for both graduate preparation programs and in-service professional learning to ensure counselors can effectively serve as advocates for ML students.

By weaving together these diverse perspectives, from the deeply personal work of self-reflection to the technical complexities of AI and interdisciplinary policy, this volume provides a holistic framework for school counselors who seek additional information about working with MLs. By integrating reflexive self-awareness, radical kinship with families, and systemic interdisciplinary collaboration, *Humanizing School Counseling for Multilingual Learners* provides the essential tools and frameworks necessary to dismantle institutional barriers and cultivate an educational landscape where equity, collaboration, and transformation ensure every student is seen, heard, and empowered to succeed.

References

de Oliveira, L. C., & Wachter Morris, C. (2015). *Preparing school counselors for English language learners*. TESOL Press.

Freire, P. (1970). Pedagogia do oprimido *[Pedagogy of the oppressed]*. Paz e Terra.

National Center for Education Statistics (2024). *English learners in public schools: Condition of education*. U.S. Department of Education, Institute of Education Sciences. https://nces.ed.gov/programs/coe/indicator/cgf

Viesca, K. M., & Commins, N. (2026). *Humanizing pedagogies with multilingual learners: Transforming teaching in the content areas*. Routledge.

Section I

Foundations of Humanizing Approaches

Chapter 2

Humanizing Approaches to School Counseling

Toward Sustained Equity for Multilingual Learners

Carrie A. Wachter Morris and Luciana C. de Oliveira

School counselors provide comprehensive support to ensure every student thrives academically, prepares for a meaningful career, and develops the social-emotional skills necessary for life. In order to address the various needs of the students in their care, school counselors develop and implement a comprehensive school counseling program promoting equity and access for all students (American School Counselor Association [ASCA], 2024). School counselors are charged with "[c]reating a plan to address any programmatic disparities or inequities that affect access and enrollment within educational programs, such as English-language learners…" (ASCA, 2024). This means that programs need to be designed that can reach and support the growth of all students, including multilingual learners (MLs), tailored to students' developmental level.

Demographic Changes in Schools and the Need to Prepare School Counselors for MLs

MLs are one of the fastest-growing student populations in the United States and will continue to grow (National Center for Education Statistics [NCES], 2024). Reflecting a significant demographic trend, the number of students identified as English Learners (ELs) in U.S. schools rose from 4.5 million in 2010 to over 5.3 million by 2021, representing one-tenth of the total student body (NCES, 2024). MLs are a diverse group of students who develop and use more than one language in their daily lives. This umbrella term includes ELs—students who are identified as needing specialized support to acquire English—as well as bilingual and multilingual students who may already be proficient in English but continue to use, maintain, and develop other languages, such as students in dual-language programs. The term is designed to be inclusive of various linguistic backgrounds:

- English Learners (ELs/ELLs): Students identified by school assessments as currently requiring English Language Development (ELD) services to access the core curriculum.

DOI: 10.4324/9781003711124-3

- Emergent Bilinguals: Students who are in the process of becoming bilingual, highlighting that they are adding a language.
- Dual-Language Learners (DLLs): Students in bilingual programs developing two or more languages simultaneously.
- Former English Learners: Students who have "reclassified" or exited EL services but remain multilingual and may still use their home language as a resource.

MLs bring a rich linguistic diversity of over 400 languages to classrooms nationwide (Migration Policy Institute [MPI], 2024). Representing almost 11% of all K-12 students, this group has expanded consistently over the last two decades, particularly across the Southern and Midwestern United States (MPI, 2024; NCES, 2023). The largest number of these students is found in California, Florida, Illinois, New Mexico, New York, Puerto Rico, and Texas. However, states such as Arkansas, Alabama, Colorado, Delaware, Georgia, Indiana, Kentucky, Nebraska, North Carolina, South Carolina, Tennessee, Vermont, and Virginia have experienced more than 200% growth in the numbers of ELLs in schools from 1995 to 2006 (NCELA, 2006). While the 1995–2006 data highlights a historical surge, current data shows that the growth of MLs is no longer just a spike—it is a sustained demographic transformation.

Recent data from the U.S. Department of Education and the Migration Policy Institute (2021–2024) highlights that this population continues to grow, particularly in states that were previously considered emerging hubs (MPI, 2024; NCES, 2024). Since the early 2010s, the national ML population has grown significantly faster than the general K-12 population. While traditional hubs like California and Texas remain large, the highest percentage increases are now occurring in the South, Midwest, and Northeast. Louisiana has experienced a 153% increase in ML enrollment between 2010 and 2021. Delaware experienced 135% growth in the same period. Kentucky continued its high-growth trend with a 128% increase and in Arkansas the ML population has more than doubled (over 100% growth) over the last 15 years, with the number of districts serving ML students jumping from 155 to over 200 statewide. States with 10% or more MLs include Texas (20.2%), California (18.9%), New Mexico (18.8%), Colorado (13.0%), Virginia (~10%), and North Carolina (~9–10%).

The need to prepare school professionals to work with these students in all U.S. states, then, is pressing. The "200% growth" of the late 90s was the beginning of a permanent shift. Today, school counselors in these regions are no longer preparing for a coming wave—they are supporting a diverse, established community. Current research (NCELA, 2024) shows that while the population has grown, access to school counselors has not always kept pace. In many districts with high ML growth, there are fewer counselors per student than the national average, making the need for humanizing counseling approaches which leverage a student's existing linguistic resources more critical than ever to address the needs of this increasing population.

Humanizing School Counseling

Humanizing pedagogies serve as a transformative framework that centers the complete selves of MLs, moving beyond mere instruction to actively sustain their diverse linguistic and cultural heritages (Paris & Alim, 2017; Salazar, 2013; Viesca & Commins, 2026). Humanizing pedagogies draw on students' whole selves in classrooms, connecting identities, knowledge, experiences, and learning, creating spaces for them to be themselves within the classroom (Hsieh, 2022).

Humanizing pedagogies and school counseling intersect through a shared commitment to centering MLs' lived experiences, ensuring that both the classroom and counseling services serve as spaces where their identities, languages, and cultures are not just recognized, but utilized as essential tools for growth. This intersection could offer ways for school counselors to come to learn more about their MLs and view them in more asset-based ways.

Humanizing school counseling is defined as a framework that intentionally affirms students' full identities, treating their diverse backgrounds as valuable assets for connection while actively fostering a culture of curiosity and understanding across social differences. For MLs in particular, humanizing school counseling celebrates MLs' languages and cultural practices—from their heritage language to their unique ways of being. By centering these personal resources, school counselors can build deeper relationships and encourage a genuine interest in understanding different perspectives. Drawing on Freire's emphasis on dialogue, agency, and critical consciousness (Freire, 1970), humanizing school counseling resists deficit framings and instead positions students as active meaning-makers within educational systems. Within this framework, the chapter identifies roles school counselors take to support MLs, including collaboration with partners and programmatic approaches that address achievement and opportunity gaps in schools and beyond.

Reflection Questions

1. How do I currently define "humanizing" in my school counseling practice? In what ways does this definition align—or conflict—with my school's structures and expectations?
2. What assumptions do I hold about MLs that may shape how I interpret readiness, engagement, or success?
3. How might adopting a more explicitly humanizing stance change how I listen to students and families?

School Counseling Roles with Multilingual Learners

Humanizing school counseling for MLs is consistent with the unified educator-counselor role, which asks counselors to hold both the identities of educator and counselor simultaneously (Levy & Lemberger-Truelove, 2021). Acknowledging this unified educator–counselor identity simply clarifies what the profession already does: teach systems, build futures, and accompany students as they make decisions that matter. It is also profoundly impactful for school counselors' work with MLs. Considering how to use the counselor identity to understand the complexities brought by the linguistic and cultural contexts of MLs in tandem with the educator role of navigating the systems of a school naturally lends itself to a humanizing stance that treats layers of complexity as context and capacity, not as deficits.

In practice, six roles tend to surface in ML-serving schools. They are not formal job duties; they are patterns of work that appear whenever school counselors focus on expanding dignity, access, and opportunity for MLs. These six roles are where the unified educator–counselor identity becomes visible in day-to-day practice.

Advocate: Challenging Gatekeeping and Expanding Access

Advocacy is central to school counseling (ASCA, 2024) and can often emerge related to work with MLs specifically during scheduling or transitions, where opportunities can open or close rapidly and potentially without MLs or their families even being aware of those opportunities. In working with MLs, advocacy around structures frequently involves four-year plans, access to dual credit, career and technical education (CTE) opportunities, accelerated coursework (e.g., honors, Advanced placement [AP], or International Baccalaureate [IB] courses), or college and career readiness (CCR) activities. Advocacy rarely involves overhauling a course registration system overnight. Rather, it might sound like a shift in frame from "are they ready?" (assuming that the answer could be "no") to "what would make this possible?" (assuming that they may be ready, but could need support specific to their context).

And school counselors know the real-world version of this:

"If not now, then when?"
"And if not at 10th grade scheduling, then how?"

VIGNETTE

A school counselor notices that despite some stated interest from MLs she serves, no MLs have enrolled in AP Computer Science. When she asks a couple teachers about that potential oversight, one of them responds, "They're still learning English—it would be too hard." The school counselor does a quick review of transcripts, revealing two of her ML students have strong math preparation and coding experience. A short planning conversation leads to their enrollment with appropriate support structures. Both students complete the course successfully.

Advocacy in this frame assumes readiness can be developed. Humanizing advocacy assumes capability first and scaffolding second—not the other way around.

Collaborator: Sharing Responsibility for Student Success

It is hard to expand access alone. School counselors can collaborate with other adults within and outside the school building to tackle larger systemic challenges–building structures and pathways for students. Collaboration with ML teachers, content teachers, interpreters, administrators, school psychologists, school nurses, school social workers, other student support service personnel, families, and community organizations builds a network of adults positioned to identify and remove barriers and improve opportunities for MLs (e.g., through shared frameworks and sustained partnerships; Davis et al., 2023).

VIGNETTE

During eighth-to-ninth-grade transition planning, the school counselor convenes ML teachers, math teachers, and a CTE coordinator to examine placements of ML students at differential levels of English proficiency. The group aligns math sequencing with language supports, and identifies logical entry points into STEM-oriented career pathways—resulting in schedules with both rigor and clarity that clearly integrate the insight from educators with multiple areas of expertise.

MTSS structures often provide natural collaboration spaces. Tier 1 supports tend to center belonging and climate; Tier 2 may involve family meetings or targeted transition supports; Tier 3 can include academic or mental health interventions. Collaboration does not guarantee perfection, but it increases the odds that MLs and their families are not feeling isolated or that they are left adrift to guess at what might be the best opportunity to pursue.

School counselors' role as collaborator is part of what makes them an indispensable member of a school leadership team. Instinctively recognizing that all students—including MLs—will be more successful if multiple adults are supporting students' trajectories. This is part of the unified educator–counselor identity: seeing that ML success improves when expertise is shared across roles rather than contained within one.

Cultural and Linguistic Mediator: Bridging Norms, Expectations, and Assets

Families and schools sometimes operate with different timelines, financial expectations, or college and career preferences. School counselors often serve as cultural and linguistic mediators, helping clarify expectations and explore futures that honor both student and family goals. Mediation is not meant to be persuasive or to convince one side of the others' position; it centers dignity, validates experiences, and elevates problem-solving.

VIGNETTE

A student expresses interest in engineering. Her family prefers that she immediately enter the workforce to support younger siblings and to increase the financial stability of the family unit. With an interpreter present, the school counselor affirms both priorities and explores scholarship, dual credit, and part-time work options that keep multiple futures open.

This kind of mediation assumes families are acting from care, even when the preferred path looks different from the students. By avoiding assumptions that families do not understand or are disregarding their students' opinions, it allows for a wider range of possible paths that could meet the needs of each individual involved.

This is the role that asks, *"Is there a version of this plan where everyone's values are seen and honored?"*

Navigator: Helping Students (and Families) Make Sense of Systems

MLs often navigate additional bureaucratic layers such as credit transfer, transcript interpretation, placement tests, FAFSA for mixed-status families, international credential conversations, and college admissions. Navigation is instructional work. The goal is empowerment rather than compliance; students learn how systems operate and how to move through them.

VIGNETTE

A junior who recently arrived from Honduras meets with the school counselor to talk about college. The student has strong math grades and an interest in computers, but his transcript includes courses that do not neatly translate to the district's graduation requirements. The family is mixed-status, and FAFSA questions raise concerns about documentation and cost. The school counselor walks him through alternative evidence for math placement, transfer of credits, and scholarship options that do not require documentation of citizenship status. Together, they map a plan that includes finishing CTE coursework, dual credit enrollment at the community college, and a transfer pathway into a four-year program in information technology. When the student leaves, he says, "Now I actually know how this works," instead of, "I guess college isn't for me."

Non-linear pathways, including CTE + dual credit + work-based learning, or early college + university transfer, can be especially powerful for MLs. Humanizing navigation names options rather than narrowing them. It expands opportunities, rather than foreclosing them.

Facilitator of Belonging: Attending to Identity and School Climate

Belonging can be tied to cultural respect and recognition, not just friendliness or general school climate (Stickl Haugen et al., 2019). Students described belonging as feeling known in context—family values, home lives, and intersecting identities—not just as individuals detached from culture. School counselors influence belonging through peer mentoring, affinity groups, multilingual communication, and partnership with families and cultural communities. Students tend to try challenging pathways once they feel seen and respected; belonging often precedes academic risk-taking, not the other way around.

Chapter 5 expands on belonging and well-being; here, it simply serves as one of the pillars of humanizing work.

VIGNETTE

A fourth-grade multilingual learner who recently arrived from Myanmar rarely speaks in class but lights up during art. The school counselor shares this with the classroom teacher during a grade-level meeting. The teacher invites the student to help create classroom labels and posters in both Burmese and English. Within weeks, classmates begin asking him how to say words in Burmese, and the student volunteers to lead a small group. During a check-in, he tells the school counselor, "They know I'm good at something." From there, participation increases in other subjects—quietly at first, then steadily.

Notice that this vignette not only speaks to Facilitating Belonging, but also Collaborator and Advocate. Many times, these roles appear most powerfully in combination.

Data User: Illuminating Patterns, Asking Better Questions

ASCA (2024) encourages data use for identifying disparities. With MLs, data are often most illuminating when examining participation, not just achievement: Who takes AP or honors? Who completes CTE concentrator pathways? Who applies to college? Who shows up to transition or financial aid nights? Patterns reveal opportunities and gatekeeping in real time. For MLs, these roles widen what counts as success and who is invited into challenging, future-oriented pathways.

VIGNETTE

During a spring data review, a school counselor notices that almost none of the MLs are participating in after-school clubs. When she asks a small group of students why, they explain that flyers only go home in English and many clubs meet on the same days as newcomer tutoring or sibling pick-ups. The school counselor works with the assistant principal to translate flyers and shift one club to a different day. The next quarter, participation triples—not because students needed convincing, but because access finally made sense in their lives.

Humanizing data use replaces simple counts—"Who's participating?" or "Who qualifies?"—with "Who isn't here yet—and why?" It invites curiosity rather than defensiveness. Data rarely answers the question by itself; it tells us where to look next. And while these roles emerge in daily practice, sustaining them requires program designs that don't depend on individual effort alone. The next step is building structures that make access and opportunity more routine—embedded in the comprehensive school counseling program rather than dependent on who happens to be asking the right questions.

Reflection Questions

1 Which of the roles described in this chapter do I enact most often? Which role feels most constrained by time, policy, or school culture?
2 Think about a recent interaction with a multilingual learner or family. Which roles were present, and which might have strengthened the outcome?
3 Where do I see opportunities for these roles to intersect more intentionally in my daily work?

Programmatic Considerations: Comprehensive and Preventive Approaches

Humanizing approaches to school counseling require attention not only to individual student interactions, but also to the design of systems that shape access, opportunity, and belonging. For MLs, many barriers are not interpersonal; they are structural–embedded in course sequencing, information flow, timeline, eligibility rules, and assumptions about who understands how school systems work. Programmatic moves that are comprehensive and preventive help reduce the burden on MLs and their families to navigate these systems independently.

Importantly, preventive programming also respects students' dignity. When MLs and their families are repeatedly required to navigate opaque systems or advocate for basic access, the message conveyed—however unintentionally—is that belonging is conditional. Humanizing programmatic moves counter this message by designing systems that assume linguistic and cultural diversity as a norm, not an exception, and that position clarity and access as shared responsibilities of the school community.

A humanizing school counseling program anticipates barriers rather than responding to them after opportunities have already narrowed. In this sense, prevention is not simply an efficiency strategy; it is an equity stance. Preventive design acknowledges that when access depends on families knowing the "right questions" to ask, speaking English fluently, or understanding unspoken norms of schooling, inequities are reproduced—even in well-intentioned systems. Humanizing programs work to make expectations, pathways, and opportunities visible and accessible *before* students encounter gatekeeping points.

By shifting attention from individual problem-solving to programmatic design, school counselors move from reacting to inequity to interrupting it. This shift does not eliminate the need for individualized support; rather, it reduces how often MLs must rely on exceptional advocacy to access opportunities that should be available by design. In doing so, comprehensive and preventive programming reframes equity work as a collective responsibility embedded within the counseling program itself, rather than as an add-on carried by individual counselors or students.

Comprehensive Program Design

Comprehensive school counseling programs aligned with the ASCA National Model (ASCA, 2025) emphasize academic, career, and social–emotional development across direct services, indirect services, and systems-level advocacy. For MLs, comprehensive programming creates the opportunity to embed support into existing structures rather than relying on case-by-case accommodations that may unintentionally isolate students or families.

What distinguishes comprehensive programming in ML-serving contexts is not the addition of separate services, but the intentional redesign of core structures so that MLs are included by default rather than by exception. When ML supports are embedded into Tier 1 programming, transitions, and CCR activities, access does not depend on individual students' ability to self-advocate or on families' familiarity with school systems. Instead, opportunity is structured into the program itself.

Examples of comprehensive programmatic moves include:

- embedding multilingual supports into Tier 1 CCR (CCR) lessons
- integrating ML-focused transition planning at key grade levels
- aligning course planning, CTE pathways, and graduation requirements early
- ensuring ML representation in career fairs, pathway nights, and leadership programs
- building consistent family communication structures across languages
- reviewing participation data across academic and extracurricular programs

Taken together, these moves shift support for MLs from reactive problem-solving to intentional design. They also signal that MLs are expected participants in future-oriented opportunities, not peripheral beneficiaries of special interventions.

VIGNETTE

A newcomer family from Eritrea enrolls a third-grade student midyear. Rather than relying on ad hoc check-ins, the school counselor invites the family to a monthly newcomer orientation that includes bilingual liaisons, visuals explaining school routines, and introductions to key staff. The family later shares that knowing who to contact about transportation, medication policies, and after-school care reduced stress and helped them feel connected early on.

This vignette illustrates how comprehensive programming can normalize access rather than personalizing need. By creating structures that anticipate common questions and barriers, the counselor reduces reliance on individual problem-solving and positions families as informed partners from the outset.

Comprehensive programming also supports collaboration. When ML supports are embedded into Tier 1 structures—such as CCR lessons, course fairs, or transition meetings—collaboration with ML teachers, interpreters, administrators, and community partners becomes a natural part of the program rather than an additional task layered onto individual counselors' workloads. In this way, comprehensive design reinforces the unified educator–counselor identity, positioning school counselors as instructional partners and system leaders as well as relational supports. Comprehensive program design positions school counselors not only as service providers, but as architects of systems that widen access and reduce inequity before it takes hold.

Preventive Programming as Equity Work

Preventive programming reduces the likelihood that MLs encounter avoidable barriers related to timing, access, or information. Many challenges faced by MLs stem from systems that assume shared background knowledge—about course pathways, postsecondary options, eligibility requirements, or school-based norms—that may not exist for families navigating U.S. schools for the first time. When these assumptions go unexamined, inequities are reproduced not through intent, but through design.

Preventive approaches often address:

- **information gaps** (e.g., unclear course implications or postsecondary options)
- **timing gaps** (e.g., interventions arriving after scheduling windows)
- **access gaps** (e.g., untranslated materials, transportation conflicts)
- **belief gaps** (e.g., who is seen as "ready" for advanced opportunities)

Viewed through a humanizing lens, preventive programming acknowledges that opportunity should not depend on families knowing how to ask the "right" questions or on students navigating opaque systems independently. Preventive design reduces the need for students to self-advocate for opportunities they were never clearly invited into, shifting responsibility from individuals to the counseling program itself.

VIGNETTE

During a seventh-grade CCR lesson, the counselor revises materials to include bilingual visuals and concrete examples of multiple postsecondary pathways. Students ask questions about apprenticeships, community college, and transfer options—topics that had not surfaced in previous years. One student remarks, "I didn't know there were different kinds of college. I thought it was just the fancy one or nothing."

This vignette illustrates how preventive programming expands possibility before students encounter gatekeeping points. By introducing pathway information early—and in accessible formats—the counselor supports informed decision-making long before course sequencing or eligibility requirements narrow options. Importantly, this shift does not lower expectations; it clarifies them.

Prevention also supports sustainability for school counselors. When ML supports are embedded into Tier 1 structures, counselors spend less time untangling preventable issues later and more time supporting students' developmental decision-making over time. A practical question many counselors recognize is, *"Do we want to spend April undoing what could have been prevented in September?"* Preventive programming answers that question by designing access upstream, where it has the greatest impact.

Transitions as High-Leverage Points

Transitions are particularly important leverage points for MLs—whether entering U.S. schools, moving between grade bands, or preparing for postsecondary transitions. These moments often concentrate multiple demands at once: new expectations, unfamiliar terminology, compressed timelines, and heightened stakes. Preventive transition supports can reduce uncertainty and widen access *before* students encounter gatekeeping points that are difficult to undo later.

For MLs, transitions are rarely singular events; they are layered processes that unfold over time. Without intentional design, students may appear to make "choices" that are actually constrained by limited information, language access, or exposure to available pathways. Humanizing transition supports aim to make options visible early enough for students to engage them meaningfully.

Examples of preventive transition supports include:

- newcomer orientations
- multilingual course catalogs

- peer transition programs
- family transition nights
- co-taught CCR sessions with ML teachers
- early mapping of prerequisite sequences

VIGNETTE

Reviewing eighth-grade course requests, the counselor notices ML students are disproportionately selecting exploratory electives rather than CTE courses that feed into high school pathways. Working with the CTE coordinator, the counselor offers short pathway demonstrations in newcomer homerooms. One student later signs up for Health Sciences, explaining, "If it starts now, I want to start now."

This vignette illustrates how exposure—not ability—often shapes opportunity. By intervening at the point of transition, the counselor expands access before course sequencing narrows future options. Rather than correcting a "mis-choice," the intervention reframes what counts as a choice in the first place.

Transitions also offer natural opportunities for collaboration. When counselors work alongside ML teachers, administrators, and pathway coordinators at transition points, responsibility for access shifts from individual students to the system itself. In this way, transitions become sites of instructional leadership as well as developmental support.

Tier 1 as the Equity Floor

For many MLs, Tier 1 programming represents their primary point of access to CCR, social-emotional learning (SEL), and academic planning supports. If Tier 1 structures are not linguistically accessible or culturally responsive, Tier 2 and Tier 3 interventions become overburdened with needs that could have been addressed earlier. When Tier 1 only works for families who already understand the system, it functions less as a universal foundation and more as a sorting mechanism.

A humanizing approach treats Tier 1 as the *equity floor*—the minimum level of access, clarity, and belonging that every student should experience. This includes not only translated materials, but also instructional practices that validate students' cultural knowledge, family experiences, and identities as relevant to learning and planning. Tier 1 is where belonging is established, expectations are communicated, and futures are first imagined.

VIGNETTE

During a Tier 1 SEL lesson, students share family traditions. A student from Guatemala talks about making tortillas with his grandmother. The teacher later displays a class map highlighting family traditions. The student becomes more participatory in class, and the counselor notes that belonging arrived quietly—well before academic planning ever would.

This vignette underscores that Tier 1 equity work often looks subtle rather than dramatic. Belonging is cultivated through everyday instructional moments that signal whose knowledge matters. When students experience belonging early, they are more likely to engage in academic risk-taking and future-oriented planning later.

Positioning Tier 1 as the equity floor reinforces the unified educator–counselor identity. Designing lessons, transitions, and structures that are accessible by default is both instructional work and counseling work—work that shapes the conditions under which students can see themselves as capable, valued, and entitled to opportunity.

Family Engagement as Preventive Infrastructure

Family engagement functions as preventive infrastructure, not simply relational outreach. Multilingual families often manage work schedules, translation needs, transportation constraints, and immigration-related stress while simultaneously learning unfamiliar educational systems. When family engagement relies on informal contact or one-time events, access becomes uneven. Preventive, family-facing structures help ensure that information, timelines, and opportunities are not dependent on families' availability, English proficiency, or prior familiarity with U.S. schooling.

Viewed through a humanizing lens, family engagement is less about attendance and more about *access to decision-making*. Preventive infrastructure shifts the question from "How do we get families to show up?" to "How do we design systems that families can realistically access?" This reframing positions families as knowledgeable partners rather than recipients of information.

Preventive family-facing structures may include:

- multilingual communication across platforms
- interpreter scheduling systems
- CCR and financial aid workshops in home languages
- family liaisons or cultural brokers
- partnerships with community organizations

VIGNETTE

At a multilingual FAFSA night, interpreters support families speaking Spanish, Dari, and Vietnamese. The counselor includes information on scholarships and pathways that do not require citizenship documentation. A parent later shares, "Now we understand the map." The student enrolls in dual credit engineering courses the following semester.

This vignette highlights how clarity—not persuasion—often drives engagement. When families receive accurate, accessible information that acknowledges legal, financial, and cultural realities, they are better positioned to support students' decision-making. Importantly, the counselor's role here is not to solve individual barriers, but to design structures that make complex systems navigable for many families at once.

Family engagement as preventive infrastructure also supports sustainability. When communication systems, interpretation supports, and community partnerships are established programmatically, counselors spend less time troubleshooting barriers on a case-by-case basis. In this way, family engagement becomes an integral component of comprehensive, preventive programming rather than an additional responsibility layered onto already full roles.

Integration Over Add-On

Humanizing programming avoids the "add-on" trap, where supports for MLs exist only as supplemental services delivered outside the core of the school counseling program. Add-on approaches often depend on individual referrals, separate meetings, or specialized interventions that unintentionally signal that MLs are exceptions rather than expected participants in the academic and career pathways of the school.

Integration—across leadership, CCR programming, MTSS, and family engagement—positions ML success as a shared responsibility rather than a specialized intervention. When ML considerations are embedded into how programs are designed, communicated, and evaluated, access becomes routine rather than remedial. Integration also reduces fragmentation: students receive consistent messages about opportunity across classrooms, counseling spaces, and family-facing systems.

VIGNETTE

The counseling team releases a multilingual course catalog with icons marking pathway-aligned courses. ML enrollment in digital design doubles in one year. A student notes, "I could finally see what the classes lead to."

This vignette illustrates how visibility shapes participation. Rather than creating a separate intervention to "encourage" ML enrollment, the team redesigns an existing structure so pathways are legible to more students. The result is not increased motivation, but increased access.

Integration reinforces the unified educator–counselor identity. Designing systems that clarify pathways, reduce ambiguity, and widen access is both instructional and developmental work. In integrated programs, school counselors are not simply responding to inequities as they arise; they are shaping the conditions under which students can imagine and pursue future possibilities.

Reflection Questions

1 Which supports for multilingual learners in my school are primarily reactive rather than preventive?
2 Where do timing, language access, or information gaps create unintentional barriers for MLs and their families?
3 What programmatic change—large or small—could I make to reduce reliance on individual advocacy?

Conclusion

Humanizing school counseling for MLs is not about adding more tasks to already full caseloads; it is about designing roles and programs that make access more visible, pathways more navigable, and belonging more likely. When school counselors hold their educator and counselor identities together, they are uniquely positioned to build systems that honor students' languages, cultures, and aspirations while widening participation in future-oriented opportunities. In doing so, humanizing practice becomes not an extra layer of work, but a more intentional way of doing the work that already matters most.

This approach requires a fundamental shift from viewing linguistic diversity as a barrier to recognizing it as a profound positive asset. By integrating multilingualism into the core of counseling services, rather than treating it as a specialized "add-on," school counselors can dismantle the systemic silos that often isolate these students from high-level academic tracks and leadership roles. This intentionality transforms counseling services into a bridge where cultural wealth meets opportunities. Ultimately, when systems are recalibrated to see the whole student, the resulting equity doesn't just benefit MLs; it creates a more empathetic and active educational environment that elevates the experience for the entire school community.

Reflection Questions

- Looking across roles and programmatic structures, where do you see the greatest leverage for creating more humanizing conditions for MLs in your current context?
- How do your school's systems, timelines, and information pathways either reduce or increase the burden placed on MLs and their families to self-advocate?
- In what ways does your current counseling program signal who belongs in future-oriented opportunities (e.g., advanced coursework, leadership, postsecondary pathways)? Who receives those signals most clearly?

- How might adopting a more explicitly humanizing stance at the program level change how success is defined, measured, or celebrated for MLs?
- What is one preventive, system-level change—not an individual intervention—that you could realistically implement or advocate for in the next academic year?

References

American School Counselor Association (2024). *ASCA Position Statements*. Retrieved from https://www.schoolcounselor.org/Standards-Positions/Position-Statements/ASCA-Position-Statements

American School Counselor Association (2025). *ASCA national model: A framework for school counseling programs* (5th ed.). Alexandria, VA: American School Counselor Association.

Davis, L., Harward, K., & Yazzie, A. (2023). Counselor-teacher collaboration in multilingual learner contexts: A qualitative case study investigating counselor-teacher partnerships. *Professional School Counseling, 27*(1). https://doi-org.proxy180.nclive.org/10.1177/2156759X231177624

Hsieh, B. (2022). Making space for ourselves, making space for each other: Humanizing practices in the ELA classroom and in teacher education. In E. Dutro & B. Pacheco (Eds.), *Trauma-informed teaching: Responsive, humanizing classrooms* (pp. 41–45). National Council of Teachers of English.

Levy, I. P., & Lemberger-Truelove, M. E. (2021). Educator-counselor: A nondual identity for school counselors. *Professional School Counseling, 24*. https://doi.org/10.1177/2156759X211007630

Migration Policy Institute (2024). *English learners in K-12 education by state*. MPI Data Hub. https://www.migrationpolicy.org/programs/data-hub/charts/english-learners-k-12-education-state

National Center for Education Statistics (2023). *Table 204.20: English learners (ELs) enrolled in public elementary and secondary schools, by state or jurisdiction: Fall 2011 through fall 2021*. Digest of Education Statistics. https://nces.ed.gov/programs/digest/d23/tables/dt23_204.20.asp

National Center for Education Statistics (2024). *English learners in public schools: Condition of education*. U.S. Department of Education, Institute of Education Sciences. https://nces.ed.gov/programs/coe/indicator/cgf

Office of English Language Acquisition (2024). *English learner educational experiences and opportunities: a report using federal datasets*. U.S. Department of Education. https://ncela.ed.gov/reports

Paris, D., & Alim, H. S. (Eds.) (2017). *Culturally sustaining pedagogies: Teaching and learning for justice in a changing world*. Teachers College Press.

Salazar, M. C. (2013). A humanizing pedagogy: Reinventing the principles and practice of education as a journey toward liberation. *Review of Research in Education, 37*(1), 121–148.

Stickl Haugen, J., Wachter Morris, C. A., & Wester, K. L. (2019). The need to belong: An exploration of belonging among urban middle school students. *Journal of Child and Adolescent Counseling, 5*(1), 1–17. https://doi-org.proxy180.nclive.org/10.1080/23727810.2018.1556988

Viesca, K. M., & Commins, N. (2026). *Humanizing pedagogies with multilingual learners: Transforming teaching in the content areas*. Routledge.

Chapter 3

Core Cultural Values Mapping Tools for School Counselors

Fostering Cultural Awareness and Self-Reflection in the Work with Multilingual Learners

Shelby Gonzales and Priscila J.B.M. Costa

Introduction

Consider the four stories below. They are based on real events although the names and identifying details are fictitious. These stories introduce this chapter by illustrating some of the complexities of cross-cultural understanding in educational settings.

> Juan's mother, from El Salvador, was called for a parent-teacher conference with Juan's American teacher because Juan did not respect his classmates' personal space. He would touch his classmates' arms or shoulders while talking and walk too close to others in line, which made his teacher and other children uncomfortable. For Juan's mom, the topic of the parent-teacher conference sounded odd, as she expected to hear about his academic needs. She did not see how his personal space could be a challenge. At the time, the teachers and interpreter present in the meeting focused on sharing the information but were not prepared to bridge the cultural gap.
>
> Jin, from China, and Mustafah, from Saudi Arabia, could not see eye to eye and started a verbal fight over gender roles in society. For each of them, the opposing points of view sounded insulting. Although they were successful young adults in their own languages, their limited proficiency in the English language did not grant them all the linguistic tools to express their perspectives on common ground, so their argument escalated fast, and their English instructor had to intervene. It would have been beneficial to follow up with a conversation about cultural differences beyond language.
>
> Fatimah, from Kuwait, could not relate to the plot of a murder-mystery fiction story read in her English class. She had never been exposed to the cultural implications of that type of story. She struggled with the reading assignment not because of her English literacy skills, but because of her diverse background

DOI: 10.4324/9781003711124-4

> knowledge. A culturally responsive lesson would have address that difference as part of the reading comprehension.
>
> Mrs. Smith complained about Emmanuel, her kindergarten student, who cried daily because his peers did not speak his home-language at school. From her perspective, the young boy was too dependent on his mom and tried to transfer that same dependence to other female figures at school. With that in mind, Mrs. Smith tried to reinforce the importance of independence and autonomy by isolating Emmanuel from other teachers who had built a rapport with him. The teacher often pointed out to other faculty and staff that Emmanuel behaved like a baby crying every day. However, Emmanuel did not cry when he encountered other teachers and students who were able to speak to him in his dominant language. A culturally aware counselor could have intervene and facilitated the teacher's understanding of child rearing practices in Emmanuel's culture and community.

These four stories have a common thread. They involve individuals who did not share common cultural backgrounds, and therefore, they depict intercultural conflicts beyond language barriers. The students (their names are pseudonyms) were multilingual learners (MLs) who had recently arrived in US schools. The teachers had to navigate differences in classroom behavior while also teaching their lessons. This chapter seeks to discuss the role of school counselors in this complex cross-cultural dynamic.

In almost two decades of teaching the English language and literacy to MLs, Priscila Costa has witnessed and been part of numerous situations marked by intercultural dissonance like the stories described above. Working with MLs requires more than just overcoming language barriers and bridging communication gaps. There may be differences in core values, beliefs, and practices as well. Echoing Hofstede et al. (2010), this chapter emphasizes that "the theme of cultural differences (…) pertains to anyone who meets people from outside his or her own narrow circle, and in the modern world this is virtually anybody" (p. xii) That includes school counselors, who must first be knowledgeable about the rich, diverse cultural backgrounds of their student caseload and the complex historical context that has led MLs to U.S. schools, so they can offer truly effective academic, social, and emotional support to MLs.

The idea for this chapter came from a course Shelby taught years ago at a large R1 university in the Southern United States. Her course focused on preparing future school counselors, social workers, teachers, and school psychologists to address the social-emotional learning of K-12 students. As she moved through course content, it was imperative for Shelby's students to begin to think about the multicultural considerations that K-12 settings demand and deserve, regardless of the professional role ahead. Priscila contributed as a guest speaker, presenting a workshop on the issues of serving MLs in American public schools.

Together, they aimed to discuss the importance of cultural sensitivity, essential for working with linguistically and culturally diverse students.

Priscila organized her lecture by highlighting several elements of MLs' teaching and learning, their strengths, barriers they face, and the various cultural aspects they navigate within the school system. The lecture ended with a task that required students to map out on their own cultural values and reflect on those implications as they prepared to enter the school system and work with the diverse myriad of K-12 learners. The cultural mapping activity opened the opportunity for rich discussions among the students, which may not have happened otherwise.

From their experiences in schools and in colleges for teacher education, Priscila and Shelby perceived that most of the concerns regarding MLs in K-12 schools focus on instructional practices, academic achievement, standardized testing, graduation rates, and classroom behavior management. For school counselors, their focus lies on the social/emotional, career, and academic development of all students which can cause school counselors to overlook the nuanced complexities that exist within cultural differences in themselves and their students. Although those aspects are of ultimate importance, they do not paint the complete picture because they lack the vital understanding of cultural values which goes beyond the racial dichotomy found in U.S. cultures. In the absence of a global and intersectional understanding of culture, counselors risk reducing students' experiences to surface-level categories that fail to capture the deeper cultural logics shaping MLs' identities, family expectations, and ways of engaging with schools.

Shelby and Priscila continued to collaborate over the years and found the value in introducing these concepts and cultural mapping tools that allow individuals to translate abstract concepts (i.e., cultural values) into concrete representations (i.e., mapping those values along a spectrum). This process has enabled students to compare and contrast how they position and engage with MLs, their families, and even their colleagues. The literature on collaboration for MLs academic success often emphasizes classroom-based practices and how instructional teams work together; however, Shelby and Priscila's interdisciplinary collaboration revealed the importance of extending this work beyond instructional contexts to enhance students' overall educational experiences. Moreover, while scholarship on cultural awareness, intercultural competence, and cross-cultural communication is well established in higher education, international education, and international business contexts, it remains comparatively underdeveloped in K-12 settings, particularly as it relates to the preparation of school counselors working with MLs. Currently, Shelby continues to use this content and these tools specifically with her school counseling students, many of whom go on to work in refugee, immigrant, and culturally diverse areas. Through this interdisciplinary partnership, it has become clear that experts from different fields are better positioned to equip future school counselors to meet the nuanced needs of MLs when they collaborate to address gaps in professional development. As the K-12 landscape continues to evolve and diversify, school counselors must be prepared to address not only academic and career development, but also the fears, concerns, and trauma that often accompany immigrant experiences and culturally diverse identities (de Oliveira & Wachter Morris, 2015). While much of the existing literature calls for collaboration among teachers across instructional disciplines, this work highlights the critical importance of collaboration that extends beyond the instructional realm.

Having MLs in our K-12 schools means much more than teaching them the English language and academic standards. School professionals are often confronted with the challenges of bridging cultural differences to reduce clashes and foster adaptation. The cultural mapping tool and activity help school professionals engage in self-reflection to understand their own positionality and cultural perspectives. For school counselors, this can often seem abstract. Defining and identifying where their cultural values lie provides a concrete way to approach understanding the holistic needs of students. The *Core Cultural Values Mapping* activity (Paige et al., 2012) for study abroad instruction, adapted here for school counselor training, serves as a tool to foster intercultural awareness. It enables pre-service counselors and teachers to reflect on their core cultural values and consider how they may differ from the diverse cultural backgrounds of the student population they will encounter in K-12 settings. This chapter discusses the roles, responsibilities, and recommendations for school counselors who are destined to work with MLs in K-12 schools. Although this chapter is written specifically for school counselors who face these challenges regularly, the content and activity could also prove beneficial for teachers, administrators, support personnel, and (school) counselor educators who seek to enhance their own understanding of cultural values through mapping and self-reflection as they aim to support and educate MLs and all of their students in the K-12 school system.

Our Positionality

It is imperative for school counselors to continually examine and deepen their understanding of their own personal and cultural contexts. Multicultural competence is an ongoing, individual journey, and culturally competent school counselors consistently strive to expand their own awareness, knowledge, and skills to engage with students and families whose cultural experiences differ from their own. Within this framework, *positionality* functions as a socio-cultural construct that acknowledges how individuals' identities, lived experiences, power relations, and social locations (e.g., language, race, nationality, immigration history, professional role, gender, and institutional context) shape how they interpret, interact with, and make meaning of others' experiences. The authors present their own positionality to model this reflective practice and to help readers consider how their backgrounds, culture, education, location, and professional training influence their perceptions, assumptions, and decision-making when working with MLs and their families.

Priscila has taught English language and literacy to MLs in various settings in Brazil and in the United States since 2007. Her academic credentials include national and international teacher certifications, a master's of arts in English for Specific Purposes, and a Ph.D. in Language and Literacy. English is her second language which she started learning as an elective extracurricular (after-school) activity in 1st grade, in Brazil. However, she did not identify herself as a bilingual person until she moved to the United States to pursue graduate studies in her early 30s. She did not feel fluent enough in English despite decades of studies. It was through international education that her self-efficacy and renewed identity were shaped. Her first-hand experience with second (or foreign) language acquisition and the impact of multilingualism on her academic achievement has informed her scholarship. She has lived many of the experiences of cultural misunderstandings and of linguistic and cultural adaptation that younger MLs endure every day. Her cross-cultural experience and qualitative research lenses on social semiotic motivate her to inform school personnel, educators, policy makers, and other stakeholders about the complexities of multilingual teaching and learning.

Shelby was born and raised in Washington state, in the United States and moved to South Carolina in her early 20s on an athletics scholarship to complete her undergraduate degree in experimental psychology. After completing her undergraduate degree, she went to complete her Educational Specialist degree in school counseling. Upon graduation, she worked as a school counselor in both North and South Carolina before completing her PhD in Counselor Education from the University of South Carolina in May of 2022. Throughout her professional education to become a school counselor, she worked with diverse student populations in the Carolinas while working to understand her own diversity, ethnicity, and multicultural self. As someone who was raised strongly in the Hispanic-Catholic culture, surrounded by her father's extended family, she never questioned her belonging. As she entered higher education, the questions began: "you're Hispanic/Latina?! You look white!", which, to be fair, is a true, face-value observation. She doesn't *look* Hispanic/Latina in the American stereotypical and racialized perspective, but she was and still is. Culture, *her* culture, runs deep; yet the surface-level perception that others have of her and who she is, is at odds. Throughout her counseling career, Shelby has used much of her own experiences, personal and professional, to inform her school counseling approach as she works with students and families within the K-12 system.

By describing their socio-cultural and linguistic background and reflecting on their intersectional positionality, the authors model for their students how they engage with the understanding of cultural values in their practices. This chapter provides a brief connection of school counseling to cultural values, an introduction to multilingual education in U.S. public schools, and how to connect these two disciplines. The cultural mapping activity found at the end of this chapter aims to help the readers map their own cultural values and reflect upon how those values influence and impact the ways they interact with people that surround them.

Connecting School Counseling to Cultural Values

An initial step in each school counselor's professional identity development must be a self-reflection of their own core cultural values and where they lie while working to understand the cultural values of the linguistically and culturally diverse K-12 MLs and their families. However, the ways in which school counseling professionals can and should do that often feel abstract. Given that ASCA (2022) calls on school counselors to continually work toward cultural competence and cultural humility to create culturally sustaining counseling programs within their school, school counselors and school counselor educators must engage with concrete activities and tools that provide ways to assess, evaluate, and reflect on their own cultural values and how those values interact with their students and their families. Creating a school climate that embraces cultural diversity helps to promote all students' academic, career, and social/emotional development. As part of this call, school counselors must commit to continually enhancing their own knowledge and awareness of prejudice, power, and oppression to meet the ever diverse and changing needs of students within the K-12 education system.

Introduction to ML Education in U.S. Public Schools

ML Identification

Services provided to MLs became federally mandated as a result of landmark legislation to ensure equitable access to education. Notoriously, the Civil Rights Act of 1964, particularly Title VI, prohibits discrimination based on race, color, or national origin in federally funded programs. Subsequently, the Bilingual Education Act of 1968, an amendment to the Elementary and Secondary Education Act (ESEA), provided federal funding to support bilingual education programs, recognizing the need for specialized instruction to help English language learners (ELLs or ELs) achieve academic success. In the *Lau v. Nichols* (1974) case, the U.S. Supreme Court affirmed that schools must take affirmative steps to support MLs, ruling that simply providing the same instruction as that offered to native English speakers violates Title VI of the Civil Rights Act of 1964. The case led to policies requiring schools to implement programs that help ELs overcome language barriers and access meaningful education. *Castañeda v. Pickard* (1981) set standards for bilingual education programs, requiring them to be based on sound theory, effectively implemented, and evaluated for success. *Plyler v. Doe*

(1982) ensured that undocumented children have the right to a free public education, preventing discrimination based on immigration status. Together, these cases reinforce the federal mandate for equitable educational access and appropriate language support for MLs. At the time when the authors are revising this chapter in 2026, social justice legislation is currently under scrutiny and being challenged by federal authorities, which can potentially affect the services provided to MLs in schools as well as their socio-emotional status in the face of growing hardships.

Nonetheless, we must emphasize that it is impossible to generalize or to determine the norms for educational policies across all 50 states because the United States is a country of continental proportions. As long as public schools follow federal laws, some policies and services can be determined by local authorities at the state, district, and school levels. Therefore, we rely on the norms we have encountered in our experiences as practitioners and scholars and hope the readers can adjust the details to the reality they find in their areas.

As of early 2026, all 50 U.S. states require a Home Language Survey (HLS) at the time of school enrollment to identify students who may need language support services. The HLS helps determine whether a student is exposed to a language other than English at home and may require further assessment of his/her English language proficiency (ELP). However, the specific questions and implementation of the survey may vary by state. For example, in South Carolina, in 2026, schools must collect a simple survey containing only three questions and do so only once for each student. The questions are listed below as found in the HLS included in the enrollment package (SCDE Early Learning, 2021):

1. "What is the language that the student first acquired?
2. What language(s) are spoken most often by the student?
3. What is the primary language used in the home, regardless of the language spoken by the student?"

If any of the answers to these questions indicates a language other than English, the student must be screened by a trained and certified ML specialist.

Terminology and Acronyms

Over the decades, several acronyms have been used to describe students identified through the HLS as someone who speaks a language other than English at home. State legislatures may use different terminology to describe services provided to students, such as English as a second language (ESL) and English for speakers of other languages (ESOL). Federal documents may still refer to linguistically diverse students as English learners (ELs) or emergent bilinguals (EBs). The nomenclature and acronyms often reflect political views on the students' status and capabilities.

The terminology above is often applied to students who have not yet achieved ELP for academic purposes according to State criteria. The criteria vary from state to state and are measured by standardized English language exams such as the WIDA *ACCESS* (WIDA, 2020). South Carolina, where both authors started their interdisciplinary collaboration, adopts the WIDA standards for MLs' English language development. The South Carolina Department of Education determines the ELP criteria for ML classification and services. ML programs' instruction and assessment comprise four language and literacy domains—listening, speaking, reading, and writing—for social and instructional purposes, English language arts, math, science, and social studies. As of 2025, the ELP assessment proficiency criteria are a composite score equal to or above 4.4 (on a scale of 1–6) on the WIDA ACCESS exams, or equal to or greater than 3 on the WIDA Alternate ACCESS for MLs with the most significant cognitive disabilities (Murphy & Corpuz, 2025).

Nonetheless, faculty and support staff, such as school counselors, must be aware that students who meet the ELP criteria on screeners or the subsequent exams will not be classified as MLs and will not receive ML services even though they *are* multilinguals and culturally diverse. After meeting the exit criteria (either on the initial screener or in the annual exams), MLs are monitored for four additional years to ensure their academic performance is not hindered by the level of their English language development. After that monitoring period, students are no longer labeled as MLs (or the acronyms used by their local schools). This classification change can be misleading for faculty and staff who are unaware of cultural differences.

Students' reclassification as monitored, former ML, or never ML does not imply that they have become monolingual or monocultural. Even after they are no longer (or never) officially identified as MLs based on their ELP, these students continue to carry with them rich multilingual and multicultural experiences that shape how they learn, communicate, and relate to the world around them. Their linguistic and cultural identities do not disappear with a change in classification, nor should they be overlooked in educational planning, counseling conversations, or school-family engagement. Counselors who acknowledge these enduring aspects of identity are better positioned to support students' long-term well-being and academic success.

Demographic Configuration

MLs are, by no means, a homogeneous group. They come from a wide range of socio-economic, cultural, and linguistic backgrounds. As explained above, U.S. public schools are not permitted to collect or report detailed information about students' immigration status due to legal and ethical considerations. Nevertheless, in our experience, we have observed that a significant portion of MLs are first-generation U.S.-born children of immigrant parents. Others have arrived in the United States through a variety of immigration pathways, each reflecting the complex and transnational nature of their lives. These pathways include:

- **Family-based immigration.** Children may enter the United States as lawful permanent residents (green card holders) through family-sponsored visas.
- **Diversity Visa Lottery.** A limited number of children enter with their families through this program, which grants green cards to individuals from countries with historically low rates of immigration to the United States.
- **Adoption by U.S. citizens.** Some international adoptees enter the United States as immigrants and may be classified as MLs.
- **Student or exchange visas (F-1, J-1, etc.).** In some cases, children come temporarily to study in the United States under specific visa programs. In other cases, children arrive as dependents of parents who are international students and scholars at the post-secondary level, mostly graduate students. This specific group of MLs often comes from highly educated backgrounds, but they still face the challenges of adapting to the host culture.
- **Refugee or asylum status.** Children may arrive seeking protection from persecution, war, or violence in their countries of origin. Refugees are different from immigrants because their relocation is forced by persecution and/or oppression (SCDSS, n.d.). This specific group of MLs has often experienced severe trauma and has waited long years for relocation.
- **Temporary Protected Status (TPS).** Children from designated countries experiencing humanitarian crises—such as natural disasters, armed conflicts, or political instability—may enter or remain in the United States legally under TPS. As of mid-2025, TPS continues to offer temporary protection and work authorization for individuals from certain countries, although beneficiaries must reapply during each extension period and face ongoing uncertainty regarding their future legal status. This program is currently under scrutiny by federal authorities.
- **Undocumented entry or permanence.** Some children arrive without documented authorization or overstay their visa's authorized duration, either with family members or as unaccompanied minors.
- **Parole programs.** Certain children are permitted temporary permanence in the United States based on urgent humanitarian reasons or significant public benefit.
- **Deferred Action for Childhood Arrivals (DACA).** Although DACA does not confer lawful immigration status, it offers temporary protection from deportation and eligibility for work permits to certain undocumented youth brought to the United States as children. As of June 2025, the program remains partially active: current recipients may continue to renew their protections, but new applications are not being processed due to ongoing legal challenges and federal court rulings.

According to the National Center for Educational Statistics, "in fall 2021, across the 50 states and the District of Columbia, the percentage of public-school students who were ELs ranged from 0.8 percent in West Virginia to 20.2 percent in Texas" (National Center for Education Statistics, 2024). More than 76% of those students spoke Spanish or Castilian as their home language. The next most commonly reported home languages were Chinese, Vietnamese, Portuguese, Russian, Haitian, Hmong, and Urdu.

This historical and demographic information is essential for school counselors because it gives a glimpse into the complex realities of MLs in U.S. public schools. They are not a homogeneous group. Nuances of their lived experiences surpass the need to learn the English language and academic content. School counselors must understand the complex historical circumstances that bring MLs into U.S. schools as well as their diverse cultural backgrounds to provide effective academic, social, and emotional support. MLs often come from diverse linguistic, cultural, and immigration experiences that shape their educational needs and personal challenges.

The location of the school district is equally significant for the immigrant experience; for instance, cultural adaptation in an urban school in large centers such as New York City or Chicago will certainly be different from that in rural schools in Alabama or Texas small towns. This is not to indicate right or wrong, good or bad, adequate or inadequate scenarios, but to acknowledge that details of the immigrant experience will be different according to the context.

Understanding historical factors, such as past and current immigration policies, civil rights cases, and educational reforms, helps counselors advocate for equitable access to support programs. Cultural awareness also allows counselors to foster an inclusive school environment, build trust with students and families, and address issues like cultural integration, stress, discrimination, or trauma from displacement. By recognizing these factors, counselors can implement culturally responsive strategies that empower MLs to thrive academically and socially.

Introduction to Cultural Values

"Two researchers in the 1960s are reported to have found over three hundred definitions of culture, and there are, no doubt, many more in existence today" (Storti, 2017, p. 1). Below, we list a few definitions that inform our understanding of culture.

"Culture is the shared assumptions, values, and beliefs of a group of people which result in characteristic behaviors." (Storti, 2017, p. 1) That is, culture is collectively constructed, and it informs how people behave.

Culture does not exist in a vacuum (Nieto, 2010). It is the "ever-changing values, traditions, social and political relationships, and worldview created, shared, and transformed by a group of people bound together by a combination of factors that can include a common history, geographic location, language, social class, and religion." Additionally, culture is "dynamic; multifaceted; embedded in context; influenced by social, economic, and political factors; created and socially constructed; learned; and dialectical" (p. 137). By *dialectical*, Nieto means that culture is a complex system and is always in interaction and tension with extrinsic factors such as historical, socio-economic, and political circumstances (Nieto, 1992, 2010, p. 136).

Culture is not predetermined by biological traits such as race and gender, although societies often form cultural constructs based on racial and gender ideologies. Culture is also not necessarily determined by the place of birth (e.g., a child born in Germany to Italian parents, who moves to France and then to the United States may or may not carry German cultural traits). Culture is not to be confused with the commonalities of human nature nor with individual personality traits. At the deepest level, as a species, all human beings are the same and have the same basic needs for food, shelter, safety, and belonging. We all feel pain, fear, sorrow, excitement, love, and other emotions regardless of culture. In that sense, all humans are inherently the "same." On the other hand, due to personality traits, every individual is unique even if two are raised by the same parents, at the same time, in the same house, and through the same experiences. In that sense, every human being is different from one another. Yet, A child starts absorbing the community's culture from the moment of birth without the need for explicit teaching. "Understanding who we are and where we belong is a developmental task for everyone that takes place in the context of the surrounding community" (Pollock et al., 2017, p. 58). The culture around us (in the communities where we are immersed) shapes our perspectives, the way we understand the world, the behaviors we perceive as desirable, our argumentation and communication patterns, the way we make decisions that seem logical and sensible, and what we consider "normal" or adequate (Meyer, 2014).

Culture is more than what someone eats, the songs they enjoy, or the clothes they wear. Culture is the underlying collection of factors that inform outward practices. We often see culture metaphorically compared to an iceberg, where the greatest part is submerged and unseen, while only the tip appears above the water. In our courses, we have used a different analogy—a tree. In the analogy of the "culture tree," Hammond (2015, p. 24) proposes that, as a tree with distinct parts, culture has three different levels that shape identity and interaction:

1 The **surface culture**, represented by the leaves and branches, consists of visible and tangible elements such as food, clothing, music, arts, language, hairstyle, games, stories, holidays, and more. These elements are exposed. Members of different cultural groups can easily access, learn about, and identify other cultures in personal interactions or from across the world through the media. Stereotypes are often formed based on the elements of surface culture.

2 The **shallow culture** (which we prefer to call *near-surface culture*, because culture is not shallow) forms the trunk, containing social norms negotiated through everyday interactions, including attitudes toward elders, perceptions of time, nonverbal communication (e.g., body language), rules about eye contact or personal space, the concept of honesty, child-rearing principles, theories of wellbeing and disease, and ways of handling emotion. These elements may or may not be overtly taught by family, educators, and other leaders to younger members of the socio-cultural group.
3 Beneath that, at the deepest level, the roots represent **deep culture**, which consists of unspoken and often unconscious beliefs, values, and worldviews that influence spirituality, ethics, health, concepts of group harmony, the concept of self, the notion of fairness, and definitions of kinship and identity. Just as a tree's strength comes from its roots, culture is deeply shaped by its foundational beliefs, guiding how people interact and interpret the world around them.

The culture tree as proposed by Hammond (2015) is a rich and tangible analogy. While not everyone has seen an iceberg, everyone we have met has seen, smelled, and touched thousands of different trees throughout their lives. We know that the outward appearance of a tree, regardless of its species, depends on its environment and the nutrients it collects from the soil through its roots, which are not always visible. Similarly, our culture depends on the environment in which we live. It is not determined by biological traits but by the community environment around us.

In our courses, we have discussed with our students how the culture-tree analogy (Hammond, 2015) can be applied to represent the multicultural nature of our classrooms. In a forest, every species of tree has unique characteristics. Some grow tall and fast while others grow slowly and deep, each drawing from distinct soil compositions and weather patterns. Yet, together, they form an ecosystem where diversity can enhance resilience. Likewise, in a school, each student brings their own cultural roots, traditions, and views from around the world. When these different "culture trees" grow side by side, they have the potential to create a vibrant, interdependent learning community. We strive to cultivate culturally diverse learning spaces where all students are honored, celebrated, and supported.

However, just like in a natural forest, not all coexistence is effortless or harmonious. Some tree species are invasive or aggressive, dominating the space, sunlight, or nutrients, and in doing so, they may limit the growth of other plants. Similarly, in multicultural school environments, certain cultural norms—often aligned with dominant or mainstream values of the larger community—can overshadow, marginalize, or even suppress the visibility and expression of less dominant cultures. Power imbalances, linguistic hierarchies, and cultural misunderstandings can lead to exclusion or assimilation pressures. Some cultural groups may develop unhealthy co-dependencies, while others may struggle for space to grow and be recognized.

In that light, MLs face some specific challenges intrinsic to their experience in U.S. institutions:

> Culturally and linguistically diverse populations are not only at higher risk for developing problems due to the many systemic challenges they face (i.e. lower socioeconomic status, language barriers, discrimination), but they also have fewer opportunities to access the care they need to address their challenges.
>
> (Staehr Fenner & Teich, 2024, p. 9)

A truly inclusive and equitable school ecosystem requires intentional action: one that not only celebrates diversity but actively monitors and prunes the dynamics that hinder mutual flourishing.

MLs bring all the elements of their culture (surface, shallow, and deep), but they are not always able to verbally explain what informs their practices. An additional analogy compares culture is like water to a fish (Meyer, 2014). Water is constantly around fish, yet the fish do not see it. Without proper instruction, we may never notice the nuances of our own culture that are always around us. However, as educators and counselors, we must be aware of the deepest elements of culture for better intercultural competence and intercultural communication. In this chapter, we use the term *core cultural values* to describe some elements of deep culture as we have used it in our courses. Paige et al. (2012) define that,

> Every human community lives by a set of values that guide how people communicate and relate to one another, interpret behavior, and evaluate each other. How do we know if someone is behaving "normally"? That concept only makes sense if we have a shared standard that frames what is normal or appropriate. Cultural values are those standards. A value system does not tell people exactly how they should behave, but it does set the standard by which they are judged. Most of the time, these standards are not written down; they are simply understood by most people in the culture.
>
> (p. 63)

Consider This Scenario

A newly arrived student from a foreign country joins a 7th-grade classroom mid-year. She rarely makes direct eye contact with the teacher, speaks only when called upon, and tends to keep her distance from classmates. Her science teacher interprets this as disengagement or defiance and reports that the student "isn't trying" or "lacks motivation." Classmates also begin to whisper that she is "weird" or "rude." What the teacher and students do not know is that in the student's cultural background, direct eye contact with adults may be seen as disrespectful, and silence in new social environments is a sign of cautious observation, not a lack of interest.

Feeling judged and misread, the student gradually begins to withdraw—not only in the classroom, but also during lunch, group work, and after-school activities. She avoids eye contact even more, keeps her head down in the hallway, and stops attending optional events. Although she is present at school, she begins to disappear socially. What began as a cultural mismatch is now layered with emotional distress, social isolation, and an increasing sense of invisibility.

This misunderstanding is a reminder that, like in a forest, some trees follow different growth patterns depending on the conditions of their native soil. When school professionals expect all students to "grow" in the same way—at the same pace, in the same direction—we risk mislabeling healthy differences as deficiencies. And when we fail to intervene early, we may inadvertently contribute to a school climate where some students shrink to survive rather than thrive.

Core Cultural Values Mapping Tool

In their courses for teachers and school counselor education, the authors have explored nine sets of core cultural values. Although they are presented in opposing pairs, they are not binary dichotomies. Each pair represents positions on a continuum. For instance, when someone asks if a given culture is collectivist or individualist, the answer is that it depends on whom they are comparing it to, because the sense of collectivism or individualism is relative. Various cultures position themselves along the continuum for each set of core cultural values, and they can only be described as more or less to a given side relative to other cultures (Meyer, 2014; Paige et al., 2012; Storti, 2017). The original mapping tool we have used in our courses can be found in Paige et al. (2012, pp. 63–68) or online in the archives of the Center for Advanced Research on Language Acquisition (CARLA) at https://archive.carla.umn.edu/maxsa/documents/CoreCulturalValues_MAXSA_IG.pdf. CARLA, at the University of Minnesota (http://www.carla.umn.edu), offers a detailed lesson plan for how to use this tool in an instructional setting aimed at study-abroad young adult students. However, we recognize that other authors also offer valuable mapping tools. Meyer (2014) provides a similar cultural mapping tool tailored for business settings, which can be adapted for working professionals in education. For more information, we recommend the tools available at https://erinmeyer.com/tools/.

In Table 3.1, the authors have adapted the *Core Cultural Values Mapping Tool* (Paige et al., 2012, pp. 64–67) aiming at school counselors. Our adaptation is informed by the scholarly literature of Hofstede et al. (2010), Hofstede et al. (2012), Meyer (2014), Nisbett (2003), Paige et al. (2012), and Storti (2017).

Table 3.1 Core cultural values mapping tool

	Continuum scale	
Individualism Prioritizes personal autonomy, self-reliance, and individual achievement. People are expected to look after themselves and their immediate families. In individualistic cultures, young adults typically leave their parents' home early to start their own independent lives. Common phrases may include: mind your own business, you do you, fend for yourself.	OOOOOOOOOO Note that in some American settings, people tend to privilege individualism when talking about their own cultural group but turn to collectivist views when stereotyping and generalizing traits of members of minoritized groups.	**Collectivism** Emphasizes group harmony, loyalty, and interdependence. People see themselves as part of a larger in-group (e.g., family, clan, organization). One person's actions honor or dishonor the whole group. In collectivist cultures, it is common to see multigenerational households. Young adults live with extended family even after marriage. Common phrases may include: it takes a village, all for one and one for all, *mi casa és su casa*.
Equality (low power distance) Views power as shared and earned. Status differences are minimized; communication is more informal and participatory. Members of a group refer to each other by first names regardless of age and social position. For instance, in a company's directory, names are listed alphabetically rather than based on rankings.	OOOOOOOOOO	**Hierarchy (high power distance)** Strongly perpetuates unequal distribution of power. Emphasizes ranking, titles, and the weight of social roles. Respects authority and expects due respect. Hierarchical structures are typically found in the armed forces, politics, schools, and corporations. Common language includes honorifics (Mr., Ms., Mrs., Sr., Dr., Pastor) and polite address terms (Sir, Ma'am)
Meritocracy Advancement and status are achieved through effort, demonstrated skills, credentials, and measurable performance. It assumes a level playing field where rewards are distributed based on objective achievements, which are often associated with individual merit, integrity, and ethics. Common elements include effort, diligence, competitiveness, credit scores, and socio-economic mobility. Common proverbs: the squeaky wheel gets the grease; the early bird catches the worm.	OOOOOOOOOO	**Ascription** Status is assigned based on age, gender, background, social connections, or family ties. Social role and identity are inherited, not earned. Common cultural examples: citizenship as a birthright, generational wealth and status, nobility titles, estate inheritance, access to educational and occupational opportunities based on social connections. Common proverb: the apple doesn't fall far from the tree."

(*Continued*)

Table 3.1 (Continued)

	Continuum scale	
Self-efficacy/internal locus of control Emphasizes personal agency and the common belief that people shape their own destiny. Believes that humans can control nature and the environment. It prioritizes self-reliance, goal-setting, and proactive problem-solving. Self-Efficacy is different from meritocracy in that it is a psychological belief about one's own capability, whereas meritocracy is a social system or philosophy about how rewards and status should be distributed. E.g., Policies to reduce global warming.	OOOOOOOOOO	**Destiny/external locus of control** Attributes outcomes to external forces that cannot be controlled by individuals. Life is shaped by fate, divine will, karma, predestination, or societal systems. Success may be seen as a blessing or luck beyond one's control. Hardships are accepted as inevitable parts of the human journey. This perspective prioritizes spiritual alignment over individual dominance. It believes that nature runs its own course as a force to be respected and adapted to, rather than controlled by human intervention.
Polychronic time Views time as flexible and circular. Interruptions are acceptable. Tardiness is tolerated. Punctuality is negotiable. Multiple activities occur simultaneously, and pacing is determined by the quality of the interaction rather than a pre-set agenda. Schedules are considered flexible guidelines. Finishing a meaningful conversation or assisting someone in need is more important than "being on time." Sample language may include "Rome was not built in one day."	OOOOOOOOOO	**Monochronic time** Perceives time as linear and segmented. It is a tangible and finite commodity that must be optimized. Schedules are prioritized. Completing tasks in the allotted time is desirable. In monochronic cultures, time is something that can be "saved," "wasted," or "lost." Adherence to a schedule is a matter of personal integrity, respect, and professionalism. Delays are often interpreted as organizational failures. Common phrases: time is money, scheduled quiet time.
Activity-oriented (doing) Values "doing" over "being." Productivity and achievement are central to self-worth. Common expectations include staying on task, meetings that are planned during meals (we should meet for coffee), and highly structured agendas. Common proverb: "Idle hands are the devil's workshop."	OOOOOOOOOO	**People-oriented (being)** Emphasizes presence, relationships, and interpersonal time. Human connection is more important than pre-determined activities. Quality time means to be together no matter what you are doing. Common expectation include delay or extend activities based on ongoing human interactions.

(*Continued*)

Table 3.1 (Continued)

	Continuum scale	
Risk-taking (low uncertainty avoidance) Risk-taking cultures exhibit a high tolerance for ambiguity and the unknown. They welcome innovation and change. Failure is perceived as a learning step. Curiosity is desirable and not perceived as dangerous. Social and geographic mobility are valued. Common elements: improvisation, last-minute plans, changing course of action to adjust to new needs.	OOOOOOOOOO	**Risk aversion (high uncertainty avoidance)** Risk-aversion cultures favor tradition, routine, familiarity, structure, and predictability. Failure is shameful, so there is a tendency toward controlling future outcomes. Uncertainty is undesirable and fearful. Common phrase: We have always done it this way, we must return to the basics, we have a contingency plan (plan B), we stick to what is on the budget.
Progress-oriented Embraces innovation, change, and forward thinking. This trait is different from "risk-taking" in its drive toward newness and advancement, which are viewed as inherently positive. This cultural value can be outwardly observed in ever-changing architecture, investment in high technology, and trending outfits. The focus is on improvement and evolution. It values the latest research and new approaches to known problems.	OOOOOOOOOO	**Tradition-oriented** Tradition-oriented cultures respect inherited wisdom, continuity, and stability. They honor the past. Change is examined cautiously and is often resisted. This trait values the elders in the community and the most experienced professionals in the field. Authority is found in people, history, and legacy. Common provers: if it ain't broke, don't fix it; and a tree without roots cannot stand.
Informality Communication and interaction are casual and egalitarian. First names, relaxed body language, and humor are common. Common example: text message language, fist bump, and slangs.	OOOOOOOOOO	**Formality** Interactions follow protocols and defined roles. Respect is conveyed through titles, formal speech, and respectful acknowledgment of status or authority. Common example: formal letters, firm handshake, and deference.
Direct communication Communication style where ideas and opinions are stated clearly and explicitly. Blunt honesty is valued over diplomacy. All the details and terms are spelled out clearly and upfront. Feedback focuses primarily on the task and what needs to be improved without unnecessary pleasantries. Common proverb: Say what you mean, and mean what you say.	OOOOOOOOOO	**Indirect communication** Meaning is conveyed subtly through tone, gestures, implied ideas, figures of speech, and anecdotal storytelling. Interlocutors use hedging as a linguistic strategy to soften the impact of a statement or to avoid direct confrontation. Preserving harmony takes precedence over bluntness. Common elements: white lies, beating around the bush, read between the lines.

(Continued)

Table 3.1 (Continued)

	Continuum scale	
Low context Communication relies on words and facts. Shared understanding comes through explicit instruction, not assumptions. Everything must be clearly stated, not implied. Common example: the signage "caution: hot beverage" written on coffee cups; lengthy course syllabus; written social contracts	OOOOOOOOOO	**High context** Meaning is embedded in relationships, body language, and shared history. Less is said, but more is meant. Members of the group share previous knowledge; therefore, they can omit words or pieces of information in their dialogue. Common example: inside jokes, inferences drawn from contextual clues.

Source: Adapted from Paige et al.'s (2012, pp. 64–67).

They do not mean to generalize or oversimplify the complexities of each cultural value. Please note that the pairs of values are contrasted here for educational purposes. They are not mutually exclusive, and they are not binary. In real life, multiple values are combined to compose a complex picture. They operate on a spectrum where there is **no** right or wrong, good or bad, desirable or undesirable. The cultural values of one group can only be analyzed in its context. Therefore, we recommend that readers use the scale in the middle column to indicate where they identify themselves leaning toward in that spectrum instead of picking one side or the other.

The definitions of core cultural values available in Table 3.1 are conversation starters. The authors recommend that course instructors and counselor educators lead a discussion to brainstorm real-life examples relevant to the educational setting. This practice reinforces why understanding core cultural values matters for school counselors when they engage with linguistically and culturally diverse students and families.

Why Is Cultural Mapping Important for School Counselors?

Intercultural Sensitivity

The term *ethnocentrism* comes from Greek and stems from the ancient Greeks' misleading belief that their ways of life were superior to that of other cultures (Nisbett, 2003). Bennett (1986, 2017) breaks down three layers of ethnocentrism as opposed to *ethnorelativism*. Bennett explains that his grounded theory based on studies conducted in educational and corporate settings is "a framework to explain how people experience and engage cultural difference"

(Bennett, 2014). His *Developmental Model of Intercultural Sensitivity (DMIS)* consist of six levels:

1 **Denial**: this stage indicates the rejection of the fact that cultural differences exist. It is often experienced by groups of people who have lived in secluded areas and have never been exposed to members of other cultures. Everything different from their cultural norms is perceived as foreign. People in ethnocentric denial may present themselves as disinterested in or even hostile to other cultural groups.
2 **Defense**: once a person is exposed to cultural differences and perceives a sense of "us versus them," he/she may feel the need to be defensive to protect what is familiar to their community. People in the defensive stage of ethnocentrism may draw stereotypical conclusions about members of other cultural groups. The "other" appears to be a threat or an abnormality while the familiar culture is identified as the norm.
3 **Minimization**: people experiencing the minimization stage downplay the effects of cultural differences. They may express it with statements such as "I don't see color" or "deep inside we are all the same." They may see cultural differences but focus on basic human commonalities that transcend cultural values and practices. On the surface, they may present themselves as culturally tolerant, but they mask the existence of social inequalities imposed by the privileges of the dominant culture.

   These first three levels represent ethnocentrism, where the dominant culture is considered the norm and the center of attention. The next three levels represent openness and the realization that multiple cultural experiences are valid.
4 **Acceptance**: people at the acceptance stage perceive cultural differences and may be curious about diversity. This stage may or may not involve negative judgments of unfamiliar cultural values and practices. It is a learning stage, where people are more open to seeing but not yet ready to adapt.
5 **Adaptation**: this stage requires empathy and the sense that multiple cultures are valuable. A person in the adaptation stage is able to experience and display appropriate behaviors according to multiple cultural contexts. For instance, a person who can handle indirect communication relayed through body language in a high context environment, but who can also communicate directly and in clear details in low context situations. This stage implies that every culture has positive and negative aspects, and it is possible to benefit from elements of multiple cultures at the same time.
6 **Integration**: A person in the integration stage navigates multiple cultural contexts seamlessly. This is a more advanced stage of ethnorelativism that only world travelers are able to attain because they experience multicultural interactions authentically. Some MLs may (although it is not guaranteed) achieve this stage as they live simultaneously in the home culture and the host culture.

Bennett (2014) offers a linear diagram to illustrate a progression from ethnocentrism (the stage of denial) to ethnorelativism (stage of integration). The visual emphasizes that as individuals move from one end of the line to the opposite side, they transition from avoidance and defensiveness against cultural differences to active empathy and integration of multiple perspectives into their own identity. While that diagram has been a helpful visual support in the authors' lessons for future school counselors, Priscila highlights that this process is not linear. It requires a recurrent exercise of reflection and awareness when individuals encounter new cultures. It is a complex movement more akin to a spiral staircase than a flat trajectory. Progress is measured not just by the distance covered but by the depth of the recursive journey. Individuals often circle back to revisit earlier stages of intercultural sensitivity when faced with new challenges, yet they do so from a higher vantage point. For school counselors and other educators, this means intercultural sensitivity is not a static achievement to be unlocked, but a continuous learning process to foster cultural integration in the educational setting.

Introducing the cultural values mapping tool is our attempt to foster *ethnorelativism* among school counselors and other school personnel. Ideally, school faculty and staff should be culturally aware and experience either adaptation or integration of cultures to support MLs. Mapping one's own cultural values is a reflective exercise that enables educators to recognize the lenses through which they interpret student behaviors, family dynamics, and educational expectations. Without this awareness, even well-intentioned practitioners may unknowingly operate from a minimization or defense perspective, masking cultural bias behind assumed neutrality. Counselors who understand their own cultural positioning are better equipped to perceive the deep cultural roots that shape students' ways of being and belonging. This self-knowledge lays the groundwork for genuine cross-cultural empathy, differentiated support, and the creation of school environments where cultural diversity is not only acknowledged but affirmed as an asset.

Collaboration with ML Specialists

Working *with* multilingual specialists within the K-12 school system is imperative when working as a school counselor to help all students find success in their social/emotional, academic, and career development (de Oliveira & Wachter Morris, 2015). Considering collaboration is a key aspect of the role of the school counselor (ASCA, 2019), it should be unsurprising that collaboration is vital when with this unique population. The ML specialists in your building are situated perfectly to help you understand the needs of the students on your caseload and your building. However, knowing where to start when working to collaborate can be a challenge. School counselors can and should take the lead on building a collaborative relationship with their ML specialists; as a member of the leadership team (ASCA, 2019), school counselors are often the first-person teachers reach out to when there is a concern about a student. Therefore, building a collaborative relationship with the support professionals in your school building is a natural necessity.

However, going about building this relationship, especially if it is new to you, can feel daunting. Consider taking the following steps to build that collaborative relationship with your ML specialist. First, build your own knowledge:

- Ensure that you have a factual understanding of school demographics
  - How many languages are spoken in the school?
  - How many different countries, nationalities, ethnicities, etc. make up the school population?
  - What current support does the school counseling program provide to these students and their families?
  - If or when you are unsure of the answers to these questions, seek them out.
- Approach your ML specialist and gain their perspective, ensuring that the data and information you have match their current and anticipated caseload.
  - In the best scenario, the ML specialist is the professional who has access to the most accurate and up-to-date information on the school's ML demographic.
  - If the data you collected does not match what the ML specialist has, explore what causes the discrepancies.
  - If and when the information matches, set up a meeting to talk through the different students and families that you both are working to serve.
    - Seek out the insight the ML specialist has on the students and families.
    - *Are there needs that aren't being met within your school's counseling program?*
    - *Are there students who are struggling to find a community or to connect with their teachers?*
    - *Is there an opportunity for you to step in and help facilitate understanding at the relational level on behalf of the students?*
    - *Which core cultural values are predominant in the MLs' cultures represented in your school?* (it requires some research)
- Establish a routine to check with your ML specialist on a quarterly basis, ensuring that you have a consistent plan to meet with them and ensure that the students that you are working with are finding the support they need within their classrooms.
  - This does not mean you do not connect through email or touch base informally when your paths cross, but intentional check-ins help ensure that the MLs within your school stay on your radar as you continually develop your comprehensive school counseling program.

In higher education, creating intentional, interdisciplinary collaborative partnerships can be modeled at the graduate/preparation level. Gonzales et al. (2022) suggest that modeling interdisciplinary collaboration for graduate-level students can aid students in their own pursuits of interdisciplinary collaboration once they work within the K-12 school system. If you are an instructor at a university, create partnerships with:

- university colleagues who are instructing the next generation of ML specialists. Invite them to your classroom. Have them speak on the needs of this unique population, talk about their personal, lived experiences in working within the K-12 system and beyond to help prepare students for the realities, celebrations, challenges, and considerations that need to be made when working with these students and families.
- international students and scholars, or international members of your community. Invite them to your classes to share nuances of their cultures and values, their experiences adapting into American culture, and their insights of what challenges children from their cultures might encounter in American schools.

If you are an undergraduate/graduate student, find the faculty members within ML education and speak to them about the concepts introduced above; build the interdisciplinary bridge, and don't be afraid to ask your instructors if they've considered building that bridge on their own. Building and facilitating the interdisciplinary bridge is a form of advocacy for your education but also for the K-12 students you will support in the future.

Lesson Outline for Counselor Educators

Within this section, we will outline how we integrated the Culture Mapping Activity into Counselor Education courses like *Introduction to School Counseling, Counseling Children and Adolescents*, and *Internship Supervision*. However, integration is not limited to these specific courses. We provide this outline and example of what worked for us as instructors; we encourage you to use what works for you and to adapt as needed based on your contextual setting.

Step 1. Introduction

Begin with highlighting the needs, challenges, barriers, and considerations of MLs (pulling content from our chapter and the entire textbook) because as school counselors (and support staff), it's our responsibility to meet the needs of MLs to ensure they have an equitable opportunity to develop socially, emotionally, academically, and their career ambitions. Additionally, CACREP (2024) aligned programs must also meet the accreditation standards listed previously in this chapter to ensure that counselors-in-training (CITs) are able to demonstrate and grow their multicultural competency.

Step 2. Framework Knowledge

The "culture tree" analogy (Hammond, 2015, p. 24) emphasizes that culture presents itself in many ways in multiple levels (surface, shallow, and deep), but first, we must understand the cultures and values we hold. As mentioned above, we have expanded the culture-tree analogy to represent the multicultural nature of our classrooms. In a forest, every species of tree has unique characteristics—some grow tall and fast while others grow slowly and deep, each drawing from distinct soil compositions and weather patterns. Yet, together, they form an ecosystem where diversity can enhance resilience. Likewise, in a school, each student brings their own cultural roots, traditions, and worldviews. When these different cultures grow side by side, they have the potential to create a vibrant, interdependent learning community. We strive to cultivate culturally diverse learning spaces where all students are honored, celebrated, and supported.

Step 3. Culture Mapping Activity

Provide each student with a copy of the *Core Cultural Values Mapping Tool* and explain how and why they will complete the activity. Provide them with the proper time and space to complete their worksheet independently. In our experience, students take their time, and many of them begin to reflect on their answers as they progress. Some may have clarifying questions. However, most students appreciate the independent work time to complete the task. Depending on the classroom and the relational dynamics, the instructor can provide the option to students to share their maps with a nearby partner if they finish mapping before the rest of the class; this can help facilitate the main, whole-group debrief that is on the horizon.

Step 4. Group Debrief

Bringing the class back together to process and discuss their experiences is both crucial and beneficial for learning. When Shelby conducts this activity with her students, she begins by modeling and sharing where she personally falls on the *Core Cultural Values Mapping Tool* to model how she discusses herself as a multicultural being and the values she has embraced throughout her life. It is worth mentioning that the cultural values she shares are not finite or written in stone. Values change, just as humans innately change. So, the authors encourage you to consider revisiting this activity from time to time to notice how your own values change through the years. Adding this tool to your own tool box as you work toward multicultural competence is beneficial. For Priscila, this reflective exercise shows how she has changed, and how her cultural values have shifted as she has progressively integrated into American culture. She often tells students which values are more strongly informed by her Brazilian culture, and which values she observes in her practices now after living in the United States for over a decade.

This use of self-disclosure by the instructor opens the door for students to share their experiences but also hear how *deep* culture presents within someone they have been getting to know throughout the class and/or program (e.g., while presenting and perceived as white, Shelby carries deep Hispanic cultural roots and values). The instructor can begin the debrief session by asking the following open-ended questions, allowing the classroom discussion to develop and progress organically based on students' responses.

1 After completing the Core Cultural Values Mapping activity, what was the easiest or most straight-forward value for you to map? What value was the most challenging?
2 After completing the Core Cultural Values Mapping activity, was there any value that was surprising to you?
3 Now that you've completed your own map, what have you learned about your own multiculturalism? Has this shifted or expanded the ways in which you view multiculturalism?
4 Moving forward, how do you see yourself applying this new insight, information, and/or cultural representation in personal and/or professional settings?

Final Considerations

The MLs we encounter in our schools can be identified as *third-culture kids (TCKs)* because they are growing up between two or more cultures. Research on TCKs, or more broadly, *Cross-Cultural Kids (CCK)*, both terms coined by Ruth Van Reken, shows how cultural differences play out in children's development. TCKs or CCKs are defined as someone who "is living/has lived in—or meaningfully interacted with—two or more cultural environments for a significant period of time during the first eighteen years of life" (Pollock et al., 2017, p. 43). The authors of this chapter recommend Pollock's and Van Reken's literature for the wealth of information they provide on the development of children who grow up in a culture different from that of their parents. Although TCKs are a highly heterogeneous group, they share common experiences of cultural shock and adjustment, and sometimes isolation, as they navigate multiple, and often conflicting, socio-cultural scenarios.

The research in the field often focuses on the children of diplomats, international missionaries, military, and businesspeople who live abroad for extended periods by choice or assignment. Nevertheless, more recently, it also includes the children of immigrants, refugees, temporary workers, locally displaced families, domestic minorities, and biracial/bicultural families who may or may not suffer more discrimination due to their cultural backgrounds (Pollock et al., 2017). In many cases, families do not have a choice but to relocate to a different culture by force, which adds a layer of complexity to their children's cross-cultural experiences. Even though many MLs are American born, they fit the description of TCK in the sense that they are raised in a culture different from that of their parents. TCKs often have a "neither/nor" experience of cultural adaptation. They may feel that they are neither a member of their parents' cultures nor fully a member of the host culture. Our role as school counselors, ML specialists, school staff, and counselor educators is to educate ourselves and those around us about diverse cultural values to help our students feel safe, welcomed, respected, and integrated into our school community.

School is a place where children learn "the values as well as the behavior of the local or other nation's culture (e.g., German International School of Silicon Valley, or Japanese International School in Singapore) in which it is embedded" (Pollock et al., 2017, p. 70). In a traditional, monocultural community, the school reinforces the deeper cultural traits shared at home. However, in cross-cultural contexts, the cultural values, practices, and orientations present in the school setting sometimes conflict with what TCKs learn from their parents at home. Such dissonance may leave children feeling socially disconnected from their peers, teachers, and caregivers. They may experience a sense of not belonging, and emotions such as grief, anxiety, and shame due to the mixed cultural signals they receive. Staehr Fenner and Teich (2024) add that schools have become more competitive and less accommodating for all, and MLs must navigate all the common pressures while also possibly dealing with trauma, financial instability, food insecurity, and the additional challenges of learning academic content in an additional language. "Because children often lack the words to express or understand what they feel or experience, it is vital for adults to help give them language and concepts to normalize what they are going through as they navigate their way into a new culture" (Pollock et al., 2017, p. 63).

Many school districts implement one-size-fits-all strategies to support students' socio-emotional learning, and do not take into consideration the unique needs of culturally diverse students and their families (Staehr Fenner & Teich, 2024). These practices stem from universalist beliefs informed by western philosophy (Nisbett, 2003) which support the idea that all humans perceive the world and interpret it in the same way. However, research in psychology shows that different values and attitudes based on core cultural values may affect our social interactions because of "deep differences in systems of thought" (Nisbett, 2003, p. xxi). That is, cultural and environmental differences influence how people perceive, resonate, make inferences, draw conclusions, and communicate. It is more than language and behavior; it is the cognitive processing of information, and as such, we understand that these differences influence the socio-emotional state of linguistically and culturally diverse learners.

By integrating the understanding of cultural dimensions into the professional identity development of school counselors, this chapter delineates the roles, responsibilities, and evidence-based recommendations for counselors working with MLs. It provides counselor educators and professional development leaders with detailed guidance on how to incorporate cultural mapping techniques into their training programs. As MLs increasingly constitute a significant demographic within K-12 schools, this chapter addresses a pressing need for our field. Existing scholarship predominantly addresses cultural training within the context of higher education, study abroad programs, and international business. This chapter situates the discussion within K-12 educational settings, providing a culturally responsive framework tailored to the socio-emotional and academic complexities that school counselors encounter when working with multilingual *children* and their families.

Through the lens of culturally sustaining pedagogy (Paris & Alim, 2017), this chapter offers a compelling argument for the intentional development of culturally competent school counseling practices. It advances the field by equipping practitioners with tools for self-reflection and by promoting a holistic approach to understanding and addressing the unique developmental needs of MLs.

Reflection Questions for School Counselors and Their Educators

1 What cultural values do I hold regarding communication, time, authority, and identity—and how might these influence my interpretations of student behavior and family engagement?

→ *Use the Core Cultural Values Mapping tool to examine your positioning on continuums such as individualism vs. collectivism or directness vs. indirectness.*

2 At which stage of the Developmental Model of Intercultural Sensitivity (DMIS) do I currently operate—and how does this affect my capacity to relate to students from non-dominant cultures?

→ *Consider whether you tend to minimize, judge, or integrate cultural differences.*

3 How might my own cultural background or institutional context unintentionally privilege certain cultural norms over others?

→ *Reflect on school-wide practices that may promote assimilation or acculturation rather than genuine integration of multiple cultures.*

4 When students from non-dominant cultures exhibit behaviors that differ from dominant norms, do I interpret these through a lens of difference or deficit?

→ *Recall scenarios where a student may have withdrawn socially or been misjudged and consider alternative interpretations.*

5 What am I doing—individually and collectively—to ensure that my school is not just a diverse space, but a thriving cultural ecosystem where all students, like trees in a forest, are nourished, protected, and allowed to grow authentically?

→ *Think of the "tree" and "forest" analogies of culture, including the complexities of unspoken deep values and the realities of dominance, co-dependence, and potential cultural suffocation.*

6 How can I help school staff recognize cultural variation in behavior, communication, and classroom participation—without defaulting to deficit-based assumptions or pathologizing differences?

→ *Consider how cultural norms around eye contact, silence, assertiveness, or deference may differ across communities.*

7 When a student's behavior deviates from dominant classroom norms, do I take a moment to pause, observe, and ask why—before intervening, disciplining, or labeling?

→ *Reflect on how cultural misunderstandings may escalate into unnecessary conflict or misdiagnosis.*

8 What support systems exist for students who express discomfort, fear, or disconnection not through words but through silence, withdrawal, or absence?

→ *Explore how culturally responsive counseling can recognize these as forms of communication rather than disengagement.*

9 In what ways does my school environment communicate belonging to all students—not just through language policies or celebrations, but through daily practices and relationships?

→ *Assess whether multilingual and multicultural students are empowered to belong on their own terms, not merely included on institutional terms.*

10 After completing your *Core Cultural Values Map*, go back to the beginning of this chapter and read the first paragraph again to answer the following question: How do I interpret and respond to each student described in those scenarios—and how might I help school faculty and staff process what is unfamiliar rather than label it as problematic?

→ *Consider how behaviors around touch, proximity, gender, storytelling, and emotional expression vary across cultures, and how your interpretations are shaped by your own cultural lens.*

Recommended Reading

Storti, C. (2017). *Understanding the world's cultures: 20th Anniversary edition of the classic figuring foreigners out* (2nd ed.). Nicholas Brealey Publishing.

Meyer, E. (2014). *The culture map: Breaking through the invisible boundaries of global business*. PublicAffairs.

While the authors do recommend all the literature cited in this chapter, we recognize that readers may want to be selective. They consider Storti's and Meyer's books two must-reads for anyone working with members of the world's cultures.

References

American School Counselor Association [ASCA] (2019). *The ASCA national model: A framework for school counseling programs* (4th ed.). ASCA.

American School Counselor Association [ASCA] (2022). *ASCA ethical standards for school counselors*. Alexandria, VA: ASCA.

Bennett, M. J. (1986). A developmental approach to training for intercultural sensitivity. *International Journal of Intercultural Relations, 10*(2), 179–196. https://doi.org/10.1016/0147-1767(86)90005-2

Bennett, M. J. (2014). The developmental model of intercultural sensitivity: Summary [Org]. *IDR Institute*. https://www.idrinstitute.org/dmis/

Bennett, M. J. (2017). Developmental model of intercultural sensitivity. In Y. Y. Kim (Ed.), *International encyclopedia of intercultural communication* (pp. 1–10). Wiley. https://doi.org/10.1002/9781118783665.ieicc0182

Counsel for Accreditation of Counseling and Related Educational Programs [CACREP] (2024). *2024 standards for accreditation*. CACREP.

de Oliveira, L. C., & Wachter Morris, C. (2015). *Preparing school counselors for English language learners*. TESOL Press.

Gonzales, S. K., Limberg, D., & Cunningham, K. M. (2022). Facilitating role understanding and collaboration between aspiring school counselors and principals. *Professional School Counseling, 26*(1c), 2156759X221134664.

Hammond, Z. (2015). *Culturally responsive teaching and the brain: Promoting authentic engagement and rigor among culturally and linguistically diverse students*. Corwin.

Hofstede, G., Hofstede, G. J., & Minkov, M. (2010). *Cultures and organizations: Software of the mind* (3rd ed.). McGraw Hill.

Hofstede, G. J., Pedersen, P. B., & Hofstede, G. (2012). *Exploring culture: Exercises, stories and synthetic cultures*. John Murray Business Academic.

Meyer, E. (2014). *The culture map: Breaking through the invisible boundaries of global business*. PublicAffairs.

Murphy, S., & Corpuz, I. (2025). ESEA, Title III, Part A/Multilingual Learner Program [Gov]. South Carolina Department of Education. https://ed.sc.gov/policy/federal-education-programs/esea-title-iii-part-a-multilingual-learner-program/

National Center for Education Statistics (2024, May). *English learners in public schools* [Gov]. Condition of Education. U.S. Department of Education, Institute of Education Sciences. https://nces.ed.gov/programs/coe/indicator/cgf/english-learners-in-public-schools

Nieto, S. (1992). *Affirming diversity: The sociopolitical context of multicultural education*. Longman.

Nieto, S. (2010). *Language, culture, and teaching: Critical perspectives* (2nd ed.). Routledge.

Nisbett, R. E. (2003). *The geography of thought: How Asians And Westerners think differently… And why*. Free Press.
Paige, R. M., Cohen, A. D., Kappler, B., Chi, J. C., & Lassegard, J. P. (2012). *Maximizing study abroad: A students' guide to strategies for language and culture learning and use* (2nd ed.). University of Minnesota.
Paris, D., & Alim, H. S. (Eds.). (2017). *Culturally sustaining pedagogies: Teaching and learning for justice in a changing world*. Teachers College Press.
Pollock, D. C., Reken, R. E. V., & Pollock, M. V. (2017). *Third culture kids: Growing up among worlds* (3rd ed.). Nicholas Brealey.
SCDE Early Learning (2021). [Gov]. South Carolina Department of Education [SCDE]. https://ed.sc.gov/instruction/early-learning-and-literacy/early-learning/
South Carolina Department of Social Services [SCDSS] (n.d.). SCDSS *Refugee resettlement program* [Gov]. South Carolina Department of Social Services. Retrieved June 20, 2025, from https://dss.sc.gov/assistance-programs/refugee-resettlement/
Staehr Fenner, D., & Teich, M. (2024). *Social emotional learning for multilingual learners: Essential actions for success*. Corwin.
Storti, C. (2017). *Understanding the world's cultures: 20th Anniversary edition of the classic figuring foreigners out* (2nd ed.). Nicholas Brealey Publishing.
WIDA (2020). *ACCESS for ELLs* [Edu]. WIDA. https://wida.wisc.edu/assess/access

Chapter 4

Navigating Microaggressions

School Counselors' Role in Advocating for Multilingual Learners

Victoria Giles-Vázquez and Brittani Level

Introduction

The role of the school counselor is to provide culturally responsive and evidence-based services that prioritize student well-being and advocate for an equitable school environment. Yet, the underlying purpose is singular to "design, implement and assess a school counseling program that improves life readiness and academic success for each and every student" (American School Counselor Association, 2025, p. 1). School counselors are essential members of the school leadership team and are tasked with fostering a school culture of success for all, including students who face barriers to success and whose barriers may not have established or manualized solutions. This responsibility invites counselors to expand their scope of leadership to recognizing and addressing systemic inequities experienced by students. In addition to systemic challenges focused on language fluency, multilingual learners (MLs) often face cultural barriers that negatively impact their socioemotional well-being, including identity-related prejudices and discrimination. Thus, a school counselor's preparation to work with multilingual populations necessitates the development of multicultural competency skills to support both the academic learning and socioemotional well-being of students.

CASE VIGNETTE

Lorena, a 14-year-old student from Venezuela, has been in the United States for less than a year and is still adjusting to her new school environment. While she is a diligent student with strong Spanish academic skills, she often hesitates to participate in class due to her developing English proficiency. Lorena has been experiencing subtle but recurring instances of exclusion and bias from both peers and teachers. One day, she visits her school counselor, Mr. Patel, feeling increasingly alienated. She shares that she overheard students making comments about her English skills and that a teacher dismissed her academic potential by assuming she needed remedial coursework. These experiences have left her feeling disrespected and unseen.

DOI: 10.4324/9781003711124-5

Specific Multicultural Competencies

School counselors are ethically responsible for developing and applying multicultural competency skills, including cultural self-awareness, cultural knowledge, and cultural skills (American School Counselor Association, 2019). *Cultural self-awareness* can be defined as the exploration of our knowledge, attitudes, and beliefs regarding working with diverse student populations. *Cultural knowledge* refers to a school counselor's understanding of students' cultural backgrounds, the challenges faced by different cultural groups and their members, and the systemic barriers affecting diverse student populations. *Cultural skills* include developing concrete strategies for engaging with and supporting students from diverse backgrounds in both individual counseling and systemic advocacy. According to ASCA (2021), these skills can be manifested through:

- Ensuring each student has access to a school counseling program that advocates for all students in diverse cultural groups;
- Addressing the impact that poverty and social class have on student achievement;
- Identifying the impact of family culture upon student performance;
- Delivering culturally sensitive instruction, appraisal, advisement, and counseling;
- Ensuring all students' rights are respected, and all students' needs are met;
- Consulting and collaborating with stakeholders to create a school climate that welcomes and appreciates the strengths and gifts of culturally diverse students;
- Using data to measure access to programs and to close disproportionate gaps in opportunity, information, and resources that affect achievement among diverse student populations (Henfield et al., 2014);
- Enhancing their cultural competence and facilitating the cultural awareness, knowledge, and skills of all school personnel (Ratts & Greenleaf, 2017; Ratts et al., 2015).

The School Counselor's Role

To effectively support Lorena, Mr. Patel recognizes that school counselors must engage in ongoing development of multicultural competence. This includes:

- *Cultural self-awareness:* Understanding his own biases and recognizing how his background shapes his interactions with Lorena and other MLs, and how his cultural background influences the way he relates to Lorena's family as well as other stakeholders. For example, Mr. Patel can mitigate his own biases by adopting a humble, mindful, and internally motivated approach to fairness.
- *Cultural knowledge:* Learning about Lorena's cultural background, the challenges immigrant students like Lorena face, and the systemic barriers

affecting MLs. For example, Mr. Patel can pursue professional development in best practices for supporting MLs and in establishing relationships with community resources that serve MLs and their families.

- *Cultural skills:* Developing concrete strategies for engaging with Lorena and other ML students at school. For example, it can involve collecting data on ML learners' academic engagement and presenting these findings to school staff, while encouraging teachers and staff to examine their own biases and develop more inclusive classroom practices. Additionally, he can learn about Lorena's personal strengths and cultural values to understand and implement coping strategies in response to microaggressions.

Identifying Microaggressions

Multicultural competency skills development is an ongoing, dynamic process that requires counselors to integrate self-awareness, knowledge, and actionable strategies to promote student safety. This developmental process is rooted in the counselor's ability to deepen their understanding of how power, prejudice, and institutional norms impact student well-being. As multicultural competence deepens, counselors are better positioned to identify and mitigate students' experiences of harm, ranging from structural inequities to subtle interpersonal interactions. Indeed, one of the clearest markers of multicultural competence is the ability to recognize and address microaggressions, which often go unnoticed, unchallenged, or normalized despite their cumulative and significant socioemotional impact.

CASE VIGNETTE: RECOGNIZING THE PROBLEM

After speaking with Lorena, Mr. Patel realizes that she is facing microaggressions that undermine her confidence and well-being. During their conversation, she shares that she often feels overlooked, unwelcome, and judged by both teachers and peers. In class, she notices that her teacher rarely calls on her compared with other students, which makes her feel invisible and undermines her academic confidence. Outside of class, she was reprimanded by a staff member for speaking Spanish with a friend in the hallway, leaving her feeling ashamed. Group projects have become particularly stressful, as her classmates express frustration about working with her, assuming that she cannot contribute effectively. Beyond these daily interactions, Lorena carries a deep and constant worry that her loved ones may be at risk of being deported by the U.S. Immigration and Customs Enforcement (ICE), making it difficult to focus on her studies and fully engage in school life. Mr. Patel validates Lorena's experiences and shares that what she is experiencing are microaggressions—subtle yet harmful comments or behaviors that convey negative messages about her identity.

Defining Microaggressions

Microaggressions are defined as "brief and commonplace daily verbal, behavioral, or environmental indignities, whether intentional or unintentional, that communicate hostile, derogatory, or negative racial slights and insults toward people of color" (Sue et al., 2007, p. 273). Individuals who enact microaggressions are often unaware that they engage in such behaviors, making them especially difficult to identify and address. The lack of insight among perpetrators of microaggressions also impedes individuals' accountability for the harm they may have caused and undermines motivation to change these behaviors, fostering defensiveness.

Microaggressions are categorized into the main forms: microinsults, microinvalidations, and microassaults. *Microinsults*, often unconscious and unintentional, are subtle verbal and nonverbal behaviors that demean a person's racial identity or heritage. For example, assuming that an Asian American person is naturally good at math, being surprised by a Latina student being articulate, and colorblind statements such as "I don't see color" are all versions of microinsults. *Microinvalidations* are verbal behaviors that negate, dismiss, or nullify the experiences of people of color, often in subtle yet insulting ways, and are usually unknown to the perpetrator. Microinvalidations can take shape through denial of racial bias, such as the statement "As a woman, I know exactly what you are going through as a person of color," or dismissing racism as an issue, such as the statement "We have had a Black president, racism doesn't exist in this country." *Microassaults*, often conscious and intentional, are explicit racial derogations characterized primarily by a verbal or nonverbal attack meant to hurt the intended victim through name-calling, avoidant behavior, or purposeful discriminatory actions. Microassaults are often what most people perceive as "old-fashioned racism" and are typically intentional. For example, microassaults can take the form of racist slurs, racist jokes, displaying a Confederate flag or swastika, and using the Nazi salute (Sue et al., 2007).

These microaggressions occur most often across interpersonal interactions, as depicted above, but they are also manifested in systemic and environmental contexts. Environmental microaggressions are reflected through institutional and systemic bias and reinforce the idea that people of color are less valued or erased in society. Environmental microaggressions can be exemplified by a lack of representation in leadership, unequal access to resources, and workplace exclusions such as dress codes that ban natural Black hairstyles.

In the school context, the impact of microaggressions becomes compounded and pervasive, resulting in a socioemotional culture of exclusion that signals who belongs and who is pushed to the margins. Referring back to the case vignette, microaggressions take shape through:

- *Microinsult:* A teacher frequently calls on her less often than other students, assuming she cannot fully engage in discussions. The teacher's behavior conveys a hidden message that she believes Lorena is less capable than her peers.

- *Microinvalidation:* When speaking Spanish with a friend in the hallway, she was told by a staff member to "speak English" at school. The staff member is effectively dismissing her linguistic and cultural identity and sends the message that her native language is unwelcome.
- *Microinsults:* During group projects, classmates express frustration about working with her, assuming she is incapable of keeping up. In this example, the microinsult is conveyed by an ascription of intelligence, assuming that Lorena is less intelligent or academically competent than her classmates because of her status as an ML.
- *Environmental microaggression:* Lorena is constantly worried at school that one of her loved ones will be removed from the country by ICE. This example reflects broader systemic issues that disproportionately impact immigrant communities, creating an ongoing sense of instability and distress.

Skills for Identification

To effectively address these issues, Mr. Patel begins to track patterns of microaggressions in the school environment. He also trains himself and staff to:

- Listen carefully to students like Lorena when they report exclusionary experiences.
- Observe classroom dynamics and interactions among students.
- Recognize coded language or implicit biases in staff conversations about MLs.
- Stay updated on laws and legislation that may disproportionately impact MLs.

Microintervention and Microaffirmation Strategies to Mitigate Microaggressions

Microinterventions and microaffirmations are strategies that school counselors can use to mitigate microaggressions through immediacy skills and affirmative practices that foster a climate of belonging. Together, these culturally competent interventions are essential to cultivating inclusion through the school system and culture. In this section, we will continue to utilize the case vignette to depict a real-life situation that school counselors may face regarding mitigating microaggressions experienced by MLs. We will then define microintervention strategies, the microaffirmation framework for implementation in schools, provide strategies for various stakeholders, and identify and apply the skills outlined at the end of the chapter.

Case Vignette Expansion: Mitigating Microaggressions

During a counseling session with Mr. Patel, Lorena shares recent experiences that have made her feel unwelcome at school. She describes how, in her history class, some classmates whisper among themselves when she takes longer to respond to questions. A few weeks ago, one student mockingly repeated her words when she mispronounced a term, causing the rest of the group to laugh. The teacher didn't address the incident, simply moving on with the lesson. Lorena tells Mr. Patel that she has started speaking less in class because she doesn't want to be ridiculed. Mr. Patel listens attentively and validates her feelings. He values a strength-based approach when working with students, so he relates to Lorena by explaining that what she is experiencing are microaggressions—subtle yet harmful comments and behaviors that can make MLs feel alienated. He reassures Lorena that she belongs and that her bilingualism and lived experience are assets, not deficits.

Recognizing that Lorena's experiences are not isolated, Mr. Patel seeks supervision and collaborates with other professionals with expertise in this area to develop a professional development presentation for teachers and school staff that helps them understand microaggressions and identify strategies to mitigate them. He provides concrete examples, including Lorena's experiences, to highlight the impact of subtle biases on students' confidence and participation. He also introduces *microintervention strategies* to help teachers respond to and prevent such occurrences in real time.

Defining Microintervention Strategies

It is important to remember that school counselors are called to act as social justice agents and must use their position of power to advocate for students and prevent further harm (American School Counselor Association, 2019). School counselors are trained and positioned to know practical, evidence-based interventions to help school communities process the negative impacts of microaggressions and daily racism (Rolón-Dow & Davison, 2018). By implementing microinterventions, school counselors build their capacity to respond effectively to students' individual needs and to model inclusive care within their respective school environments.

Sue et al. (2019) developed a strategic framework for addressing microaggressions that provides concrete action steps and dialogues that targets of microaggressions, allies, and bystanders can perform. These strategies are known as microinterventions, or interpersonal tools that are intended to counteract, change, or stop microaggressions by subtly or overtly confronting and educating the perpetrator. Microinterventions also communicate to the person experiencing microaggressions that their experiential reality is valid, that their value as a person is affirmed, that their racial or group identity is affirmed, that support and encouragement are provided, and that they are not alone (Sue et al., 2019). There are two main strategies used when implementing microinterventions. The first is to enhance psychological well-being and provide those using microinterventions a sense of control and efficacy. Second, microinterventions are also used to provide a concrete action plan for responding that can directly disarm or counteract the effects of microaggressions by challenging those who engaged in the microaggression. There are four goals when engaging in microinterventions: Make the "Invisible" Visible, Disarm the Microaggression, Educate the Offender, and Seek External Intervention.

Making the "Invisible" Visible focuses on identifying and articulating a microaggression to bring it to the attention of the person who committed it. This action also highlights potential subconscious metacommunication of which the offender may be unaware and provides an opportunity for others in the social space to raise their awareness of microaggressions and to model appropriate responses. For example:

- *Microaggression:* A teacher consistently mispronounces a student's name or uses a nickname the student hasn't chosen.
- *Microintervention (Making It Visible):* "I've noticed the student has corrected their name a few times—would it help to practice it together so we're saying it right?"
- *Disarming the microaggression* includes a more direct and confrontative approach to mitigating microaggressions. This goal is realized by stopping or deflecting the comments or actions through expressing disagreement, challenging what was said or done, and/or pointing out its harmful impact (Sue et al., 2019). In other words, it is about addressing microaggressive behavior to prevent further harm while maintaining professional conduct and respectful communication. For example:
    - *Microaggression:* A student says to another, "You don't even look Mexican."
    - *Microintervention (Disarming):* "Hey, that's not okay—comments like that can be hurtful, even if you didn't mean it that way. Let's talk about it."

Microinterventions are intended to be educational, not punitive. As school counselors, social-emotional learning is a core component of our work, supporting students' well-being and promoting a more supportive school climate. This aligns with the third goal of microinterventions, *Educating the Offender*, where the ultimate hope is to educate the person being held accountable by engaging them in a dialogue about what they have done that has proven offensive, what it says about their beliefs and values, and have them consider the worldview of marginalized group members (Goodman, 2011). This action promotes the tenets of social-emotional learning, including fostering self-awareness in the person who caused harm, strengthening social awareness for all involved, developing relationship skills by confronting ruptures and creating opportunities to repair harm, and supporting responsible decision-making. For example:

- *Microaggression:* A teacher says to an immigrant parent, "It's just hard when families don't value education."
- *Microintervention (Educating the Offender):* "Actually, research shows immigrant families often highly value education—it's just that they may express it differently or face more systemic challenges in participating."

Lastly, seeking external reinforcement or support may be necessary to mitigate harmful microaggressions. The fourth goal of microinterventions, *Seeking External Intervention,* is used when a situation escalates, the harm is consistent or severe, or when someone in a position of power needs to be involved to ensure safety and accountability. Involving institutional authorities may be necessary when (a) a strong power differential exists between perpetrator and target, (b) the microaggression is blatant and immediately harmful (microassault), (c) it would be risky to respond personally, or (d) institutional changes must be implemented (Sue et al., 2019). It is important to center the focus on impact, not intention, and to emphasize the responsibility to protect students, not punish staff. Furthermore, it is essential to be mindful of how our engagement in *Seeking External Intervention,* especially when seeking accountability, so we do not unintentionally uphold a punitive mindset or authoritarian disciplinary approach for students and instead promote restorative practices and opportunities for social-emotional learning. For example:

- *Microaggression (microassault):* A student previously disciplined for racist behavior bars another student of color from using the bathroom while making racist remarks and posing in a threatening manner.
- *Microintervention (Seeking External Intervention):* The counselor meets with the student individually to explore what led to the comment and its impact. The principal initiates disciplinary action in accordance with the student's behavioral action plan. The student is invited to a restorative circle (with consent from the harmed student) to hear the impact, take responsibility, and co-create repair.

Additionally, this goal highlights seeking support from others as an aspect of self-care for those engaged in this work. Some essential actions that can be taken are to find a support group, utilize community services, engage in a buddy system, or seek advice and counseling from understanding professionals. These external sources are intended to enable advocates to express their emotions safely, connect with others who validate and affirm their being, and receive advice and suggestions. Ultimately, the goal is also to prepare advocates for anticipated challenges and to build capacity to manage the stresses of social justice work (Sue et al., 2019).

Considerations for Microintervention Strategies

It is important to note that microaggressions are often invisible to both the perpetrator and the recipient. Moreover, most White Americans experience themselves as good, moral, and ethical, and hold the illusion of subjectivity. Thus, it can be difficult for individuals to believe they possess biased racial attitudes and are capable of engaging in microaggressions (Sue, 2004). This tendency toward ethical blind spots promotes experiential avoidance of reckoning with the harm caused and resists accountability by the initiator of the microaggression. Due to this moral superiority bias, microaggressive acts can often be rationalized as seemingly unbiased and valid, leaving the recipient of the aggression with a nagging question: *"Did it really happen?"* (Crocker & Major, 1989).

It can be challenging to identify a microaggression when other explanations seem plausible and more socially accepted. Therefore, it is imperative to amplify the voices of those who are on the receiving end through cultural humility. *Cultural humility* can be defined as "a lifelong commitment to self-evaluation and self-critique, to redressing the power imbalances… and to developing mutually beneficial and non-paternalistic partnerships with communities" (Tervalon & Murray-García, 1998, p. 123). Additionally, cultural humility is reflected in ethical and professional standards that call for ongoing self-reflection, recognition of power and privilege, and commitment to lifelong learning to honor and affirm the diverse cultural identities of clients and students (ASCA, 2014; ASCA, 2022; Ratts et al., 2016). Thus, school counselors must uphold a commitment to self-awareness, cultural humility, and a willingness to learn about cultures that are different from their own. Through this process, one can be better positioned to both identify and avoid microaggressions and to rectify harm if they occur, rather than engaging in harmful denial or avoidance of the subject.

Another consideration in the context of engaging in microinterventions is that, at times, it is "often problematic to ask people of color to educate or confront perpetrators when the sting of prejudice and discrimination pains them" (Sue et al., 2019, p. 131). When possible, it is best practice for an ally or bystander to mitigate the microaggression, especially considering the harmful impacts of marginalized stress. *Marginalized stress* refers to the additional stress that individuals from marginalized groups experience due to their minority status, often resulting from actual and/or anticipated discrimination, prejudice, and social stigma (Sue et al., 2019). To support students experiencing marginalized stress, school counselors can also support MLLs by helping them identify and implement coping strategies for those who have been harmed (see Sue et al., 2019, for a list).

Defining and Implementing Microaffirmations

It has been shown that students as young as those in middle school have expressed awareness of microaggressions from peers and teachers (Banks et al., 2020). Additionally, the negative consequences of microaggression in youth have been studied and include sleep disturbances, low self-esteem, and trauma-related symptoms, including anxiety and depression (Burleigh & Wilson, 2021; Steketee et al., 2021). One strategy to prevent and mitigate microaggressions is the practice of *microaffirmations,* which are "small acts of active listening that encourage feelings of inclusion and shared cultural intimacy" (Boyce-Rosen & Mecadon-Mann, 2023, p. 2). Thus, effectively implementing microaffirmations is essential for school counselors to buffer against the adverse effects of microaggressions in school settings.

Layered Framework for Implementing Microaffirmations in Schools (LFIMS)

To mitigate the impact of microaggressions in the school setting, Boyce-Rosen & Mecadon-Mann developed a layered framework for implementing microaffirmations into everyday K–12 practice named the Layered Framework for Implementing Microaffirmations in Schools (LFIMS) (2023). The framework comprises four layers, including microrecognitions, microvalidations, microtransformations, and microprotections. In the LFIMS, each layer identifies a level of microaffirmation that builds on the preceding layer.

The first layer, *Microrecognitions*, is the recognition of presence or identity, and can be visual, verbal, or through action. For example, inclusive signs and symbols in the classroom, such as a "Black Lives Matter" sticker or a "Safe Space" poster, can signify a sense of welcome and belonging (Rolón-Dow & Davison, 2018). They are also practiced verbally by using students' correct pronouns, avoiding deadnaming, and pronouncing names correctly (Anzani et al., 2019; Rolón-Dow & Davison, 2018). Microrecognitions also involve eliminating marginalization within a group, such as removing gender from classroom games and competitions (Pérez Huber et al., 2021; Rolón-Dow & Davison, 2018).

Next, *Microvalidations* involve recognition of presence or identity through active listening, appreciative inquiry and shared cultural intimacy. Educators and providers create classrooms or student spaces where students can work collaboratively to understand and celebrate diversity (Molina et al., 2019; Pérez Huber et al., 2021; Rolón-Dow & Davison, 2018). It is necessary to provide socio-emotional learning opportunities for students to develop the skills needed to engage in culturally intimate conversations in the classroom (Betters-Bubon et al., 2022).

Microtransformations focus on creating and facilitating a sense of belonging (Boyce-Rosen & Mecadon-Mann, 2023). This layer includes initiating welcoming conversations about race, identity, and prejudice, seeking opportunities for mentorship for marginalized students, and encouraging students to connect with community groups that celebrate their shared identity (Boyce-Rosen & Mecadon-Mann, 2023). For example, a school counselor may consider organizing a small-group lunch-and-learn session for MLs to build mentoring relationships with immigrant professionals in the community. Another consideration is supporting students in finding or forming student groups that celebrate a shared identity, such as a Black Student Union, a Gender and Sexuality program for multilingual students student organization (Pérez Huber et al., 2021; Rolón-Dow & Davison, 2018). Lastly, *Microprotections* are tools for stepping in to interrupt or counteract racist, ableist, or homophobic words and actions (Boyce-Rosen & Mecadon-Mann, 2023). This last layer comprises the microinterventions discussed at the beginning of this section: making the invisible visible, disarming microaggressions, educating the offender, and seeking external intervention. In addition to implementing microaffirmations, multiculturally competent school counselors initiate ongoing, intentional dialogue about culture and identity with students, a core multicultural counseling skill known as broaching.

Broaching, a multicultural clinical skill coined in 2007, is a method for counselors to explore cultural differences in session (Day-Vines et al., 2007). Broaching is a process by which counselors bring the cultural characteristics of the client and the counselor into the room and invite clients to explore the relevance of those characteristics (Jones & Welfare, 2017). School counselors can use this skill as an invitation to learn more about the students they work with to increase their sense of belonging within the school community. For example, school counselors can invite students to engage in dialogue about their cultural backgrounds and explore similarities and differences within social-emotional learning student groups.

Evidence-Based Practice

Evidence-based practice for school counselors is a crucial tool for building comprehensive school programs (Zyromski & Dimmitt, 2022). The evidence-based school process includes: (a) assessing a school's areas of strength and growth, (b) identifying an appropriate and needs-aligned approach, and (c) evaluating outcomes to determine implications for practice (Zyromski & Dimmitt, 2022). Engaging in the evidence-based school counseling approach ensures appropriate and personalized implementation of microaffirmations in the school setting.

The following examples demonstrate how microaffirmations and microinterventions can be implemented to support MLs (MLLs) based on stakeholder roles (Zyromski & Dimmitt, 2022):

Teachers:

- *Microintervention—Making the Invisible Visible:* Provide training on recognizing and interrupting microaggressions.
- *Microvalidation—Active Listening & Cultural Intimacy:* Encourage culturally responsive teaching practices.
- *Microrecognitions—Recognizing Linguistic Diversity:* Normalize linguistic diversity in the classroom.

Peers:

- *Microintervention—Disarming the Microaggression:* Establish student-led cultural competency initiatives.
- *Microtransformations—Creating a Sense of Belonging:* Create inclusive group work guidelines.

Administrators & Staff:

- *Microintervention—Policy-Level Change & Seeking External Support:* Implement policies that promote linguistic inclusivity (e.g., allowing students to use their home language in non-instructional settings).

- *Microprotections—Educating & Preventing Harm:* Provide structured opportunities for teachers to reflect on biases.

Skills for Identification

A few weeks later, while observing a history class, Mr. Patel, the school counselor, sees an opportunity to apply what was discussed in training. Lorena hesitates before answering a question, and a classmate rolls their eyes and mutters, "This is taking forever." The teacher glances at Lorena but hesitates, unsure how to respond. Recognizing the moment as a learning opportunity, Mr. Patel immediately intervenes.

Microinterventions:

- *Disarm the microaggression:* "Let's be mindful of how we treat our classmates. Everyone deserves respect in this space."
- *Educate the offender:* "It's important to be patient when working with multilingual learners. Being bilingual is a strength, not a weakness."
- *Support the teacher:* After class, Mr. Patel speaks privately with the teacher, offering strategies to foster an inclusive classroom environment and providing resources on responding to microaggressions effectively.
- *Seek external support:* Mr. Patel follows up with Lorena's other teachers, ensuring they are aware of ways to support MLs and prevent similar incidents.
- *Broaching:* Mr. Patel initiates the disclosure that he is aware of how the current socio-political climate is impacting Lorena's community and invites Lorena to process this topic only if she consents to do so. Mr. Patel also shares with Lorena that he is a first-generation immigrant who also needed in-school support as an MLL and invites Lorena to dialogue about similarities and differences between their identities.

Microaffirmations:

- *Microrecognition—Visibility & Representation:* Mr. Patel collaborates with the history teacher to incorporate diverse perspectives, including the contributions of multilingual historical figures, reinforcing the value of linguistic diversity.
- *Microvalidation—Active Listening & Appreciation:* After class, Mr. Patel checks in with Lorena: "I noticed you were taking your time to think through your answer, which is a great skill. I want to make sure you know that your voice matters, and I appreciate your contributions."
- *Microtransformation—Creating a Sense of Belonging:* Mr. Patel connects Lorena with a peer mentoring program for multilingual students and organizes a schoolwide initiative celebrating linguistic diversity, encouraging students to share words from their home languages during morning announcements.

- *Microprotection—Preventing Future Harm:* Mr. Patel advocates for professional development sessions focused on linguistic inclusivity and implicit bias, ensuring teachers feel empowered to intervene in similar situations.

Advocating for MLs in the Context of Subtle Transgressions

CASE VIGNETTE EXPANSION: ADVOCACY IN ACTION

Lorena's experience highlights the need for systemic change. Mr. Patel takes steps to advocate for her and other MLs by:

- Educating staff on the impact of microaggressions and promoting inclusive language policies.
- Creating a school-wide initiative that celebrates linguistic diversity, including hosting a Multilingual Student Awareness Week.
- Developing peer mentorship programs where MLs are paired with supportive peers.

What Does Advocacy Look Like?

Advocacy in schools can take many forms for school counselors. At the *individual level,* school counselors support students like Lorena in building resilience and confidence through individual and group counseling services, advocate for their socioemotional needs within the context of individualized education plans, and conduct microvalidations. School counselors can provide advocacy at the *classroom level* through partnering with teachers to implement inclusive pedagogical strategies, engaging in microtransformations to create a sense of belonging (ex. peer mentoring program for multilingual students, organizing a schoolwide initiative celebrating linguistic diversity, etc.), and engaging school leadership in implementing the microintervention "seeking external intervention" to mitigate harm caused by microaggressions in school. At the *school-wide level,* school counselors may engage in microprotection by promoting policies that support MLs' rights as part of their advocacy work. Finally, school counselors enact advocacy at the *community level* by engaging parents and families in discussions about cultural inclusivity.

Conclusion: Lorena's Growth and Schoolwide Change

Over time, Lorena becomes more confident at school. With Mr. Patel's support, she joins a student advocacy group that promotes linguistic diversity. Teachers have become more mindful of their language and interactions, and the school now has clearer policies on addressing microaggressions. This vignette illustrates how school counselors can move beyond merely identifying microaggressions to implementing meaningful interventions and advocacy. By prioritizing multicultural competence, actively mitigating harm, and championing multilingual students, school counselors can create an environment where all students feel seen, valued, and empowered.

References

American Counseling Association (2014). *2014 ACA code of ethics*. https://www.counseling.org/docs/default-source/default-document-library/2014-code-of-ethics-finaladdress.pdf

American School Counselor Association (2019). *ASCA national model: A framework for school counseling programs* (4th ed.). ASCA.

American School Counselor Association (2021). *The school counselor and cultural diversity*. American School Counselor Association.

American School Counselor Association (2022). *ASCA ethical standards for school counselors*. American School Counselor Association. https://www.schoolcounselor.org/Standards-Positions/Position-Statements/ASCA-Position-Statements/The-School-Counselor-and-Cultural-Diversity

Anzani, A., Morris, E. R., & Galupo, M. P. (2019). From absence of microaggressions to seeing authentic gender: Transgender clients' experiences with microaffirmations in therapy. *Journal of LGBT Issues in Counseling*, *13*(4), 258–275. https://doi.org/10.1080/15538605.2019.1662359

Banks, B. M., Cicciarelli, K. S., & Pavon, J. (2020). It offends us too! An exploratory analysis of high school-based microaggressions. *Contemporary School Psychology*, *26*(2), 182–194. https://doi-org.libproxy.uncg.edu/10.1007/s40688-020-00300-1

Betters-Bubon, J., Pianta, R., Sweeney, D., & Goodman-Scott, E. (2022). Antiracism starts with us: School counselor critical reflection within a multitiered systems of support framework. *Professional School Counseling*, *26*(1a). https://doi.org/10.1177/2156759X221086747 (Original work published 2022)

Boyce-Rosen, N., & Mecadon-Mann, M. (2023). Microaffirmations: Small gestures toward equity and advocacy. *Professional School Counseling*, *27*(1a). https://doi.org/10.1177/2156759X231160722

Burleigh, C. L., & Wilson, A. M. (2021). Teachers' awareness in identifying microaggressive behaviors within the k-12 classroom. *Social Psychology of Education*, *24*(1), 143–116. https://doi-org.libproxy.uncg.edu/10.1007/s11218-020-09604-9

Crocker, J., & Major, B. (1989). Social stigma and self-esteem: The self-protective properties of stigma. *Psychological Review*, *96*(4), 608–630. https://doi.org/10.1037/0033-295X.96.4.608

Day-Vines, N. L., Wood, S. M., Grothaus, T., Craigen, L., Holman, A., Dotson-Blake, K., & Douglass, M. J. (2007). Broaching the subjects of race, ethnicity, and culture during the counseling process. *Journal of Counseling & Development*, *85*(4), 401–409. https://doi.org/10.1002/j.1556-6678.2007.tb00608.x

Goodman, D. J. (2011). *Promoting diversity and social justice: Educating people from privileged groups* (2nd ed.). Taylor & Francis. http://public.ebookcentral.proquest.com/choice/publicfullrecord.aspx?p=683962

Henfield, M. S., Washington, A. R., & Byrd, J. A. (2014). Addressing academic and opportunity gaps impacting gifted Black males: Implications for school counselors. *Gifted Child Today*, *37*(3), 147–154. https://doi.org/10.1177/1076217514530118

Jones, C. T., & Welfare, L. E. (2017). Broaching behaviors of licensed professional counselors: A qualitative inquiry. *Journal of Addictions & Offender Counseling, 38*(1), 48–64. https://doi.org/10.1002/jaoc.12028

Molina, R. L., Ricciotti, H., Chie, L., Luckett, R., Wylie, B. J., Woolcock, E., & Scott, J. (2019). Creating a culture of micro-affirmations to overcome gender-based microinequities in academic medicine. *The American Journal of Medicine, 132*(7), 785–787. https://doi.org/10.1016/j.amjmed.2019.01.028

Pérez Huber, L., Gonzalez, T., Robles, G., & Solórzano, D. G. (2021). Racial microaffirmations as a response to racial microaggressions: Exploring risk and protective factors. *New Ideas in Psychology, 63*, Article 100880. https://doi.org/10.1016/j.newideapsych.2021.100880

Ratts, M., Singh, A., Nassar-McMillian, S., Butler, S., & McCullough, J. (2016). Multicultural and social justice counseling competencies: Guidelines for the counseling profession. *Journal of Multicultural Counseling and Development, 44*, 28–48.

Ratts, M. J., & Greenleaf, A. T. (2017). Multicultural and social justice counseling competencies: A leadership framework for professional school counselors. *Professional School Counseling*. https://doi.org/10.1177/2156759X18773582

Ratts, M. J., Singh, A. A., Nassar-McMillan, S., Butler, S. K., & McCullough, J. R. (2015). Multicultural and social justice counseling competencies. Retrieved from https://www.counseling.org/docs/default-source/competencies/multicultural-and-social-justice-counseling-competencies.pdf?sfvrsn=8573422c_20

Rolón-Dow, R., & Davison, A. (2018). Racial microaffirmations: Learning from student stories of moments that matter. *Diversity Discourse: CSD Research Briefs, 1*(4), 1–9. http://udspace.udel.edu/handle/19716/23723

Steketee, A., Williams, M. T., Valencia, B. T., Printz, D., & Hooper, L. M. (2021). Racial and language microaggressions in the school ecology. *Perspectives on Psychological Science, 16*(5), 1075–1098.

Sue, D. W. (2004). Whiteness and ethnocentric monoculturalism: Making the "invisible" visible. *American Psychologist, 59*(8), 761–769. https://doi.org/10.1037/0003-066X.59.8.761. https://doi.org/10.1037/0003-066X.59.8.761

Sue, D. W. (2005). Racism and the conspiracy of silence: Presidential address. *The Counseling Psychologist, 33*(1), 100–114.

Sue, D. W., Alsaidi, S., Awad, M. N., Glaeser, E., Calle, C. Z., & Mendez, N. (2019). Disarming racial microaggressions: Microintervention strategies for targets, White allies, and bystanders. *American Psychologist, 74*(1), 128–142. https://doi.org/10.1037/amp0000296

Sue, D. W., Capodilupo, C. M., Torino, G. C., Bucceri, J. M., Holder, A. M. B., Nadal, K. L., & Esquilin, M. (2007). Racial microaggressions in everyday life: Implications for clinical practice. *American Psychologist, 62*(4), 271–286. https://doi.org/10.1037/0003-066X.62.4.271

Teachers College, Columbia University (2024, July). Education's future for English learners must start now. Retrieved from https://www.tc.columbia.edu/articles/2024/july/educations-future-for-english-learners-must-start-now/

Tervalon, M., & Murray-García, J. (1998). Cultural humility versus cultural competence: A critical distinction in defining physician training outcomes in multicultural education. *Journal of Health Care for the Poor and Underserved, 9*(2), 117–125. https://doi.org/10.1353/hpu.2010.0233

Zyromski, B., & Dimmitt, C. (2022). Evidence-based school counseling: Embracing challenges/changes to the existing paradigm. *Professional School Counseling, 26*(1a), 2156759X2210867. https://doi-org.libproxy.uncg.edu/10.1177/2156759x221086729

Chapter 5

Fostering Belonging and Well-Being among Multilingual Learners

Strategies for School Counselors Through an Equity Lens

Bruno Andrade

Social-emotional Learning as Not the End-Point

The counselors' meeting was unusually quiet that afternoon, the kind of quiet that settles after a long day of holding other people's emotions. Around the table, six school counselors from an international school in São Paulo gathered for their monthly roundtable—a space meant for professional exchange, but one that had slowly become a place to exhale. "Sometimes," one counselor began, "I feel like my students become invisible the moment English enters the room."

She shared a recent group session in which a multilingual learner (ML) described feeling "invisible." When she gently asked why, the student hesitated, then said, "Because I don't know how to feel in another language." The table fell still. Heads nodded. Eyes dropped. There was recognition in the silence.

Another counselor, who had been listening closely, added her own story. A child in her care, still new to the school, had begun drawing elaborate scenes during social-emotional learning (SEL) circles—forests, oceans, spirals of color—illustrations that carried emotions he could not yet name in English. "We're supposed to help them identify their feelings," she said softly. "But whose feelings are we teaching them to name? In whose language? On whose terms?"

A third counselor recalled a Grade 6 student who had recently moved from Seoul. During an SEL session on naming emotions, the student remained quiet while classmates offered words like happy, frustrated, worried. Only later, in a private moment, did he offer a Korean word: 정 (jeong). "It's when you feel something strong for people you know… not just love, but something warm and deep," he explained. "I feel it for my grandmother. But there's no word for it in English."

This counselor began inviting all students to contribute emotion words from their home languages—terms for feelings English does not quite reach, like *saudade*.[1] Slowly, a multilingual lexicon grew on the classroom wall. Students pointed to it during SEL sessions, sometimes switching languages mid-sentence, sometimes tracing a word with their fingers instead of speaking it aloud. The circle shifted: less about fluency, more about belonging.

DOI: 10.4324/9781003711124-6

Across the room, there was a collective exhale—the kind that comes when someone has articulated something everyone has been carrying. These stories, woven together, revealed a shared truth: MLs navigate emotional geographies far more complex than any SEL checklist could capture. And the counselors supporting them do so within systems that often fail to see the full weight of that complexity.

This chapter, thus, begins with the subtle tensions and ethical dilemmas that MLs navigate in the emotional geographies of Brazil's international schools. It begins with a simple observation: that SEL, as it is commonly implemented, often assumes emotion is universal, and belonging is neutral. In São Paulo, a city built through layered migrations and racial hierarchies, students arrive carrying not just multiple passports, but multiple grammars of being. For them, feeling safe, seen, or supported cannot be reduced to behavioral competencies or English-only checklists. Their emotional lives are mediated by language, race, class, and memory.

The international school sector in Brazil has long been positioned as a gateway to global citizenship, social capital, academic excellence, and linguistic prestige. But beneath its cosmopolitan veneer lies a pedagogical terrain structured by epistemic erasures, colonial inheritances, and deep inequities. The SEL frameworks widely used in these schools are often imported wholesale from the Global North,[2] rarely interrogating the power relations they carry or the forms of cultural translation they require. Language is not simply a medium; it is a site where identity, agency, and exclusion are constantly negotiated (Arthur, 2004; Cummins, 2000). Ignoring this is not neutral; it is violent.

This chapter, therefore, explores how school counselors, often positioned at the intersection of care, compliance, and cultural brokerage, navigate such tensions. It asks: How can SEL be reimagined as a space where MLs are not asked to leave parts of themselves at the door? What would it mean for school counseling to treat linguistic plurality not as a barrier to emotional development, but as its very foundation?

Drawing on a small-scale qualitative study conducted between March and May 2025, the chapter presents the voices and experiences of nine counselors working in international schools in São Paulo. These are not intended as representative samples, but as situated knowledges—testimonies that emerge from the everyday pedagogical and ethical labor of making students feel seen, heard, and thus valued. Methodologically, the chapter follows a narrative and relational approach, treating interviews not as data extraction but as moments of co-construction. Counselors are not neutral technicians; they are feeling, interpreting, improvising subjects within institutions that demand performance but rarely offer structural support.

Rather than offering a technocratic model for "inclusive" SEL, the chapter foregrounds discomfort, contradiction, and emergence. It examines the ways counselors make space for mother tongues in moments of crisis, reframe emotional literacy in contexts of linguistic hybridity, and confront the institutional pushback that often arises when race, language, and belonging are named in the same sentence. The São Paulo context which is rich in diversity, but rife with inequalities, demands such interrogation.

In doing so, this chapter contributes to a growing body of work that reframes SEL not as a universal solution, but as a culturally contested practice. It joins calls to reimagine school counseling as a site of linguistic and social justice (Asempapa, 2019; Martin et al., 2017), particularly in Global South contexts, where dominant frameworks too often obscure the voices and needs of racialized, marginalized and multilingual students. Here, SEL is not the endpoint. It is the terrain. And multilingual students are not problems to be solved, they are theorists of their own experience. This chapter simply tries to listen.

Listening Otherwise: Method, Ethics, and Positionality in Motion

This chapter is not a neutral report. It is a response to a field saturated with global scripts and local silences. To research school counseling for MLs in São Paulo's international schools is to step into a terrain shaped by language hierarchies, racialized expectations, and institutional discomfort. It demands not detachment, but ethical involvement; not objectivity, but situated listening. In this section, I outline the methodology, ethical stance, and positionality that shape the inquiry, not as prefaces to the "real" data, but as constitutive elements of the knowledge produced.

Walking the Edges: Design as Inquiry, Not a Blueprint

This study adopts a qualitative, exploratory design, grounded in narrative inquiry and critical interpretive frameworks. Data collection unfolded in two phases: first, an open-ended questionnaire to identify key practices, perceptions, and tensions related to counseling MLs; second, semi-structured interviews with nine school counselors working in international schools in São Paulo. Participants were selected through purposive sampling, based on their direct involvement in SEL and their experience navigating culturally and linguistically diverse school environments.

The research design is intentionally situated, non-linear, and reflexive. Instead of seeking generalizability, it aims for contextual, relational, and affective dimensions. In this spirit, analysis was guided by diffractive methodology (Barad, 2007), a framework that resists simple reflection or categorization. Diffraction (Barad, 2007; Mazzei, 2014; Ulmer, 2016) encourages the researcher to notice how knowledge emerges through entanglement between theory and data, self and other, voice and silence. It asks: how do institutional forces, emotional labor, and positionalities interfere with what is said, how it is said, and what remains unsaid?

This methodological approach is especially relevant for a study that explores school counseling practices in the context of equity, inclusion and multilingualism. In counseling, as in research, meaning is rarely clear-cut. Counselors often listen for what is beneath the surface: a hesitation, a contradiction, a shift in language (see de Oliveira & Wachter Morris, 2015, for a discussion of school counselor's roles and responsibilities). Diffractive reading mirrors this ethical and analytical disposition. It allows the researcher to attend not only to what participants say, but to how they navigate institutional discourses, linguistic hierarchies, and emotional risk when doing so.

In São Paulo's international schools, where English is often positioned as the dominant or legitimate language, and where race and class shape students' access to recognition, traditional thematic coding risks flattening participants' situated knowledges. By contrast, diffractive analysis makes space for ambiguity, for fragmented reflections, and for narratives that do not fit into predefined categories. This is vital in a study that centers professionals who are themselves working within systems that may reward silence over critique.

Furthermore, diffraction resonates with feminist and decolonial traditions that view research as a relational and political act (Dillard, 2000; Mignolo & Walsh, 2018). It offers an alternative to extractive research models by treating participants as co-constructors of knowledge and honoring the epistemic weight of emotion, partiality, and contradiction. In a field like counseling, where relationships are foundational, diffractive methodology affirms complexity rather than seeking to resolve it.

Ultimately, diffraction was not only a method for reading the data; it was also a way of being in relation with participants. It shaped how interviews were conducted and how analysis was approached: not as pattern-seeking, but as interference-tracing. This makes diffraction an ethically and analytically sound choice for a study situated at the intersection of counseling, language, and social justice.

Ethics of Proximity: Consent, Silence, and the Right to Hesitate

In elite, often global school environments, where counselors are expected to perform neutrality, speaking about race, language, belonging, and exclusion can be risky. Counselors have to often be concerned about surveillance, institutional backlash, or professional isolation. This research therefore adopts an ethics of proximity and care (Collins, 2000; Dillard, 2000; González-Rosario & Davis, 2025), treating consent as a relational process rather than a one-time form. Anonymity was preserved not only to protect participants, but to honor the political significance of what was offered and withheld.

Epistemic violence operates not only through what is said, but through the invalidation of who is allowed to speak and how (Carneiro, 2005). In the context of epistemic racism (Carneiro, 2005), silence is not absence; it is strategy, resistance, or trauma. The data collected was read, analyzed, and interpreted with this in mind. Discomfort, hesitation, or even refusal were treated as data and traces of institutional power at work.

Moreover, drawing on work on whiteness in Brazil (Schucman, 2014), this study recognizes how silence can serve the reproduction of dominance. In international schools, that silence often takes the form of institutional "neutrality," which codes any mention of race or linguistic injustice as political or disruptive. This research refuses that frame.

I Am in This: Researcher Positionality as Method

This work is written from within the field it critiques. I am a brown, gay, Brazilian educator and curriculum writer, whose career is heavily shaped by both international education and critical pedagogy. My own experiences in international schools inform not just the questions I asked, but the way I hear the answers. This is not a view from nowhere.

Acknowledging one's position is not about self-centering, but rather it is about accountability (Ribeiro, 2017); therefore, I do not claim objectivity. I claim implication. Following the tradition of endarkened feminist epistemology (Dillard, 2000), I approach the research as someone enmeshed in the field both professionally and emotionally struggling to hold space for complexity without collapsing it into easy narratives.

This positionality allowed participants to speak with nuance. Our shared language, geography, and institutional realities enabled moments of resonance and co-theorizing. Yet this closeness also required caution. Power circulates even in shared spaces. I worked to remain reflexive, not extractive; to listen with, not listen for.

What Is Missing Also Speaks: Constraints and Silences as Findings

Access to participants, their time, trust, and willingness to speak was shaped by the same conditions that structure educational life in Brazil: institutional pressures, racial and linguistic hierarchies, and uneven levels of comfort with topics like inclusion and multilingualism. Not all counselors felt safe enough to speak. Others spoke carefully, always aware of what could be misunderstood or weaponized. These constraints are not footnotes to the research. They are the research.

Following a map of the linguistic hegemony of English in Brazilian education (Santos & Gouvêa, 2019), this study recognizes how language access and legitimacy are racialized. The dominance of English in international schools means that even within "multilingual" spaces, certain kinds of speech are more valid than others. Some participants switched between Portuguese and English in the same interview, searching for the words that felt safest or most precise.

It is important to note that digital access and academic participation in Brazil remain uneven across race, region, and class. The testimonies here reflect those tensions. What is absent or unsaid in this research should not be corrected. It should be read. These silences are evidence of institutional boundaries that still govern what can be spoken, and by whom.

Building Emotional Infrastructure through Equity and Inclusion

The emotional well-being of MLs cannot be detached from the politics of identity, language, and power. If school counseling is to be genuinely inclusive, it must move beyond a behavioral understanding of SEL to describe it as a relational, situated, and justice-oriented practice (Dillard, 2000; hooks, 1994). For MLs, the need for care and belonging is inseparable from the conditions under which their identities are heard, translated, or silenced.

In this sense, the work on equity and inclusion is not an initiative. It requires the construction of emotional infrastructure: not just support systems, but an institutional ethos that centers equity, belonging, and linguistic legitimacy. Emotional infrastructure, therefore, refers to the set of relational, institutional, and symbolic conditions that shape how students are allowed to feel, belong, express themselves, and become.

Too often, inclusion efforts in elite international schools remain confined to celebratory events, elective workshops, or image-driven campaigns. Meanwhile, counseling programs operate with frameworks imported from the Global North, presuming a universal emotional subject: one who names feelings in standardized English, expresses vulnerability through "appropriate" behaviors, and regulates affect in ways legible to dominant norms. These assumptions risk pathologizing students who do not (or cannot) perform emotion in these ways. Institutional diversity often functions as a form of emotional management rather than structural change (Ahmed, 2012). The challenge is not simply inclusion, but the redistribution of attention, of care, of legitimacy.

In international schools in São Paulo, where English often functions as both medium and measure of success, multilingual students navigate not only linguistic barriers but affective hierarchies. Brazil's racial democracy myth obscures the ways in which social-emotional expression and recognition are racialized (Carneiro, 2005). What is read as "confidence" in one student may be read as "aggression" in another. Similarly, the inability to name emotions in the dominant school language is often misinterpreted as lack of emotional maturity rather than as linguistic exclusion. School counselors must therefore be equipped to decode these misreadings and to affirm the full humanity of students whose ways of being fall outside dominant norms.

Constructing emotional infrastructure through an equity lens involves more than incorporating celebratory multicultural content. It involves systemic change: interrogating which emotions are sanctioned, which languages are legitimized, and which students are afforded the space to be complex, contradictory, and whole. Racial and linguistic identities in Brazil are historically marked by exclusion and epistemic violence (Gomes, 2012). A truly inclusive SEL program must account for this.

Rather than treating linguistic diversity as an obstacle, counselors must recognize it as an asset. Students' emotional worlds are shaped in and through their home languages. Denying this link impairs both identity development and academic potential (Cummins, 2000). Culturally sustaining pedagogies (Peristeris, 2017) reinforce this view, calling for schools to create space for students' full linguistic repertoires. In Brazil, there is a direct connection between language justice and racial equity (Gomes, 2012), urging educators to challenge linguistic hierarchies that invisibilize Afro-Brazilian and Indigenous ways of knowing and feeling.

International school counselors must train for affective literacy that recognizes cultural and racial contexts because emotion is culturally mediated. What counts as emotional regulation in one context may signal repression or distress in another (González Rey, 1999). counselors must develop affective literacy that is attuned to the racialized and classed norms shaping emotional expression. Schooling often suppresses the emotional life of marginalized students under the guise of discipline or neutrality (hooks, 1994). In Brazil, this manifests in the racialized interpretation of Black children's emotional expressions often deemed "disruptive," "immature," or "excessive" within private elite school settings (de Souza et al., 2018; Gomes, 2012). These misreadings are rooted in colonial legacies that continue to frame Black affect through a deficit lens (Carneiro, 2005). Not all emotional responses are easily legible within SEL's prevailing models. Silence may be strategic. Anger may be justified. Emotional contradiction may signal resistance, not dysfunction.

Discomfort is not a problem to be fixed, but a sign of tension that must be named and understood (Ahmed, 2012; Anzaldúa, 1987). In the context of counseling, this means reading hesitation, code-switching, or emotional dissonance not as deficits, but as meaningful responses to institutional pressures. While code-switching has often been interpreted through a compensatory or assimilationist lens (Canagarajah, 2006), recent work on translanguaging,[3] especially in contexts of racialized multilingualism, offers a more agentive and decolonial framing. Translanguaging recognizes how multilingual speakers mobilize their full linguistic repertoire to make meaning, express emotion, and assert identity (García & Wei, 2014; Otheguy et al., 2015). In counseling spaces, this shift matters: it reframes linguistic plurality not as interference or confusion, but as emotional strategy and epistemic resistance.

Echoes in Practice: Tracing Feeling across Power

School counseling in international education is often imagined as a space of care, neutrality, and support. Yet, as this chapter has already argued, care is never neutral. When practiced in international schools structured by racialized hierarchies, linguistic prestige economies, and epistemic exclusions, counseling becomes entangled with the very systems it seeks to soften. For those who approach the work from an equity-informed lens, especially those who themselves speak, look, or think from the margins, the task is not simply to "support" students, but to survive the institutional contradictions of that support.

This chapter turns to the voices of nine school counselors in São Paulo who navigate these contradictions every day. Drawing from open-ended questionnaires and in-depth interviews, their responses are not presented here as data to be categorized, but as traces of tension and affective signals of the friction between what schools say about inclusion and how they actually manage equity and promote a sense of belonging.

What emerges is not a neat narrative of best practices. It is a field of intertwined pressures: institutions that celebrate inclusion and equity on paper but censor conversations about race; SEL frameworks that demand emotional regulation without questioning who decides what "regulated" looks like; multilingual students asked to narrate their trauma in a dominant language, then praised for their "resilience" while their difference remains unacknowledged.

For counselors committed to inclusion and well-being, especially those who embody marginalized identities, this work is costly. It often requires institutional willfulness (Ahmed, 2012): the courage to speak when silence is safer, to name power when "neutrality" is expected, and to hold space for students whose emotions, grammars, and grief do not fit institutional scripts. Inclusion without a shift in power is not inclusion; it is containment (Gomes, 2012; Ribeiro, 2017).

In what follows, three interwoven tensions are traced: the discomfort institutions exhibit when race and language are named together; the emotional burden of implementing SEL through frameworks that erase difference; and the micro-resistances counselors enact to carve out space for students to be seen, felt, and held. These are not offered as universal truths, but as situated insights into what it means to do inclusion and well-being work from within systems still structured to disqualify it.

Institutional Discomfort: When Inclusion Meets Its Limits

Despite institutional narratives of "global citizenship" and "embracing inclusion," participants described a pervasive discomfort when conversations moved beyond celebration into critique, particularly when connecting race, language, and belonging. This discomfort was not incidental; it was structural. Counselors recounted moments where they were encouraged to "stay positive," "focus on universal values," or "avoid controversy"; coded ways of discouraging deeper engagement with inclusion and equity.

> We're told to make students feel seen, but when I bring up how race or language affects who feels welcome, I'm seen as making things political. Inclusion is fine as long as it doesn't challenge the way things already work.
>
> In-depth interview

> The school says it's diverse, and in many ways it is. But when I tried to suggest a workshop on racialized language in peer conflict, it was quickly reframed as a 'parental sensitivity' issue. The fear wasn't the topic—it was who it might implicate.
>
> Questionnaire respondent

This strategic avoidance aligns with Ahmed's (2012) critique of institutional diversity work, where naming inequality becomes the problem, not the inequality itself. Counselors who attempted to introduce language around racism, linguistic hierarchies, or exclusion were often redirected toward "safe" themes, such as empathy or kindness; concepts easily detached from structural inequities. This refusal to name race and power reproduces whiteness not just as phenotype, but as institutional normativity (Carneiro, 2005). As one participant reflected during the in-depth interview, "Inclusion here means not making anyone uncomfortable. But discomfort is part of healing, and it's part of being real with students."

The Emotional Cost of Normative SEL

The emotional burden of working within imported, behaviorist SEL frameworks surfaced across multiple interviews. Counselors reported feeling constrained by curricula that prioritize regulation over relationship, and English fluency over affective depth. They shared how this limited their ability to respond meaningfully to students' needs, particularly when those needs were shaped by cultural or linguistic differences.

> The curriculum requires: 'Can the student name their feeling?' But what if the word they need doesn't exist in English? Or doesn't feel right in that context? I've seen students shut down, not because they don't feel, but because they don't feel in the way the school expects them to do so.
>
> In-depth interview

> We're encouraged to track students' emotional progress through worksheets and metrics. But those tools weren't made for kids whose experiences aren't standardized. I worry we're confusing adaptation with wellbeing.
>
> Questionnaire response

This critique resonates with the argument that culturally sustaining pedagogies must center the emotional and linguistic realities of students, not demand assimilation into dominant affective codes (Asempapa, 2019). For MLs, expressing emotion in a dominant language may require emotional translation, flattening, modifying, or silencing affect in order to be understood. This form of linguistic adaptation often comes at the cost of identity, particularly in contexts where home languages are tacitly devalued (Cummins, 2000).

A counselor described the toll of being caught between institutional expectations and their own ethical convictions. *"Sometimes,"* one said, *"I feel like I'm being asked to fix students when what they really need is someone to listen to them. I often ask: do you want my advice or do you want me just to listen?"*

Micro-resistances and the Possibility of Otherwise

Despite these pressures, many participants described subtle but powerful acts of resistance: bending the curriculum, making space for silence, inviting students to switch languages, or reimagining "regulation" as relational safety rather than behavioral control. These interventions were rarely celebrated, but they mattered.

> I stopped translating students' emotional responses into English when I write notes. I started recording them as they were said. Even if I'm the only one who understands it, it feels like I'm respecting their voice instead of filtering it.
>
> In-depth interview

> We made an emotion journal that didn't have words. Just colors, drawings, symbols. Some students opened up in ways they hadn't before. I realized we'd been asking them to feel on my terms, not theirs.
>
> Questionnaire respondent

In weekly group sessions, counselors at one São Paulo international school piloted a "translanguaging SEL circle," where students could express their emotions using any language or symbolic system they preferred: spoken words, gestures, color cards, or drawings. Sessions began with a multilingual mood board. Instead of "I feel ___," students selected from emotion words in Portuguese, Korean, Arabic, or Spanish often followed by storytelling in a mix of languages.

Counselors noted a clear shift: students previously described as "quiet" or "withdrawn" began taking ownership of their emotional expression. The space became more relational, less performative. These adaptations, small, context-bound, yet powerful, demonstrated that emotional safety emerges not from standardization, but from linguistic legitimacy.

This kind of relational design affirms what this chapter argues throughout: that MLs are not emotionally underdeveloped; they are navigating complex systems of translation, legitimacy, and power. And they are doing so with remarkable creativity and resilience.

These practices resonate with the concept of endarkened feminist epistemology (Dillard, 2000): holding space for knowledge that is emotional, partial, and situated. They also align with the theory of translanguaging as both a pedagogical and affective act (García & Wei, 2014). In these instances, counselors chose not to translate students into institutional legibility, but to expand what care could look like.

Importantly, these micro-resistances were not framed as heroic. They were often quiet, improvised, and constrained by broader institutional demands. Yet they signal a call for a pedagogy of possibility (Freire, 1996): the insistence that another way is always possible, even within the margins of compliance.

Holding the Line: Professional Isolation and the Politics of Voice

For counselors working within international schools in São Paulo, engaging in equity work is not simply a matter of practice; it is a matter of positionality, risk, and resistance. Many of the participants in this study spoke of the profound isolation that accompanies efforts to challenge institutional silence around race, language, and systemic exclusion. This isolation is not only interpersonal; it is structural. This reflects the idea that in contexts marked by structural inequalities, the right to speak and be heard is not equally distributed (Ribeiro, 2017), and silence itself often results from systemic exclusion.

Counselors who themselves inhabit marginalized identities whether racialized, queer, or linguistically marked described how their presence was often welcomed as representation, but their voice was discouraged when it disrupted dominant narratives. This paradox aligns with the notion of the "diversity worker" as one who is tolerated as a symbol, but punished when speaking from experience (Ahmed, 2012).

> I was hired in part because of my background, and I was proud of that. But when I started raising concerns about how certain students were being read emotionally, I was told I was being too sensitive. I guess my difference became a liability.
>
> In-depth interview

> There's an unspoken rule: you can embody diversity, but don't speak about it. Especially if what you're saying challenges how the school sees itself.
>
> Questionnaire respondent

This institutional ambivalence reveals the tension between margin and center which refers to the expectation that those from the margins perform legitimacy without questioning the systems that marginalize them (hooks, 1994). Several participants shared that while they were encouraged to attend inclusion-related training or represent the school in external initiatives, they received little support when advocating for changes in internal policy or curriculum. The labor of inclusion fell on them, but the power to implement it remained elsewhere.

The emotional toll of this position was evident. Counselors described second-guessing their language in emails, hesitating before naming race or coloniality in meetings, and feeling surveilled in ways their peers were not. This form of precarity is not incidental; it is part of how institutions maintain hegemonic norms under the guise of neutrality (Collins, 2000).

> I've been asked to 'tone it down' when discussing equity in team meetings. However, my white colleagues can suggest the same things and be seen as innovative. It's frustrating.
>
> In-depth interview

This dynamic also extended to the affective labor of advocacy. Counselors of color, particularly women and LGBTQ+ counselors, reported being seen as the "go-to person" for inclusion and equity issues who are expected to advise, mediate, or educate others, often without recognition or compensation.

> When anything related to inclusion comes up, I'm called in. But when it's time to write policy or evaluate practice, I'm not at the table. I'm consulted, but never included.
>
> Questionnaire respondent

These findings echo the premise that equity work, when divorced from power, can become another form of institutional extraction (Dillard, 2000; Gomes, 2012; Matias & Zembylas, 2014). Emotional labor becomes normalized, while critical voice is demonized.

And yet, amidst this isolation, the counselors in this study were not silent. They reflected, adapted, and resisted. Some formed informal networks of support with trusted colleagues; others documented the exclusions they witnessed, creating a quiet archive of institutional memory. Voice is not only about speaking, it is about naming from a place of implication (Ribeiro, 2017). And in these acts of voice, however precarious, lies a radical commitment to care.

> Sometimes it feels like I'm the only one saying these things. But I still say them. Because if I don't, then LGBT students like me won't hear it from anyone else.
>
> In-depth interview

These stories remind us that inclusion and equity are not departments. They are a demand for ethical relations. In counseling, this means recognizing that well-being cannot be separated from dignity, and dignity cannot be achieved without institutional accountability. Educational justice is not about access alone; it is about transforming the spaces we gain access (Gomes, 2012).

The professional isolation described by participants is not an argument against equity and inclusion in counseling but rather an argument for its necessity. Without equity-informed practices, school counseling risks becoming complicit in emotional assimilation, epistemic erasure, and the reproduction of whiteness and cis-heteronormative practices as the norm. But when practiced relationally, structurally, and reflexively, counseling can become a space of radical accompaniment, where counselors not only help students navigate institutions, but slowly and intentionally transform those institutions from within.

Braiding Voices and Holding Spaces for Growth: Toward a Radical Ethics of Belonging

This chapter has sought to trace the complex intersections between multilingualism, emotional well-being, and the political imperative of equity and inclusion in international schools. Through an equity-informed lens and grounded in the lived experiences of school counselors in São Paulo, the analysis affirms that the emotional health of MLs is not an isolated outcome but a socially structured phenomenon. It is shaped by institutional norms, linguistic hierarchies, racialized expectations, and uneven access to recognition.

Identities are never singular; they are layered, intersectional, and contextually produced (Collins, 2000; Crenshaw, 1991). In international schools where English often functions as a gatekeeping tool, multilingual students frequently navigate hidden curricula of exclusion, even within spaces that profess inclusion. Counselors working to support them do so while negotiating these same tensions, often from within minoritized subject positions themselves. The affective labor of educators is not equally distributed; those who embody difference are often asked to perform inclusion without institutional power to enact it (Miller & Howell, 2019).

This work, then, is not only pedagogical, but it is also profoundly political. Supporting MLs' demands more than programmatic SEL interventions; it requires a reconfiguration of what and who is considered central to the life of international schools. Drawing on the decolonial critiques (Mignolo & Walsh, 2018), we see that transforming school culture involves more than diversifying voices; it means challenging the logics of whiteness, cis-heteronormativity, linguistic supremacy, and affective regulation that often structure belonging.

Truly liberatory educational spaces must begin with an epistemic shift that moves toward "endarkened" ways of knowing that recognize the wisdom, histories, and emotional truths of Black, Indigenous, LGBTQIAP+, and racialized communities (Dillard, 2000). This is particularly urgent in Brazil, where linguistic and racial identities are deeply entangled, and where silence around race and sexuality often masks deep-seated inequities (Gomes, 2012; Ribeiro, 2017). In this context, counselors must be supported not only as professionals but as knowledge holders and change agents whose work is vital to justice-oriented education.

Rather than offering a resolution, this chapter gestures toward a horizon. One in which school counseling is seen as part of a broader emotional infrastructure of equity. An infrastructure that does not shy away from discomfort, contradiction, or complexity. One that makes space for students to bring their full selves whether it be linguistically, racially, or emotionally into the classroom, and for counselors to do the same without penalty.

To move in this direction is to understand that well-being is not a checklist; it is a commitment. A commitment to cultivating schools that feel different because they are different. Where belonging is not scripted, but lived. Where care is not conditioned on conformity. And where the emotional lives of MLs are not treated as ancillary, but as central to the future of education.

Reflective Tool: Building Emotional Infrastructure: A Checklist for Counselors at International Schools

This is not intended to be a tool for measurement, but a compass for reflection:

- Are students allowed and encouraged to name emotions in their home languages?
- Do your SEL materials reflect cultural and racial variation in emotional expression?
- Are silence, hesitation, translanguaging or code-switching understood as meaningful data, not deficits?
- Have you mapped how disciplinary patterns correlate with race, language, and emotion?
- Do your sessions create room for non-verbal affect: color, story, song, metaphor, gesture?
- Are there systems in place to debrief with staff when institutional resistance is encountered?

Emotional infrastructure is not about perfectly inclusive programs. It is about making relational, linguistic, and institutional space for complexity. These questions can help counselors align their daily practices with a radical ethics of belonging.

Notes

1 Saudade is a word in Portuguese that describes a deep, poignant feeling of longing for someone, something, or a moment that is absent—often accompanied by affection, nostalgia, and the awareness that the object of longing may never fully return. It blends yearning, emotional memory, love, and loss into a single sentiment that has no direct equivalent in English.

2 The *Global North* refers to countries that hold disproportionate economic, political, and cultural power—largely due to histories of colonialism, extraction, and racialized inequality. It is less a geographic category and more a positional one, describing nations whose worldviews, institutions, and knowledge systems are treated as universal, often marginalizing perspectives from the Global South.

3 *Translanguaging* is the dynamic use of a multilingual speaker's full linguistic repertoire, challenging the idea that languages exist as separate, bounded systems. It highlights how learners flexibly draw on all their semiotic resources to make meaning, resist linguistic hierarchies, and disrupt monolingual norms rooted in colonial language ideologies.

References

Ahmed, S. (2012). *On being included: Racism and diversity in institutional life*. Duke University Press.

Anzaldúa, G. (1987). *Borderlands/La Frontera: The new mestiza*. Aunt Lute Books.

Arthur, N. (2004). *Counselling international students: Clients from around the world*. Springer.

Asempapa, R. S. (2019). Culturally responsive mentoring: Frameworks for supporting prospective teachers of color. *Journal of Education and Learning*, *8*(3), 1–10. https://doi.org/10.5539/jel.v8n3p1

Barad, K. (2007). *Meeting the universe halfway: Quantum physics and the entanglement of matter and meaning*. Duke University Press.

Canagarajah, A. S. (2006). Negotiating the local in English as a lingua franca. *Annual Review of Applied Linguistics*, *26*, 197–218.

Carneiro, S. (2005). A construção do outro como não-ser como fundamento do ser. [The construction of the other as non-being as the foundation of being]. In J. Bento (Ed.), *Pensamento negro em educação* [Black thinking in education] (pp. 15–25). Fundação Cultural Palmares.

Collins, P. H. (2000). *Black feminist thought: Knowledge, consciousness, and the politics of empowerment* (2nd ed.). Routledge.

Crenshaw, K. (1991). Mapping the margins: Intersectionality, identity politics, and violence against women of color. *Stanford Law Review*, *43*(6), 1241–1299.

Cummins, J. (2000). *Language, power and pedagogy: Bilingual children in the crossfire*. Multilingual Matters.

de Oliveira, L. C., & Wachter Morris, C. (2015). *Preparing school counselors for English language learners*. TESOL Press.

de Souza, I. S., Leite De Souza, L. E., Alves, L. T. Q., De Souza Mendes, L. A. N., & Do Vale, V. P. (2018). Do silêncio do lar ao silêncio escolar: Racismo, preconceito e discriminação na educação infantil. [From the silence of home to the silence of school: Racism, prejudice, and discrimination in early childhood education]. *Revista Em Favor De Igualdade Racial*, *1*(1), 137–146. Retrieved from https://periodicos.ufac.br/index.php/RFIR/article/view/2000

Dillard, C. B. (2000). The substance of things hoped for, the evidence of things not seen: Examining an endarkened feminist epistemology in educational research and leadership. *International Journal of Qualitative Studies in Education*, *13*(6), 661–681. https://doi.org/10.1080/09518390050211565

Freire, P. (1996). *Pedagogy of the oppressed* (M. B. Ramos, Trans.). Continuum. (Original work published 1970)

García, O., & Wei, L. (2014). *Translanguaging: Language, bilingualism and education*. Palgrave Macmillan.

Gomes, N. L. (2012). Relações étnico-raciais, educação e descolonização de currículos. [Ethnic-racial relations, education, and the decolonization of curricula]. Currículo sem Fronteiras, *12*(1), 98–109.

González Rey, F. L. (1999). La afectividad desde una perspectiva de la subjetividad. [Affectivity from a subjectivity perspective]. Psicología: Teoría pesquisa, *15*(2), 127–134.

González-Rosario, L., & Davis, E. (2025). School counseling social justice advocacy: A resistance story of navigating micropolitics at the state level. *Journal of Progressive Human Services*, 1–14. https://doi.org/10.1080/10428232.2024.2448922

hooks, b (1994). *Teaching to transgress: Education as the practice of freedom*. Routledge.

Martin, A. J., Papworth, B., Ginns, P., & Liem, G. A. D. (2017). Motivation and engagement: Same Or different across school transitions? *Contemporary Educational Psychology*, *49*, 1–12.

Matias, C. E., & Zembylas, M. (2014). When saying you care is not really caring: Emotions of disgust, whiteness ideology, and teacher education. *Critical Studies in Education*, *55*(3), 319–337. https://doi.org/10.1080/17508487.2014.922489

Mazzei, L. A. (2014). Beyond an easy sense: A diffractive analysis. *Qualitative Inquiry*, *20*(6), 742–746. https://doi.org/10.1177/1077800414530258

Mignolo, W. D., & Walsh, C. E. (2018). *On decoloniality: Concepts, analytics, praxis*. Duke University Press.

Miller, R. A., & Howell, C. D. (2019). "Constantly, excessively, and all the time": The emotional labor of teaching diversity courses. *International Journal of Teaching and Learning in Higher Education*, *31*(3), 491–502. http://www.isetl.org/ijtlhe/

Otheguy, R., García, O., & Reid, W. (2015). Clarifying translanguaging and deconstructing named languages: A perspective from linguistics. *Applied Linguistics Review*, *6*(3), 281–307.

Peristeris, K. (2017). Culturally sustaining pedagogies: Teaching and learning for justice in a changing world. *Journal of Teaching and Learning*, *11*. 10.22329/jtl.v11i1.4987.

Ribeiro, D. (2017). *O que é lugar de fala?* [What is a place of speech?]. Letramento.

Santos, B. S., & Gouvêa, R. (2019). *Para além do pensamento abissal: Das linhas globais a uma ecologia de saberes*. [Beyond abyssal thinking: From global lines to an ecology of knowledges]. In B. de S. Santos (Ed.), *A gramática do tempo: Para uma nova cultura política [The grammar of time: Towards a new political culture]* (pp. 237–281). Cortez.

Schucman, L. V. (2014). *Entre o encardido, o branco e o branquíssimo: Branquitude, hierarquia e poder na cidade de São Paulo*. [Between dirty-white, white, and whitest: Whiteness, hierarchy, and power in the city of São Paulo]. Annablume.

Ulmer, J. B. (2016). Writing slow ontology. *Qualitative Inquiry*, *22*(4), 273–283. https://doi.org/10.1177/1077800415615619

Section II

Collaborative and Interdisciplinary Practices

Chapter 6

Acompáñame

Kinship and Authentic Cariño in the Counseling Profession

Socorro G. Herrera, Lisa Porter, and Katherine Barko-Alva

School counseling is, at its core, a relational profession. Individuals enter the field because they believe in young people and they carry a conviction that every student deserves to be supported, guided, and championed (Sharma et al., 2023). School counselors choose this work not only to respond to academic and social concerns, but also to cultivate conditions in which children can thrive as whole humans. This requires counselors across the country to reflect upon the increasing number of families and students featuring a diverse array of languages and cultures. According to the National Center for Education Statistics (2024), in 2021, there were 5.3 million multilingual learners (MLs) in K-12 schools across the United States. Such diversity requires school counselors to be prepared to shift and continually reflect upon the biographies of students and families they serve. Shi and Watkinson (2019) found that school counselors did not feel adequately prepared to support MLs. Often, school counselor preparation programs emphasize a broad understanding of K-12 students, including attention to development across the lifespan, crisis prevention, career development, and multicultural contexts (CACREP, 2023). Yet, within that preparation, there may not be sufficient time to develop the frameworks and strategies that would support understanding the different family ecologies and collective cultural forms of care when working with MLs and their families, particularly when there is not a shared linguistic background. As a result, school counselors often find themselves navigating situations in which their professional training has not fully prepared them to partner with multilingual families in ways that cultivate trust and partnerships (de Oliveira & Wachter Morris, 2015; Hilliard et al., 2025).

The crux of this challenge is that supporting MLs requires strategies grounded in reflection requiring an understanding of the differing biographies of families. This necessitates "stepping outside of the box" by using authentic cariño (Bartolomé, 2008; Herrera et al., 2020; Valenzuela, 1999) and radical kinship (Boyle, 2017) to learn strategies our preparation programs may not have offered. Both concepts refer to the notion of intentionally attending to cultivating connections that create a sense of belonging and responsibility for one another

DOI: 10.4324/9781003711124-8

both inside and outside the school. Authentic cariño and radical kinship must be informed by the historical and linguistic context of ML families and students while maintaining the expectations set forth from school counseling preparation programs. These concepts go beyond a purely relational posture; rather, they represent a political, ethical, and humanizing commitment to students and families, one that naturally challenges deficit paradigms, standardized systems, and a limited definition of family engagement. Furthermore, it centers on an understanding of the biographies and narratives of both the ML students and their families. These stories are shaped by migration, hope, sacrifice, linguistic dexterity, and the navigation of complex and competing systems (Herrera et al., 2020). To understand the milieu of the ML students and their families, school counselors must continue to reflect on their own narratives to prevent making assumptions based on their socio-cultural histories, linguistic backgrounds, educational pathways, and lived experiences.

In this chapter, we situate the need for biography-driven school counseling within our own personal and professional journeys. We highlight how families, students, and school counselors uncover and attend to the fears that disconnect cultural, linguistic, and community ties. This sets the stage for the conceptual grounding and frameworks that follow as we move deeply into authentic cariño and kinship as lenses for school counseling.

A Personal Entry Point: "Mire Señora"

After teaching for many years, I (Herrera) decided my impact would cast a wider net if I could sit in high-stakes meetings and have a deeper knowledge of the assessments, family dynamics and the emotional dimension of the learner. As a teacher, I was constantly battling a tension that resulted from observing how school counselors, school psychologists, and educators communicated and interacted with the families I served. I wondered if coursework would provide me the insights to support families in making decisions that were in the best interest of their children. This inner tension, along with the voices of mothers who approached me quietly each day seeking clarity, reassurance, and dignity, led me to the profession of school counseling. Years later, I pursued my doctorate in educational psychology. Four decades later, many of those initial tensions I experienced early in my career still hold true today.

Reflection on Parent Perspective

> "Mire señora… yo no sé qué esperan de mí. Me hacen preguntas que no entiendo. Luego me piden papeles imposibles de conseguir."/"Look, ma'am… I don't know what they expect of me. They ask me questions I don't understand. Then they ask for papers that are impossible for me to get."

This mother was not confused, disengaged, or resistant. She, like many parents, was fearful. She spoke from a place of invisibility and vulnerability, aware that the wrong answer or simply the inability to provide a school-requested document could determine her child's educational trajectory. In her trembling voice, one can hear not only anxiety, but *deep love*. She wanted to be seen as a partner in educating her child and participate fully. What she encountered instead was a system that evaluated, diagnosed, and recommended before it listened, learned, and understood. Interactions such as these shaped what it meant for me to be a school counselor. Beyond the multicultural coursework, training, and my own shared culture and language with the families, I needed to step back and understand not from textbooks or theoretical constructs, but rather from a humanistic perspective. I had to humbly unlearn, even as a woman of color, the paths families had traveled and how those journeys influenced their understanding of navigating an unfamiliar educational system. To do so, critical questions must be asked of oneself, the school community, and the professionals within school counseling:

- How many educational decisions are made without understanding a family's history, language, or humanity?
- How often do professionals lean on expertise, while families carry knowledge no assessment can capture?

These questions have remained my focus throughout my career as a school counselor and in my present role within higher education. After years of serving communities, I learned to respond to the changing landscape of what it means to be a school counselor and authentically engage with families. School meetings with families can become compliance checkpoints, referrals can become labels, and engagement can become documentation. In these instances, caring has the potential of becoming procedural. Alternatively, meetings can become spaces where educators and school counselors practice acompañamiento, that is walking alongside families (Ruiz Malagon, 2025), expressing a deep sense of care and responsibility as school counselors enter in community with families. Such spaces value a humanistic, family, and student-centered ecology that understands the biography and biopsychosocial history of the communities they serve (Herrera, 2022).

When Care Is Contextual and Conditional: The Limits School Counseling

Modern schooling, influenced by policy changes and competing agendas, has the potential of creating school contexts where school counselors are tasked with attending to the emotional and relational, while at the same time trying to attend to the mandates, packaged curricula, testing, and socio-political contexts in which they practice. This continual balancing act can often be overwhelming and lead to significant burnout (Niles et al., 2024). At its core, the foundation of school counseling is about guidance and management. However, depending on context and culture, often school counselors feel trapped by the endless management tasks (i.e., maintaining case load documentation, completing screening and overseeing assessment protocol) that can be reactive in nature rather than the emotional work of establishing rapport and proactively fostering relationships with students and families.

Management tasks required by school counselors are not inherently problematic. In fact, they are often necessary. But when they become primary, they displace the humanizing work that sustains belonging and hope (Niles et al., 2024). In response to the growing demands and complex agendas, school counseling can become transmittal. School counselors meet families primarily when:

- There is a concern or referral
- A student needs placement or assessment
- A schedule must be arranged
- A crisis occurs (such as a behavioral incident)

This reactive model positions families as objects of intervention, not co-constructors of student success. It leaves little room for understanding the biopsychosocial histories of the families through which trust, advocacy, and shared decision-making emerge (Herrera, 2022).

The Consequence

When we lead with paperwork, protocol, and placement before relationship, biography, and belonging, we create counseling encounters characterized not by empowerment, but by:

- Invisible fear
- Deficit assumptions
- Misinterpreted silence
- Pathologized difference
- De-valued cultural capital

Toward a Humanizing School Counseling Stance

To serve MLs, school counselors must adopt a stance that recognizes families not as cases but as kin, not as clients, but as collaborators. We must shift from "How do I fix this situation or place this student?" to strategies that uncover their biographies. Core to humanizing within the school counseling profession is expanding on the notion of understanding the socio-cultural dimension of the student. 1) ***Sociocultural Dimension:*** Every student arrives with their own life experiences, has a place that offers joy and hope, and possesses both internal and external sources of resilience. It is imperative to move beyond point and time (i.e., surveys, interviews) toward gathering information in authentic ways through radical kinship. This begins by exploring and understanding the support networks the student already has (within and beyond their school community) and then determining how to leverage those networks to address their goals and challenges. 2) ***Linguistic Dimension:*** Often, ML students and families integrate into new communities where they are seeking ways to express their hardships as well as goals, but the open spaces where such conversations are possible are limited. Simply getting a translator is not opening the space for conversation. A lot of what we do in the name of relationship building is often scripted/constrained (i.e., Tuesday Taco Night, sanctioned cultural events). Instead, school counselors could promote and foster authentic listening sessions and family gatherings where parents and caregivers are interacting with each other at a relational level embracing their humanity. Being in a counseling office or meeting in large groups might not support family sharing. Large gatherings can be great, but they must not be school-centric where information is disseminated preventing authentic conversations to occur.

The core for school counselors is to ask questions about what conditions need to exist for students and families to feel supported as they navigate challenging learning and living spaces. We must build on strategies that serve as conduits between community, family, school, and students. This begins by intentionally listening and seeking guidance from families using authentic cariño. Understanding the greater community and places where such interactions are already happening is paramount. Who are the community leaders? Where are the organic community gathering spaces? This involves embracing discomfort and encountering the community where they are at.

Reflection on the Power of Community Leaders

Atifa and her family came to the United States as Muslim refugees from Sudan. Upon arriving, Atifa's children began attending public school while she helped her family acclimate, find employment, and learn English. Atifa is a henna artist, event planner, and retail supplier. Her community knows she is creative, resourceful, and views her as a key contact for navigating daily life.

As more Christian Sudanese relocated to the area, she noticed increasing tension between Christian and Muslim Sudanese especially at broader cultural events that involved both groups. Because both groups utilized her event-planning services and henna artistry, she became instrumental in working toward peace between the two groups. As a result, she is respected by both Christian and Muslim Sudanese and is often called on if problems arise or when incoming families arrive. Despite Atifa's significant influence, no one at her children's school was aware of the assets she brought to the community or the leadership role she offered to immigrant families enrolled at their school site.

- What efforts are made by schools to learn about community leaders, such as Atifa?
- How might school counselors build relationships with community leaders?
- How could Atifa's skills, knowledge, and community respect help to support the school counselor?

Cognitive and Academic Dimensions

Understanding and leveraging the social cultural and linguistic dimensions of the student provides school counselors with the knowledge and tools that support conditions for open dialogue and reflection guided by authentic cariño and radical kinship. This knowledge and the actions we take in addressing the needs and utilizing the assets the student brings, allow for school counselors to engage and support the cognitive processing and academic aspirations of the student.

School counselors can remove hierarchical dynamics that distance the multiple participants within a school culture by fostering radical kinship. This enables all to see themselves as part of a community bound by responsibility to one another. It asks educators to authentically walk alongside families and students. Together, the frameworks of authentic cariño and radical kinship demand a counseling model rooted in compassion, relational justice, and cultural reciprocity.

Engaging with Multilingual Learners and Their Caregivers

We recognize the mounting pressures school counselors are facing. Ever-changing expectations, increasing amounts of documentation and caseloads, and limited access to time and resources often prevent us from supporting students in meaningful ways (Shi & Brown, 2020). Confronted with this problematic landscape, intentionally creating sustainable learning spaces, wherein families-students-school-community relationships (Herrera et al., 2020) are cultivated, supported, and affirmed, seems to be far-reaching. Actions bound in authentic cariño and radical kinship shift the paradigm toward connection, cooperation, and collaboration that can lead to a better learning environment for multilingual students and their families. The following story about Catalina's journey reminds us how expediency and limiting our view of what is possible can change the trajectory of a student's life. A vast chasm exists for many families between the "hopes and dreams" they have for their children and what school counselors know to make their dreams come true. Families' limited understanding of the college application process, counselors' narrow understanding of students' cultural and linguistic backgrounds, and limited access to financial resources and/or information (Jiang & Harklau, 2024; Kanno & Cromley, 2013; Purgason et al., 2024).

Catalina's Story: Diverting from the Dominant Narrative

Catalina had been in the United States for five months. Her parents, siblings, and grandmother emigrated, fleeing from political and social upheaval shattering their home country. While she understood English to a certain degree, Catalina was not prepared to face the academic, linguistic, and socio-cultural challenges she would encounter in U.S. schools. It was Catalina's dream to attend college and become a lawyer. Catalina's school in her home country had been academically rigorous; her grades had always reflected her attention and responsibility toward school. Her love of learning and desire to become a lawyer remained strong as she transitioned to school in the United States. The buzz among her peers in the US was focused on future aspirations, "Which school is your top choice? What about your SAT/ACT scores? At home, too, that was all her family would talk about, "*Cuando vayas a la Universidad.../When you get to college...*". Her family had uprooted their entire lives so that she could attend college and set the example for her brothers and sisters.

Reflection Questions

1 What do we know about the socio-cultural and linguistic dimensions of Catalina's life?
2 How can this knowledge inform the conversations and school counselors share with Catalina and her family regarding attending college?
3 What questions could the school counselor pose regarding next steps knowing what you know?

With excitement about the future, Catalina decided to make an appointment with her school counselor to begin the application process. Catalina needed clarification in terms of SATs/ACTs, letters of recommendation, GPA, application waivers, FAFSA, and the overall process of college application. While meeting with the school counselor, she realized that when her grades were transferred from her country to the U.S system, they were not transferred correctly, thus rendering her GPA lower than she expected. Using all her linguistic resources, she tried to explain to the school counselor that her GPA needed to be adjusted to accurately reflect her grades. Catalina had made the honor roll multiple times, she had won several debate awards, and she had even competed in an international science fair representing her country. Her grades did not reflect her academic prowess as a student.

Reflection Questions

1. In what ways could the school counselor respond using strategies grounded in authentic cariño to reduce the anxiety thwarting hope?
2. How might a school counselor be innovative in looking at policies pertaining to grades and how these policies vary between U.S. institutions?
3. What letter/documents/evidence could be retrieved to illustrate Catalina's academic strengths in her home country for usage in the US college application process?

Catalina's school counselor mentioned that she would need to revalidate her grades with a certified letter from a valid U.S. education agency, and this process might be lengthy. She proceeded by asking what her plans were after graduation. Catalina said, "College…I am going to Saint Francis University." Given the limited information, the school counselor had to inform her response regarding Catalina's next steps; she followed the protocol most familiar in these situations. The school counselor informed Catalina that her school of choice was not feasible given its level of difficulty (i.e., extremely low acceptance rate), and the fact that she (Catalina) did not speak English sufficiently to attend a four-year institution. Instead of going to St. Francis University, the school counselor suggested alternatives to explore such as trade school or the local community college. Catalina was devastated. Was attending university not an option? How would she tell her parents?

Supporting ML Students and Families Using Authentic Carino and Radical Kinship

Acompañamiento is a theoretical construct that has been used in the Latino/a/e community as a way of creating genuine relationships of care that challenge fossilized systems/ways of doing (Ruiz Malagon, 2025). Although Catalina's counselor may not have a shared experience, this theory helps create the groundwork for addressing and resisting systems that prioritize expediency and efficiency over the individual's biography (Herrera, 2022). School counselors, like Catalina's, sometimes find themselves reacting to the constant systemic demands. In theory, school counselor preparation and practice espouses centering the student's biography. However, in school contexts, deeply embedded assumptions about what is attainable may be clouded by the scripts and cultural biases that are often normalized within the system.

Acompañamiento in Practice

1. Find opportunities to meet with parents to learn and document the student's socio-cultural, linguistic, and academic background to support the goals the student has for the future.

2 Framed by authentic cariño and radical kinship, spend more time reaching out to schools where immigrant students previously attended to facilitate conversations related to the academic dimension of the learner.
3 Debrief all information with the student to provide a sense of security and radical kinship to help eliminate barriers and walk alongside the student.

Prioritizing Student and Familial Assets and Embracing Community Ties

Taking a stance of acompañamiento guided by authentic cariño reframes our mindset for embracing the possibilities for every student based on their own realities. School counselors can begin to address systemic barriers by recognizing familial assets as well as reaching out to community members who support and uplift students and families. School counselors have the responsibility of considering the cultural (aspirational wealth), linguistic (strong content knowledge), and cognitive (conscious decision) strengths that lead to success. Often, learning about these assets requires going beyond the immediate family unit to seeking out community leaders, such as Atifa, to help create a network of support and care. Sometimes, school counselors shy away from the potentialities of community networking for fear of confidentiality. The intent of community networking, however, is to uncover the intertwined systems of support within immigrant communities that can be understood through dialogue and time together with families and community leaders. The goal isn't to seek specific details from community members outside of the family but rather to understand this intertwined system. It is precisely here where radical kinship and authentic cariño situate our work and bring everything together. They are the heart and fundamental linchpins of what we do, but often are what gets the least attention (Bartolomé, 2008; Boyle, 2017; Herrera et al., 2020; Valenzuela, 1999).

Overcoming Systemic Paralysis: Authentic Cariño as an Agentive Tool

For decades, multilingual students and their families, such as Catalina's, have been viewed through a deficit perspective. Sometimes this is due to poor counselor preparation programs, unavailable professional development or working in a system that does not attend to the needs of MLs. Although one's initial response to Catalina's story is to place blame on the school counselor, we must consider how political, economic, and social systems limit the potentialities of the school counseling profession and reinforce deficit thinking and societal biases (Mayes & Byrd, 2022). Increasing administrative demands coupled with the quest for efficiency within societal systems have created a false consciousness and diminished the connection between school counselors, families, and students (Porter et al., 2021; Prattico, 2022). Scripted conversations for relaying information to students/families along with completing forms, recording data, and writing reports to demonstrate "progress" have become normalized routines within the profession (Niles et al., 2024).

These systematized routines can be found in K-12 educational spaces across the United States. Schools, after all, are the product of society and are often referred to as "mirrors" or microcosms of society (Calkins, 2023; Dewey, 1899; Sellars & Imig, 2023). Issues that are happening within society-at-large shape the priorities, policies, and overall climate within K-12 education. School counselors know this firsthand. However, the limitation of this perspective of schooling is that it does not prioritize the humanity behind the systematized policies and priorities.

Authenticating Socio-Emotional Dimension of the Learner

When examining today's educational system, measuring learning gains and losses and assessing "academic" gaps fuel the priorities and narratives within the U.S. K-12 schools (Dianis et al., 2015; Kyles-Smith, 2023). When standardized performance takes priority, societal issues facing families are often siloed causing ruptures in family communication, student well-being, and authentic human connections rooted in relational trust (Bryk & Schneider, 2003). Systems and those who serve MLs when not biography-driven close the door for opportunities and impact levels of fear of the system itself (Herrera, 2022). Educators often seek to address the socio-emotional dimension of the learner through mass produced kits that take the students through activities devoid of their own history and experiences (Stearns, 2019).

Even when opportunities emerge that attempt to elevate the humanness of participants within a system, such as the prioritization of socio-emotional learning (SEL), they can become overly rigid or structured. Rather than elevating authentic opportunities for self-awareness, positive mental health, and collaborative community building that are culturally relevant, a one-size-fits-all approach to SEL has been packaged, repurposed, and celebrated with little to no connection to larger societal issues, diverse perspectives, and/or family contributions (Clark et al., 2022; Free & Križ, 2022; Gupta, 2024). Self-regulating strategies are helpful in reducing stress and enhancing clarity, yet such practices don't address the situational knowledge our children are bringing to school (Camangian & Cariaga, 2022). Realities pertaining to secure housing, family employment, and political safety are brought to school by children every day. Support for emotional well-being might not be in curricula packages but rather strategies rooted in authentic cariño and radical kinship such as a lunch date with a small group of students, care packages for students and families, playtime at an apartment complex's play area, walking to school with families, or coffee meetings with community leaders to build relational trust.

The current socio-political climate in the United States is extremely divisive and impacting families across the country, particularly tensions surrounding immigration and deportation (Gonzalez et al., 2025; Rogers et al., 2025). Changes within U.S. immigration policy have always created a notion of fear for many in this country, especially for ML families (Gallo & Link, 2015; Gonzalez et al., 2025; Johnson, 2022). Although there have been moments when this fear has either intensified or lessened based on the policies in existence at a given time (i.e., Immigration Control and Reform Act of 1986 granting amnesty, Deferred Action for Child Arrivals (DACA) of 2012 protecting undocumented individuals who came as children, U.S. Zero Tolerance Policy of 2018 prosecuting undocumented migrants as criminals, and the One Big Beautiful Bill of 2025 that heavily funds mass deportation and increased enforcement), such laws have significant implications for the day to day operations within a school setting as well as children's politicized funds of knowledge (Ee & Gándara, 2020; Gallo & Link, 2015). School counselors are often the first to address the fall-out when such policies impact families. Several in the school counseling profession, for example, are at a loss in how to pivot around the uncertainty of the DACA program that assists undocumented students in accessing US higher education. For years, school counselors working in high schools with high immigration populations have utilized this program as a way for entry to college for many of their students (Bernal-Arevalo et al., 2021; Diaz-Strong, 2025). At present, there is increasing fear that applying would expose students and their families to immigration enforcement or that the program might soon cease to exist as a viable option (Najarro, 2025).

Melissa's Determination to Make a Difference

Melissa is a school counselor at a local high school in a mid-size town in North Carolina. Her school district is composed of immigrant and refugee families with over 100 languages represented. 53% of her school's population are native Spanish speakers with the majority of students coming from multi-status immigration households. When current immigration policies began to ramp up in 2025, she and her colleagues found the attendance of her Latino/a/e students was greatly affected. Even when students came to school, they were preoccupied thinking about the safety of their families and discussing the current moment among themselves. Her school counseling team discussed ways to support families affected by mass deportation as well as ensure the safety of students arriving at school. Melissa and her colleagues were determined to assist their families despite the overwhelming obstacles. Although staunch supporters and advocates for families, Melissa, like many generations of school counselors who've come before her, has borne witness to immigrant families having to navigate vulnerable spaces with varying degrees of empathy, care, and respect. Still, she felt that this moment is paramount. She and her colleagues struggled to find institutional mechanisms to stop the current wave of destruction separating families who've lived in their community for decades. Wanting to do something, her school counseling team began to actualize how their positions and voices could help create safe spaces for their ML students and families.

Reflection on How to Create Safe Spaces in This Moment

- Identify multiple ways of ongoing communications that offer resources and ongoing support such as hosting sessions (virtually and in-person) that inform ML families on knowing their rights, connecting people to people contacts, and networking with third-party community partners that support ML families.
- Discuss and collect emergency plans with families (i.e., Designation of Person in Parental Relationship forms and/or steps for expediting emergency guardianship).
- Utilize Asset mapping as a tool for identifying and documenting organizations, individuals, and general resources that provide ML families with key information, specifically who, what, and when to contact should critical situations arise. Often, networks of support are all that is left for families and students to rely on. Such tools move beyond fight or flight responses to mindfully creating agentive tools that help families feel a sense of hope.

These actions provided much needed knowledge for families living in constant fear. Yet, Melissa, like many who serve as school counselors during this time, continues to feel that her contributions are solely reactionary to the powers that be without any long-term changes to positively heal and improve the current climate of her school. She goes to bed each night feeling despair, fear, and hopelessness wondering if she will receive a call informing her that another student's parent has been detained. She wants her school to do more but what? Melissa, like the author's story at the beginning of the chapter, deeply feels the realities her students and families are facing. Although Melissa and her colleagues have proactively found ways to inform and assist families, the work at times feels overwhelming and hopeless. We, as authors, urge those like Melissa to lean into the feelings that permeate rather than having them buried by systemized ways of doing because these emotions serve as an entry point to reaching authentic cariño.

Authentic Cariño and the Human Connection

This is a pivotal moment that requires re-engagement by recognizing how the paths of least resistance and fossilized ways of doing within the profession are not working. No longer is it about roles and routines that have always been followed but relationships and radical change rooted in kinship. The sense of urgency that is being felt elevates the human connection and poses possibilities for working alongside families to ensure safe and caring spaces of mutual reciprocity and respect.

To some degree, many of the stories in this chapter validate the idea of schools being referred to as "mirrors" or microcosms of society. Societal biases and socio-political tensions are embedded in the daily operations of a school, both overtly and covertly, as seen with the señoras' alienation by the system, Catalina's dream being dismissed by her school counselor, and even Melissa's feelings of despair worrying about the outcome of many of her ML families. Yet, like Herrera (seen in the author's narrative), Atifa, Melissa, and her team of colleagues, it begins with authentic cariño. Hope exists, and people are change agents when bounded by radical kinship. Schools reflect the happenings of society at large. However, this idea underestimates how families, students, school counselors, educators, and community leaders working together can create substantive and authentic change that radically alters the path and priorities for schools and communities. As school counselors, community members, and human beings, it is important to reflect on what connects us. Authentic cariño is where it begins. It guides the mindset, motives, and advocacy in our daily endeavors and is the foundation for radical kinship and inclusive change.

Conclusion

Ensuring the success and well-being of students and their families are essential pillars of the school counseling profession (de Oliveira & Wachter Morris, 2015). If the care and assurance of our students and family's well-being are rooted in authentic cariño and radical kinship, these pillars can withstand anything. Supporting ML students and their families requires more than training; it requires a renewed commitment to the reasons for becoming a school counselor. Schools can often be marginalized spaces for ML families and students, but they also have the power to support and uplift their own communities. School counselors stand at the intersection of this crossroad and are needed more than ever.

In this chapter, we have introduced authentic cariño and radical kinship in counseling contexts, situated biography as a tool for culturally grounded school counseling, discussed how school structures can distance school counselors from relational work, and analyzed the role of school counselors amidst current socio-political stressors facing multilingual (ML) families. Additionally, we wove stories into the chapter meant to contextualize a multiplicity of voices and experiences all leading to the concepts of authentic cariño and radical kinship. Lastly, we offered reflective tools and practices for school counselors committed to humanizing their work.

The long hours, extensive demands, and countless needs can weigh heavy on school counselors. It is a profession that demands much and sometimes feels overwhelming. We applaud the instrumental role school counselors play in the field. It is difficult to return to what is most fundamental when feeling pulled in multiple directions. It is precisely at this moment when pause and recognition for the amazing richness within a diverse and vibrant school community is most critical. We end this chapter by returning to its beginning in remembering the tensions Herrera felt during her early years as a school counselor. We urge school counselors to lean into the discomforts and uncertainties to lead with authentic cariño and radical kinship as they work with ML students and families in navigating unfamiliar spaces. Prioritize the rich and diverse family biographies as fundamental, listen to the community members and parents (such as the señoras) wanting to contribute, and trust that small efforts can lead to lasting change.

Review of Recommendations

1 Re-center the role of the counselor to embrace the biographies of the family and student.

- Understand how systems as well as our own biographies impact our perceptual lens on the families and students served.
- Create familial listening sessions where pathways are open for communication without fear or judgment.
- Find school personnel who serve as pivotal entry points for opening dialogue with families. Work as allies within the school to create lines of communication with families.

2 Expand your toolbox to identify ways to create building blocks that help students attain their social and academic goals.

- Move beyond limits of standardized assessments and the scripts they create silos and limit student potentialities.
- Draw upon cultural community wealth to bring to light the overlooked familial and student assets.
- Listen with authentic cariño to the student as they navigate the system to achieve their goals.

3 Stay current to the socio-political moment which heavily influences the day-to-day norms of the school.

- Understanding how national, state, and local policies impact ML learners.
- Provide a safe and professional response to advocate for all learners.
- Extend community networks that diminish traditional notions of "the expert" in order to better reach families while finding ways to create supportive spaces that aren't based on fossilized ways of doing.

References

Bartolomé, L. I. (2008). Authentic cariño and respect in minority education: The political and ideological dimensions of love. *International Journal of Critical Pedagogy*, *1*(1), 1–17. https://res2.weblium.site/res/5fe40a3e4360cf0021845259/602cd8acfb57dd0021 43887a

Bernal-Arevalo, K. E., Pereyra, S., Griffin, D. M., & Sharma, G. (2021). "They're in the shadows": School counselors share the lived experiences of Latino/a undocumented students. *Journal of College Access*, *6*(2), 94–108. https://scholarworks.wmich.edu/jca/vol6/iss2/8/

Boyle, G. (2017). *Barking to the choir: The power of radical kinship*. Simon & Schuster.

Bryk, A. S., & Schneider, B. (2003). Trust in schools: A core resource for school reform. *Educational Leadership*, *60*(6), 40–45. https://rmcgrathprofessionalportfolio.wordpress.com/wp-content/uploads/2021/03/trust-in-schools-a-core-resource-for-school-reform4.pdf

Calkins, A. (2023, May 23). *Why transforming education is so damn hard*. NGLC: Next Generation Learning Challenges. https://www.nextgenlearning.org/articles/why-transforming-public-education-is-so-damn-hard

Camangian, P., & Cariaga, S. (2022). Social and emotional learning is hegemonic miseducation: Students deserve humanization instead. *Race Ethnicity and Education*, *25*(7), 901–921. https://doi.org/10.1080/13613324.2020.1798374

Clark, C. T., Chrisman, A., & Lewis, S. G. (2022). (Un)standardizing emotions: An ethical critique of social and emotional learning standards. *Teachers College Record: The Voice of Scholarship in Education*, *124*(7), 131–149. https://doi.org/10.1177/01614681221111432

Council for Accreditation of Counseling and Related Educational Programs [CACREP]. (2023). *2024 CACREP Standards*. https://www.cacrep.org/for-programs/2024-cacrep-standards/

de Oliveira, L. C., & Wachter Morris, C. (2015). *Preparing school counselors for English language learners*. TESOL Press.

Dewey, J. (1899). *The school and society: Being three lectures*. University of Chicago Press.

Dianis, J. B., Jackson, J. H., & Noguera, P. (2015). High-stakes testing hasn't brought education gains. *Phi Delta Kappan*, *97*(1), 35–37. https://doi.org/10.1177/0031721715602235

Diaz-Strong, D. X. (2025). Nested contexts of support: How the local context shapes school agents' support of undocumented students. *Children and Youth Services Review*, *170*, 108130. https://doi.org/10.1016/j.childyouth.2025.108130

Ee, J. J., & Gándara, P. (2020). *Under siege: The disturbing impact of immigration enforcement on the nation's schools* (Issue Brief Series No. 2). Immigration Initiative at Harvard. https://immigrationinitiative.harvard.edu/wp-content/uploads/2020/01/brief_2_english.pdf

Free, J. L., & Križ, K. (2022). The not-so-hidden curriculum: How a public school system in the United States minoritizes migrant students. *Equity & Excellence in Education*, *55*(1–2), 50–72. https://doi.org/10.1080/10665684.2022.2047409

Gallo, S., & Link, H. (2015). Diles la verdad": Deportation policies, politicized funds of knowledge, and schooling in middle childhood. *Harvard Educational Review*, *85*(3), 357–382. https://doi.org/10.17763/0017-8055.85.3.357

Gonzalez, D., Bernstein, H., Haley, J. M., & Kenney, G. M. (2025, May 29). *Shifting immigration policies jeopardize immigrant families with children: Challenges to basic needs and health care* (Brief). Urban Institute. https://www.urban.org/research/publication/shifting-immigration-policies-jeopardize-immigrant-families-children

Gupta, A. (2024). *Do we dare disturb the status quo?: A critical discourse analysis of CASEL's social and emotional learning (SEL) framework (T)* [Master's thesis, University of British Columbia]. Open Collections, University of British Columbia Archive. https://open.library.ubc.ca/collections/ubctheses/24/items/1.0443551

Herrera, S. G. (2022). *Biography-driven culturally responsive teaching: Honoring race, ethnicity, and personal history* (3 ed.). Teachers College Press.

Herrera, S. G., Porter, L., & Barko-Alva, K. (2020). *Equity in school-parent partnerships: cultivating community and family trust in culturally and linguistically diverse classrooms*. Teachers College Press.

Hilliard, C., Goodman-Scott, E., Edirmanasinghe, N., & Smith Durkin, S. (2025). The experiences of multilingual-learning-focused school counselors: A phenomenological investigation. *Professional School Counseling, 29*(1). https://doi.org/10.1177/2156759X251386815

Jiang, L., & Harklau, L. (2024). Multilingual learners' access to college: Students, school counselors, and institutional doxa and hysteresis. *TESOL Journal, 58*(2), 881–908. https://doi.org/10.1002/tesq.3260

Johnson, K. R. (2022). Systemic racism in the U.S. immigration laws. *Indiana Law Journal, 97*(4), 1145–1170. https://www.repository.law.indiana.edu/ilj/vol97/iss4/4/

Kanno, Y., & Cromley, J. G. (2013). English language learners' access to and attainment in postsecondary education. *TESOL Quarterly, 47*(1), 89–121. https://doi.org/10.1002/tesq.49

Kyles-Smith, K. (2023). To address learning gaps, go deeper. *Educational Leadership, 81*(1). https://www.ascd.org/el/articles/to-address-learning-gaps-go-deeper

Mayes, R. D., & Byrd, J. A. (2022). An antiracist framework for evidence-informed school counseling practice. *Professional School Counseling, 26*(1a). https://doi.org/10.1177/2156759X221086740

Najarro, I. (2025, February 26). What to know when advising college-bound, undocumented students. *Education Week*. https://www.edweek.org/teaching-learning/what-to-know-when-advising-college-bound-undocumented-students/2025/02

National Center for Education Statistics (2024). *English learners in public schools*. U.S. Department of Education, Institute of Education Sciences. Retrieved February 2, 2026, from https://nces.ed.gov/programs/coe/indicator/cgf.

Niles, J. K., Dorais, S., Cashwell, C. C., Mullen, P. R., & Jensen, S.. (2024). School counselors' burnout, hope, and self-efficacy: A sequential regression analysis. *Journal of Counseling & Development, 102*(4). https://doi.org/10.1002/jcad.12530

Porter, L., Barko-Alva, K., & Herrera, S. G. (2021). Plexiglass: How power, policy and politics create a mirage of equitable family engagement. *Journal for Multicultural Education, 15*(3), 330–342. https://doi.org/10.1108/JME-08-2020-0086

Prattico, E. (2022). Can democracy survive without the voice of experts? With an interview with Kenneth Baynes. In E. Prattico (Ed.), *Habermas and the crisis of democracy: Interview with leading thinkers* (pp. 100–119). New York, NY: Routledge. https://doi.org/10.4324/9781003144519-6

Purgason, L. L., Johnson, G., Vallecillo, O., Covington, C., Parker, R. H., & Airhart-Larraga, S. (2024). English ass a second language teachers' perspectives on interprofessional collaboration with school counselors: Supporting emergent bilingual students. *Journal of Educational and Psychological Consultation, 34*(2), 168–197. https://doi.org/10.1080/10474412.2023.2240304

Rogers, J., Kahne, J., La Torre, D., Castro, C., Stern, S., Bronstein, M., & Ishimoto, M. (2025). *The Fear is Everywhere: U.S. High School principals report widespread effects of immigration enforcement*. UCLA's Institute for Democracy, Education, and Access. https://idea.gseis.ucla.edu/publications/files/fear-is-everywhere-report

Ruiz Malagon, J. C. (2025). Acompañamiento as a Latine critical race theory approach to community public health research. *Latino Studies, 23*, 350–358. https://doi.org/10.1057/s41276-025-00520-7

Sellars, M., & Imig, S. (2023). Mirror, mirror on the wall? Is there anything fair in here at all? Examining the current relationship of school and society. *Discourse: Studies in the Cultural Politics of Education, 44*(5), 713–726. https://doi.org/10.1080/01596306.2022.2120456

Sharma, G., Yukhymenko-Lescroart, M., & Bernal-Arevalo, K. (2023). Counseling students' experiences and interpretations of purpose development. *Heliyon, 9*(3), e13760. https://doi.org/10.1016/j.heliyon.2023.e13760

Shi, Q., & Brown, M. H. (2020). School counselors' impact on school-level academic outcomes: Caseload and use of time. *Professional School Counseling, 23*. https://doi.org/10.1177/2156759X20904489

Shi, Q., & Watkinson, J. (2019). English language learners and school belonging: Implications for school counselor practice. *Professional School Counseling, 22*(1b). https://doi.org/10.1177/2156759X19834442

Stearns, C. (2019). *Critiquing social and emotional learning: Psychodynamic and cultural perspectives. Lexington Books*. http://doi.org/10.5040/9781666992472

Valenzuela, A. (1999). *Subtractive schooling: U.S.-Mexican youth and the politics of caring*. State University of New York Press.

Chapter 7

Developing and Maintaining Collaborative Partnerships with Key Personnel to Support Multilingual Learners

Malti Tuttle, Lucy Purgason, Leonissa V. Johnson, and Alexis Dowdell

Introduction

Multilingual learners (MLs) represent one of the fastest-growing student populations in the United States, a trend projected to continue (National Center for Education Statistics, 2020). Often MLs are underserved and overlooked due to the belief that students are being served by the ESOL teacher. This poses a challenge in that the MLs' holistic needs are not being met through a comprehensive school counseling program or school-wide focus. Further exacerbating this service gap is the low number of school counselors who themselves are MLs or have training in skills to serve MLs. Former U.S. Secretary of Education, Miguel Cardona, during the National Association for Bilingual Education was quoted asking, "Why is it that in 2023, in many school systems in our country, we treat our English learners as students with deficits-rather than assets in a globally competitive world?" (Najarro, 2023). School counselors who are equity minded and focused recognize MLs as assets and vital to the nation. Therefore, the role and practice of collaboration with key personnel to support the development of MLs in school settings is critical. This chapter invites school counselors to address the critical call to action to collaborate and advocate for supporting MLs.

School counselors are trained to collaborate with key personnel within the school setting to support students' success. Through collaborative partnerships, school counselors leverage their power and influence to advocate for MLs and their families by building a community of support focusing on academic development, career preparation, and social-emotional learning. This chapter highlights how school counselors can develop collaborative partnerships with administration, teachers, ESOL teachers, school nurses, interpreters, and community agencies to access resources for the unique needs of MLs. This chapter is grounded in an adapted version of Wachter Morris' (2025) collaboration framework which includes joining forces amongst key personnel to drive change through collaborative practices to address challenges faced by MLs, collaboration opportunities with invested partners, and roles and responsibilities for each

DOI: 10.4324/9781003711124-9

identified partner. Ethical considerations and recommendations will be included to guide collaboration and decision-making.

Role of School Counselors Collaborating through an Equity and Access Lens

In April 2022, the Office of English Language Acquisition (OELA) published a document titled "Addressing the Impact of COVID-19 on Multilingual Learners and Their Social and Emotional wellbeing" that focused on MLs and their families. OELA outlined how the consequences from the pandemic resulted in "disproportionate and inter-related consequences for their economic stability, educational opportunities and outcomes, and social, emotional, physical, and mental well-being" (2022, p. 1). The four specific areas of impact addressed by OLEA focused on school attendance; economic, community, and society; supports and resources; and physical and mental health. During the pandemic, MLs experienced the most disruptions to learning and education even though schools pivoted to online learning formats (Catalano et al., 2021; Sugarman & Lazarín, 2020). Even now, it is imperative to recognize that the academic and mental health needs of MLs continue to arise and present themselves post-COVID-19 within the school settings (Purgason et al., 2024). The American School Counselor Association (ASCA) strongly calls for school counselors to serve as "advocates for equitable treatment of all students and strive to establish inclusive and welcoming learning environments in which all students can thrive and reach their full potential" in *The School Counselor and Equity for All Students* position statement (2024). Therefore, school counselors are called to advocate and collaborate with and on behalf of MLs to ensure that equitable access to educational, mental, and physical health, and post-secondary opportunities are available to students.

Collaboration

Collaboration between school counselors and invested partners is vital in the role of supporting, advocating, and working with and on behalf of MLs (Tuttle et al., 2021). School counselors encounter many individuals in the school setting and engage in various activities involving collaboration of students. Therefore, school counselors are in the position to be mindful of what is discussed during these conversations and ensure that they are advocating ethically on behalf of students. This is especially important in regard to MLs since they may fall under vulnerable populations.

The American School Counselor Association (ASCA, 2022) Ethical Standards for School Counselors mentions *collaboration, collaborate,* and *collaborators* throughout the entirety of the ethical standards which highlights the immense role school counselors have in maintaining ethical dispositions throughout the collaboration process. Furthermore, as school counselors collaborate to support MLs, they must keep the ethical standards at the forefront. Specific ethical standards pertaining to MLs fall under the B.2 Responsibilities to the School (ASCA, 2022) section focusing on collaborating to remove barriers to promote equitable student outcomes (B.2.e) and to advocate to ensure that bilingual/multilingual interpreters are vetted to represent the cultures and languages of the student, families and guardians, and community (B.2.j). These specific ASCA Ethical Standards underscore the ethical responsibilities and obligations school counselors have in collaborating with invested and critical parties to support the success and well-being of MLs.

School-Family-Community Partnerships Model

One approach to collaboration with multiple stakeholders is the school-community-family partnerships model. This model, developed by Bryan and Henry (2012), has evolved and been utilized with various populations and contexts in recent years (Bryan et al., 2020, 2022; Cook et al., 2016; Henry et al., 2017). The model involves a seven-stage process that begins with counselors considering their worldview and attitudes regarding students, families, and communities. This step allows counselors, school faculty, and staff to reflect on stereotypes, biases, or deficit-based narratives that could hinder strengths-based and equitable partnerships and collaboration with ML families and communities. Next, counselors assess the needs and strengths of the school community by listening to and centering diverse voices, including MLs, families, communities, and stakeholders. This stage may highlight relevant needs, generate goals, and identify key partners and resources to include in future collaboration. Additionally, skills such as community asset mapping may draw attention to people, resources, and institutions that can help meet pertinent needs (Griffin & Farris, 2010).

As counselors continue with the model, they develop a partnership leadership team that includes relevant collaborators such as administrators, ESOL teachers, nurses, ML families, and community members. At this stage, intentional outreach and invitations to ML parents and relevant cultural brokers are critical. Once a leadership team is established, a shared vision for collaboration and partnership can begin. The team identifies new, non-traditional, and culturally appropriate ways to partner (Bryan et al., 2022). Centering the suggestions and perspectives of MLs team members is critical to ensure community-informed and culturally relevant solutions (Betters-Bubon & Schultz, 2018). Additionally, centering family and community voices may yield collaboration with community-trusted leaders and organizations (Cook et al., 2016). Once a plan is in place, partners take action (Bryan & Henry, 2012). Infusing welcoming and inviting practices, such as timely invitations, prepared interpreters, and relevant content, may yield successful initiatives. Furthermore, recruiting multilingual families and community members to both participate in developed activities and lead by sharing their perspective, expertise, and resources can positively impact engagement. Completing the partnership model involves evaluating partnerships and maintaining ongoing communication to sustain collaborative efforts and ensure that they evolve and grow in meaningful ways. Components of the school-family-partnership model will be further employed in later sections of this chapter.

Collaboration with School Leaders

School counselors along with administrators are uniquely and well positioned to collaborate with school administrators to improve instructional equity since both professionals possess leadership roles within the school setting (Bryant et al., 2024; Lashley & Stickl, 2016). As educational leaders, school administrators are in the role to influence policies and programs that have significant implications for the learning environment which impact ML (Mavrogordato & White, 2020; Phillips et al., 2023). Therefore, the school administrator can lean into the school counselor to work to support MLs by reviewing policies, data, and engaging in strategic planning to create an inclusive school environment. Both professionals are trained in leadership and together are able to harness their specific roles to develop and identify practices that will support success for ML students which may include scheduling culturally informative training for teachers and staff, assessing family needs and hosting coffee talks to build community, leveraging on positionality and power to advocate at the district office for the services of vetted and trained interpreters if needed (Tuttle et al., 2022).

Collaboration with Classroom Teachers

Classroom teachers are an integral part of a student's academic journey, playing a vital role in the academic and social development of MLs through daily direct instructional interactions. Because of this, teachers can have a powerful impact on MLs' academic success and eventual educational attainment. Teachers' perception of their students' ability to succeed academically has been connected to MLs feeling more supported and more willing to engage in behaviors beneficial to their learning (Hersi & Watkinson, 2012). Specifically, teachers' positive beliefs about their ML students and personal investment in their success can have a significant positive impact on MLs' academic achievement. Facing barriers like large class sizes, insufficient access to interpreters, and time constraints of a busy school day, teachers can be left with few resources or time to implement targeted interventions for these students. Thus, it becomes essential that school counselors collaborate with classroom teachers to support and cultivate the learning experiences of MLs with a multi-tiered approach.

To address the individual needs of each specific ML student, it is imperative that counselors and teachers working with MLs understand that each student comes to the school with a unique combination of languages, customs, skills, and needs that will impact their learning experiences and shape the challenges they face in the school environment. In addition to the stressors that come with learning a new language, often while adjusting to a new country, MLs may also struggle to form friendships with non-ML students and may feel disconnected from their school community and lack a sense of belonging (Duff, 2001). Consequently, teachers have noticed that these challenges can prevent MLs from interacting and engaging in the classroom (Shi & Watkinson, 2019). Research has highlighted the importance of teachers utilizing targeted instructional strategies to support MLs in ways that honor their identities, yet it can be harder to put this in practice as a lone instructor (Nieto, 2017). Therefore, it is necessary that teachers and counselors work together to address and cultivate a tailored learning experience for MLs that is centered on increasing student connections inside and outside of the classroom and validation of their identities. A needs-assessment targeted to MLs could be an effective tool to learn about the specific needs of these students and the details of each subgroup of MLs. The data from this assessment could be shared between teachers and counselors to increase shared knowledge about the school's ML population, inform collaborative efforts, and facilitate the development of targeted interventions to address the unique needs of each ML student in their classrooms.

A key initial step in addressing the needs of MLs in a school is becoming well informed about evidence-based practices and data-driven strategies tailored to support the ML population. Collaboration between school counselors and teachers is most effective when both parties possess a strong understanding of strategies specifically designed to support MLs within their school context (Davis et al., 2023). The impact of this collaboration can be multiplied across the school when more educators receive targeted training that equips them with the skills necessary to effectively support MLs (Davis et al., 2023). The need for more training on teaching and supporting MLs is apparent as research has also underscored teachers' perspectives on feeling unprepared to meet the needs of their MLs (Hong et al., 2019). When school counselors and teachers collaborate to understand the cultural and linguistic backgrounds and experiences of MLs, they are better positioned to cultivate inclusive learning environments that promote both a sense of belonging and academic success for MLs (Villegas & Lucas, 2002). Advocating for more professional development opportunities and the intentional sharing of resources between counselors and teachers can enhance both groups' confidence and capacity to effectively support MLs.

Although the process to facilitating effective partnerships and collaboration between school counselors and teachers may seem a bit daunting given the specific barriers that exist within a school to inhibit this kind of collaboration (e.g., time constraints, role ambiguity, lack of a resource-sharing system), teachers and counselors can work together to leverage existing systems in the school to foster this collaboration. For example, counselors and teachers can implement scheduled collaboration times during Student Success Team (SST) meetings or during staff meetings to overcome time constraints and create a consistent communication system. This kind of structured, action-focused collaboration is critical for identifying unmet needs, sharing evidence-based resources, and designing culturally responsive strategies (Davis et al., 2023). By working together to implement scaffolded Tier II and Tier III interventions – such as creating inclusive onboarding protocols for new MLs – counselors and teachers can streamline efforts and create a smooth transition for new ML students. Moreover, research supports that collaboration across roles in core content areas is more effective when both counselors and teachers bring their unique knowledge and skillsets to the partnership (Gibbons et al., 2010). Joint initiatives like co-teaching classroom lessons and integrating SEL concepts into core curricula can help integrate academic, social-emotional, and career development goals in ways that are inclusive of MLs' needs (Mariani et al., 2016). These collaborative efforts enable teachers and counselors to create a robust system of support that is tailored to the needs of the diverse cultural and academic experiences of MLs while leveraging and strengthening schoolwide systems already in place. These integrated approaches and intentional, action-focused collaboration initiatives between counselors and teachers can foster a holistic educational experience to enhance the learning and improve the academic outcomes of MLs.

Collaboration with ESOL Teachers

English for Speakers of Other Languages (ESOL) teachers possess a unique skillset within the K-12 school setting. ESOL teacher endorsement requires coursework specifically in instructional approaches and pedagogical considerations for MLs, linguistics education, and the processes of learning a new language, and culturally responsive learning considerations (Linville, 2020). ESOL teachers serve MLs using a variety of instructional models including pull-out instruction in a separate classroom or push-in instruction and co-teaching with the classroom teacher. In addition to supporting MLs in academic instruction, ESOL teachers often spend the most time with MLs and their families, developing rapport and establishing strong relationships (Vera et al., 2022). MLs' immigration stories vary from harrowing journeys of fleeing armed conflicts to resettlement in the United States for parents' educational or job opportunities. Regardless of the circumstances of arrival in the United States, the acculturation and transition stress of resettlement can take a physical, emotional, and financial toll. Through connections made in the ESOL program, with students who speak the same language or share similar experiences, MLs may share their stories, providing insights important for school counselors to consider when developing comprehensive school counseling programs (Johnson & Cain, 2019).

Whether through involving ESOL teachers in pre-planning to help design curriculum lessons that increase accessibility of the content for MLs, consultation with ESOL teachers ahead of SST meetings to better understand a student's strengths and experiences, or utilizing ESOL teacher's social capital with families to share information about the school counseling program, collaboration with ESOL teachers is critical to ensuring that the needs of MLs are identified, understood, and supported. Though ESOL teachers view collaborations with school counselors positively (Tuttle et al., 2021), they often report being overlooked for conversations involving MLs (Johnson et al., 2019); therefore, it is incumbent upon the school counselor to intentionally invite or advocate for ESOL teacher involvement in things like student support team meetings, school counseling advisory boards, and professional learning communities. Involving ESOL teachers in these spaces creates a foundation of comprehensive supports to facilitate and enhance learning experiences and academic outcomes for ML students (Davis et al., 2023).

Case Study

Korina is an elementary school counselor working in a rural district with a student population in her building of just over 500 students. Prior to her arrival, the school counseling position was vacant for two years, as there was a statewide school counselor shortage, especially in her rural area. The town where the school is located has seen an increase of immigrants and asylee seekers from Venezuela and El Salvador. She is the sole school counselor and has been implementing a comprehensive school counseling program since starting five years ago.

Korina was proud of the efforts she had made to integrate an evidence-based SEL curriculum. She was able to deliver at least one unit in each grade level based on classroom teacher completed needs assessments and school-wide screener data. Unfortunately, her high student caseload prevented her from delivering more lessons. In most years, she ran at least two sets of counseling groups (one set in the fall and one in the spring) on topics such as coping skills, friendship skills, and academic skills, but time spent meeting individually with students in crisis was impeding her ability to deliver counseling groups.

Korina's principal recently approached her regarding reports from the lunch duty teachers regarding students visibly upset on the playground during lunch recess. The duty teacher reported that four out of five days of the week one or two students at each lunch recess were alone and crying. One teacher attempted to intervene, but the students were Spanish speakers, and the teacher was not fluent. The principal asked Korina to check in with the students to find out about what support they might need. Korina learned that each of the students was a ML and newcomer to the United States. It occurred to Korina that given their shared identities the students might benefit from meeting together in a small group.

Finding time to re-dedicate to group counseling interventions would require multiple forms of advocacy. First, Korina knew that she needed to find a way to carve out more time in her schedule for Tier II interventions. Teachers were familiar with the evidence-based SEL curriculum, as Korina had been implementing it in classrooms for two years. Korina realized that she could use data-driven strategies to identify the topics and then curate the units for delivery by classroom teachers. With teachers delivering these lessons, students would have greater access to curriculum related to conflict resolution, coping skills, empowerment, and leadership, and Korina would have more time to run groups.

Korina brought this forward to the principal, using pre-post data regarding the current impact of SEL lessons and the subsequent increase in groups she could offer as rationale. The principal and Korina collaborated to identify two staff meetings dedicated to planning for this transition. In the first meeting, Korina would present logistics including the plan that she and the principal developed for delivering the lessons during a dedicated time during the school week. The second meeting would be devoted to strategies for teaching SEL, including best practices for presenting curriculum to MLs. In preparing for these meetings, Korina consulted with the ESOL teacher, who agreed to partner with Korina to present instructional strategies for ML at the school-wide meeting. One idea they developed was doing a brief experiential activity where content for the lesson would be provided to teachers in Spanish, as an empathy-building exercise to demonstrate the difficulties language learners encounter, and to highlight this linguistic strength.

Once the details of the SEL curriculum were determined, Korina turned her attention to starting the newcomer group. As a monolingual speaker, Korina experienced hesitancy and concern that this would limit her ability to facilitate. Not only did she not have the personal experience as a newcomer, but she had never successfully learned another language and worried this would hinder her ability to effectively communicate with students. Korina researched and identified a technology using an I-pad and earbuds to translate from English into a student's first language. The technology could translate to the specific dialect of a language, important for students at Korina's school who were from Venezuela and El Salvador. Although the ear buds were more expensive than hand-held translators, Korina requested funds from the parent-teacher association to purchase.

Korina began to search for a group curriculum to cover topics such as adjusting to a new environment, navigating school in the United States, identifying cultural strengths, and coping with transition-related feelings. Unfortunately, her initial search did not yield any elementary group counseling curriculum designed for ML but after consulting with colleagues she learned about Supporting Transition Resilience of Newcomer Groups (STRONG), a 10-session group curriculum available in an elementary version to support newcomer immigrant and refugee youth (strongforschools.com, 2024). Collaborating with the ESOL teacher provided Korina with insights on how she could present the group curriculum to better ensure language access. In addition, the ESOL teacher shared information she knew about the students' transition experiences based on what she had learned from students and their families. She also offered to translate the group permission form to share with families and introduce Korina on a phone call.

Korina was excited to begin the groups, yet she also recognized that she had not been able to proactively address the needs of the burgeoning newcomer population in her school and community. To ensure that these student need gaps did not occur in the future, she committed to routinely consulting with teachers about newcomer needs during their professional learning community time and auditing the student needs assessment and screeners they complete to ensure that concerns would be identified.

Reflection Questions

1. What language supports are currently available in your school and community? (e.g., bilingual staff, translation devices, language learning programs)?
2. What ML classroom strategies are you familiar with, and how can these inform your group counseling approach?
3. What resources and supports are available in your setting for students with trauma histories?
4. What opportunities do you have to engage administrators in your setting in advocating for the needs of MLs and families?
5. What community agencies, non-profits, and/or faith-based groups could be potential collaborators?

Collaboration with Parents/Caregivers/Families

Parents, caregivers, and families are critical stakeholders in students' lives. As the original microsystem, MLs are a part of, parents and families possess a wealth of information regarding student history, backgrounds, and culture (Johnson et al., 2019). Parents can influence student outcomes, including grades, motivation, course placement, and retention rates. Further, guardians impact student goal setting and behaviors (Hoover-Dempsey et al., 2005). It is imperative, therefore, that school counselors collaborate with parents, caregivers, and families.

Styles of parent collaboration or involvement vary. Historically, participation in U.S. schools by middle and upper-income parents has included volunteering, Parent Teacher Association engagement, and ongoing support with homework. Parent involvement amongst multilingual families may look different, especially due to work schedules, language acquisition, and efforts to understand the U.S. education system (Gonzalez et al., 2013; Mitchell & Bryan, 2007). Additionally, schools may inadvertently exclude multilingual families from engagement by using only monolingual communication and limited outreach to multilingual families (Gonzalez et al., 2013).

Before engaging in parent/caregiver/family collaboration, school counselors and other personnel must consider their own beliefs and perceptions about multilingual families. Deficit-oriented perspectives may lead to assumptions about multilingual parents' interest, capacity, and ability to be meaningfully involved in their children's education (Gonzalez et al., 2013). Bryan and Henry (2012) explained the importance of centering family voices and utilizing strengths-based approaches when collaborating with parents and caregivers.

Hoover-Dempsey et al. (2005) noted several factors that influence parent involvement, including parent motivation, invitations, and life contextual factors. Other researchers have expounded on these factors within multilingual parent contexts when engaging multilingual families and offered recommendations including partner-focused engagement, intentional invitations, and flexibility (Betters-Bubon & Shultz, 2018; Gonzalez et al., 2013; Mitchell & Bryan, 2007). For example, Gonzalez et al. (2013) described the concept of *respeto*, a high esteem that Latino families may hold for adults and professionals working with youth in the community. Similarly, Mitchell and Bryan (2007) detailed an authority figure perspective held by some Caribbean immigrant parents. As a result, multilingual families may have a deference for educator expertise and choose not to interfere with their children's education out of a sense of respect. Communicating expectations about family involvement is essential to ensure ML family participation. Intentional invitations from the school and school counselors are an important step. These invitations should communicate specific details about events, content that will be shared, and how families can anticipate being involved (Gonzalez et al., 2013).

School counselors should also offer families flexible options for participation. Soliciting feedback from families about their preferences for contact (i.e., phone calls, text messages, etc.) and the ways they are most interested in collaborating (i.e., learning, volunteering, providing resources, etc.) is critical. School counselors can use this feedback to identify meaningful opportunities for multilingual family participation that allow ML parents to contribute knowledge, expertise, or perspective. Counselors should also solicit ideas from families about the best places to connect (i.e., school groups, home visits, community-based locations, etc.) to foster engagement or connection (Betters-Bubon & Shultz, 2018; Gonzalez et al., 2013). Finally, invitations and other outreach activities should include and make explicit language support services, such as interpreters or translation services. Making clear that families will have communication access fosters family collaboration and involvement.

Collaboration with Interpreters/Translators

Differences in language can impede parent and family collaboration or partnership (Gonzalez et al., 2013). Language access refers to providing written or verbal information to parents or guardians in a language they can understand (Gardner & Love, 2025). Schools may have several multilingual staff members who support their day-to-day activities and bridge language gaps across the school community. Multilingual staff are essential to building and sustaining relationships with ML families and communities (Gardner & Love, 2025).

Interpreters, however, are distinct from multilingual staff as they have formal training in interpretation/translation and the legal and educational contexts wherein they interpret (Gardner & Love, 2025). Interpreters should be employed when impartial parties are needed to communicate critical information between families and school staff, such as formal meetings disclosing student-related data/concerns or events presented to the broader school community. Challenges with interpreters include conflicts with confidentiality, omitting or shifting language used by the speaker, role ambiguity, misinterpreting personal reactions, and lacking contextual knowledge about the school, policies, or student/family contexts (Paone & Malott, 2008).

Scholars have recommended that counselors facilitate pre- and post-session briefings to avoid and work through potential interpreter challenges (Paone & Malott, 2008). Edirmanasinghe et al. (2022) proposed that during the pre-session briefing, school counselors explain "a) the interpreter's role, b) the purpose/goal of the meeting, and c) expectations of school counseling sessions in general" (p. 65). Additional topics to discuss during the pre-session briefings include interpreter knowledge about school counseling, confidentiality and its limits, and content that may be emotionally or topically difficult for families or the interpreter (Paone & Malott, 2008). School counselors can also use the pre-briefing session to rehearse, discuss event logistics (i.e., where the interpreter will sit or stand), and solicit interpreter input about cultural factors that may influence the event (Edirmanasinghe et al., 2022; Paone & Malott, 2008).

School counselors should be mindful that utilizing interpreters may impact the length of the event. Further, speakers should use clear sentences to support audience understanding (Paone & Malott, 2008). Finally, once events are over, school counselors should engage in debriefing sessions to review interpretation-related issues, process interpreter reactions, and reinforce confidentiality (Paone & Malott, 2008). Successful collaboration with interpreters can yield positive outcomes for ML and their families.

Collaboration with School Nurses

School nurses also interact and engage with students to support their physical and mental health well-being. Often students might seek the services of the school nurse to address social-emotional, health, and economic needs (Tuttle et al., 2018). These specific needs may encompass coordination of care, hearing and vision screening, access to glasses and medical referrals, and promotion of wellness activities. The role of the school nurse intersects with the school counselor in that each addresses various student concerns such as child abuse, neglect, community outreach, bullying, social anxiety, and barrier to health care (Tuttle et al., 2018; Whitman et al., 2010). Furthermore, Whitman et al. (2010) recognized that the increase of immigration led to "unique challenges for school health services with the subsequent introduction to new cultures and languages" (p. 209).

The school nurse has an integral role in collaborating with school counselors to support the wellness of all students, including MLs. Tuttle et al. (2018) developed the School Counselor and School Nurse Collaboration Model, which outlined four steps to collaboration: 1) Mutual Understanding of Professional Role in the School Setting, 2) Respect for Ethical Considerations, 3) Establishing Guidelines for Collaboration, and 4) Ongoing Communication and Consultation. These four steps provide a framework to guide the collaboration between school counselors and school nurses to ensure that both professions' training, expertise, and roles are in the forefront. Specifically, ensuring that ethical and professional dispositions are maintained to prevent overstepping of boundaries or ethical violations (Figure 7.1).

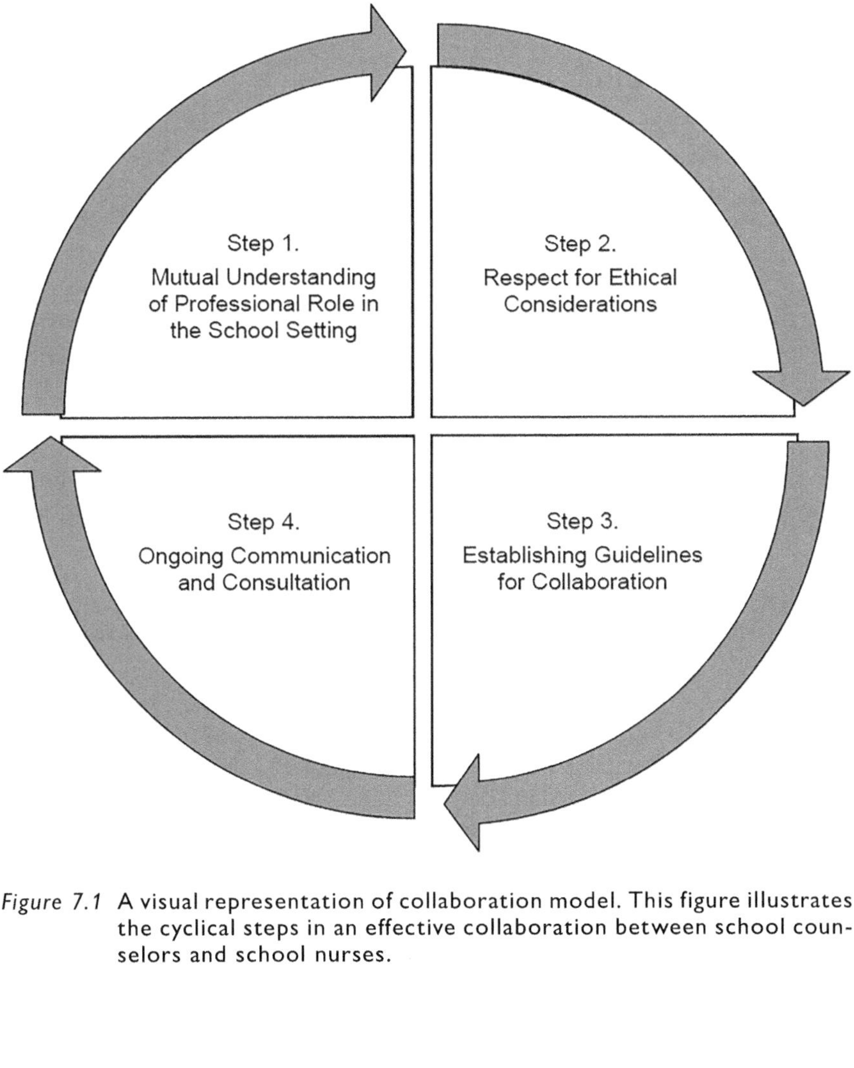

Figure 7.1 A visual representation of collaboration model. This figure illustrates the cyclical steps in an effective collaboration between school counselors and school nurses.

School nurses provide education services to students and families pertaining to physical and medical health. Furthermore, school nurses are prepared to assist in educating vulnerable populations, which may include MLs and immigrants, by ensuring their education delivery is accessible to everyone (Tuttle et al., 2018). The school counselor can collaborate with the school nurse to ensure ethical considerations are made when connecting MLs with outside referral resources, seeking vetted interpreters to avoid students engaging in language brokering, and bridging communication gaps when language may be a barrier (Tuttle & Johnson, 2018; Whitman et al., 2010). School counselors and school nurses who collaborate to address the needs of ML students and families through linguistically appropriate means "can significantly reduce the barriers to access, eliminate disparities, and improve health and academic outcomes" (Whitman et al., 2010, p. 212).

Collaboration with Community

From an ecological systems perspective, school counselors increase their ability to provide wrap-around and holistic support to MLs and families by working with faith-based institutions, non-profit and community agencies, and mental health providers. Partnering with these groups can help school counselors identify and allocate resources that can help increase educational access and participation for MLs, as communication, transportation, and financial challenges for many MLs can limit their ability to participate in school and school-affiliated activities. This can also impact their ability to navigate systems such as the college application process, often requiring knowledge of post-secondary supports (e.g., Federal Financial Aid, scholarships, college and career technology platforms) and financial resources for associated costs of application and testing fees.

School counselor community collaboration can provide MLs access to cultural brokers and translators sharing their linguistic and cultural backgrounds and may be able to assist with financial and basic needs resources. Beyond resource provision, community partners can establish mentoring relationships with MLs and connect on shared cultural identities. For example, Arriero and Griffin (2019) engaged in community asset mapping to identify resources and guest speakers from the Latinx community for a career and college readiness program for Latinx high school students. Topics were identified by the students themselves, offering a platform for self-advocacy and empowerment.

Given the rise in mental health needs impacting MLs, especially in the wake of the COVID-19 pandemic and current national and global socio-political factors, school counselors' ability to connect families to community mental health resources is critical (Purgason et al., 2024). Cultivating a vetted list of bilingual mental health providers accepting a variety of payment options is important. Some schools have a person in the position of a family-community liaison who can act on behalf of families to help coordinate services, but in the absence of this position school counselors can develop and maintain relationships with key community partners to advocate for the needs of MLs and families.

Case Study

Leslie is a school counselor in a mid-sized, suburban *middle* school. She is one of two school counselors in a school with 1,100 students and a large ML population. The majority of MLs are Spanish-speaking, but in recent years, a growing number of Haitian MLs have enrolled at her school who primarily speak Haitian-Creole.

Since the COVID-19 pandemic, the school's state-wide achievement test scores have dropped. This year, the School Improvement Plan includes a goal to increase state-wide math test scores by ten percent. To help reach the goal, the school hosted a Math Night. While teachers facilitated math activities with students, Leslie hosted a test-prep information workshop for families to share details about the upcoming statewide test cycle, school technology tools that offer access to students' daily assignments, and strategies to support students at home during the testing window. Leslie requested a school district-provided interpreter to support this workshop and met the interpreter 10 minutes before the program began.

When reviewing the Math Night sign-in sheets at the end of the meeting, Leslie noticed that very few Haitian families attended. *When she mentioned this to a teacher colleague, the teacher said that families did not always prioritize attending these events.* Leslie was frustrated by this response and wanted to take action to better connect with the Haitian families at her school but was not sure where to begin.

Leslie began by reflecting on her own knowledge, attitudes, and implicit biases about the Haitian students and families in her school community. She considered what she knew about the experiences of the families that arrived at her school. Many Haitians came to her state after a natural disaster over 15 years ago. More families relocated due to ongoing political unrest. Over the last decade, a growing number of Haitian churches, businesses, and a Haitian-American Chamber of Commerce emerged in her area. Leslie also reflected on how harmful attitudes by school staff could impact Haitian family engagement. Leslie recognized that she alone did not have all the resources to meet student needs, but partnering with school stakeholders, families, and the broader community could make a positive difference for students.

Leslie gathered data to assess the needs and strengths of the Haitian students and families in her school. Leslie started by reaching out to Haitian MLs and parents for listening sessions. The ESOL teacher invited Leslie to talk with the Haitian students in her class about their experiences at school. Leslie worked with the Parent Liaison to connect with Haitian families. She began with the Haitian families who attended her Math Night workshop. She called and thanked them for participating in the workshop and asked if they would be open to talking with her about their experiences in the school. She also asked if there were other parents they believed she should connect with to better understand their experiences and the best methods to contact and engage in the future. Parents shared that communication by text and meetings after school hours would be most helpful. Leslie and the Parent Liaison scheduled listening sessions to hear families' stories about their experiences at school.

During the listening sessions, Leslie learned that several parents of Haitian students appreciated the Math Night but expressed concern about the event and other school activities. Some parents did not realize they were expected to attend since teachers had "expertise" regarding math teaching and requirements. Other parents were frustrated that they were not informed about the meeting until a few days beforehand and had difficulty navigating work and family schedules. Additionally, the content shared during the session was difficult to understand due to the interpreter's different dialect. Parents also noted the interpreter's lack of familiarity with the session content. Parents shared that while they were a growing community in their school, the technology platforms and resources used for day-to-day communications did not have content available in Haitian Creole. Leslie recognized the need for better communication resources. She asked families if they would be open to participating in these efforts to find solutions or if they were aware of any individuals from the local Haitian community who might be a helpful advocate or resource. Parents shared information about a local Haitian church that engaged in outreach in the community.

Leslie shared the listening session data with her principal and co-counselor. She was encouraged to facilitate a multidisciplinary team to develop partnerships. Haitian parents and cultural brokers from the community were invited to participate on the team. School personnel such as the ESOL teacher, Parent Liaison, Math teacher, school nurse, and school counselors were also on the team. Needs expressed during the listening sessions were shared. Together, the Partnership team identified needs and community resources including people, civic associations, and institutions with resources to potentially address needs. Additionally, the school nurse shared community health resources in case illness impacted attendance causing students to miss school and academic instruction which is crucial to learning.

The team identified a key goal for communication resources and supports for Haitian families and other multilingual families. The team also believed that strategic outreach to help Haitian students and families feel connected to the school was important. The team developed a plan for updated licenses for school technology, local interpreter outreach and development, and a parent welcome initiative for Haitian families and students to feel connected to the school and learn about the school community. The committee shared the plan and goals with the school community and solicited feedback.

The school administrator and technology lead connected with the district regarding the school technology license update. Counselors met with the local church leaders and the Haitian-American Chamber of Commerce to identify individuals who spoke the relevant dialect. Individuals were invited to participate in the district-led interpreter training program. A Welcome group was established that paired new Haitian families with parents who had been at the school for two or more years. A Kick-off meeting occurred at the school for families to connect and hear about topics of interest from Haitian families. The group held monthly meetings at the Haitian church since families already participated in weekly church-related events. The school counselors, administrators, nurse, teachers, and other personnel rotated as speakers for these sessions and provided updates about school resources, technology, and upcoming activities. One grade level of teachers was also invited each month to greet families. Reminders were texted to families with information about the upcoming session. Locally trained interpreters participated in each of the sessions, and pre-briefing meetings were held with the relevant speaker a week ahead of the event. Over time, a Pan-Caribbean club from a local university provided childcare and math tutoring to MLs during the monthly sessions to earn volunteer hours. Parents and Pan-Caribbean club members were also invited to spread the word and apply to the district-led interpreter training program. The Partnership team evaluated the progress made from the original goals.

Reflection Questions

1 What are the histories and geo-political contexts of the MLs in your school and community?
2 What are the narratives about MLs, their families, and their communities in your school? Who informed those narratives? Do they need to be challenged?
3 Who are the trusted cultural brokers for ML communities in your school and community? How might you identify and engage with those brokers?
4 What might help you work most effectively with the interpretation/translation supports at your school/community?
5 How can you identify and build relationships with relevant partners at your school and within your community?

Conclusion

School counselors are uniquely trained and positioned to support the success and well-being of ML students within the school setting by collaborating with invested key personnel and partners. An approach through an equity lens extends into the ethical obligations school counselors are responsible for in their work to meet the needs of all students. Collaboration with administrators, teachers, ESOL teachers, school nurses, families, and communities builds partnerships to keep MLs at the forefront in the decision-making process, ensuring equity and access are considered, and maintaining an asset-based lens.

Guiding these efforts are models such as the School-Community-Family Partnerships Model (Bryan & Henry, 2011), which offers broad applicability across interprofessional and interdisciplinary school-based collaborations. For school counselors in particular, models like the School Counselor and School Nurse Collaboration Model (Tuttle et al., 2018) provide customized approaches for working with specific collaborators and critical partners. These two models and approaches, referenced throughout this chapter, serve as essential guides for fostering meaningful collaboration aimed at enhancing the educational experiences of MLs. School counselors and school counselors in training can seek professional development opportunities such as attending conferences, reading books, and consulting recent research to keep current on the needs of ML students and communities.

References

American School Counselor Association (2022). ASCA ethical standards for school counselors. https://www.schoolcounselor.org/getmedia/44f30280-ffe8-4b41-9ad8-f15909c3d164/EthicalStandards.pdf

American School Counselor Association (2024). *The school counselor and equity for all students*. ASCA Position Statements. https://www.schoolcounselor.org/Standards-Positions/Position-Statements/ASCA-Position-Statements/The-School-Counselor-and-Equity-for-All-Students

Arriero, E., & Griffin, D. (2019). Adelante: A community asset mapping approach to increase college and career readiness for rural Latinx high school students. *Professional School Counseling*, *22*(2), 1–9. https://doi.org/10.1177/2156759X18800279

Betters-Bubon, J., & Shultz, J. W. (2018). School counselors as social justice leaders: An innovative school–family–community partnership with Latino students and families. *Professional School Counseling*, *21*(1b), 1–11. https://doi.org/10.1177/2156759X18773601

Bryan, J., & Henry, L. (2012). A model for building school-family-community partnerships: Principles and process. *Journal of Counseling and Development*, *90*(4), 408–420. https://doi.org/10.1002/j.1556-6676.2012.00052.x

Bryan, J., Henry, L. M., Daniels, A. D., Edwin, M., & Griffin, D. M. (2022). Infusing an antiracist framework into school-family-community partnerships. In C. Holcomb-McCoy (Ed.), *Antiracist counseling in schools and communities*. American Counseling Association.

Bryan, J., Williams, J. M., & Griffin, D. (2020). Fostering educational resilience and opportunities in urban schools through equity-focused School–Family–Community Partnerships. *Professional School Counseling*, *23*(1_part_2), 1–14. https://doi.org/10.1177/2156759X19899179

Bryant, J. C., Tuttle, M., Birdsong, D., & Mecadon-Mann, M. (2024). Principal and school counselor partnerships: Aligning leadership roles to support the school mission and student success. *Southeast Journal on Educational Administration, 23*(1), 1–17. https://www.srcea.co/journals

Catalano, A. J., Torff, B., & Anderson, K. S. (2021). Transitioning to online learning during the COVID-19 pandemic: Differences in access and participation among students in disadvantaged school districts. *The International Journal of Information and Learning Technology, 38*(2), 258–270. https://doi.org/10.1108/IJILT-06-2020-0111

Cook, A. L., Hayden, L. A., Bryan, J., & Belford, P. (2016). Implementation of a school-family-community partnership model to promote Latina youth development: Reflections on the process and lessons learned. *International Journal of Research on Service-Learning and Community Engagement, 4*(1), 101–117. https://journals.sfu.ca/iarslce/index.php/journal/article/view/189

Davis, L., Harward, K., & Yazzie, A. (2023). Counselor–teacher collaboration in multilingual learner contexts: A qualitative case study investigating counselor–teacher partnerships. *Professional School Counseling, 27*(1), 2156759X231177624.

Duff, P. (2001). Language, literacy, content, and (pop) culture: Challenges for ESL students in mainstream courses. *The Canadian Modern Language Review, 58*(1), 103–132. https://doi.org/10.3138/cmlr.58.1.103

Edirmanasinghe, N. A., Attia, M., Brant-Rajahn, S., & Staton, R. A. (2022). Working with immigrant children in schools: Applying a multi-tiered approach. *Journal of Child and Adolescent Counseling, 8*(2), 59–71. https://doi.org/10.1080/23727810.2022.2074771

Gardner, L., & Love, J. (2025, May 22). *Equity through language access: Best practices for collaborating with interpreters.* National Education Association. https://www.nea.org/resource-library/equity-through-language-access-best-practices-collaborating-interpreters

Gibbons, M. M., Diambra, J. F., & Buchanan, D. K. (2010). School counselor perceptions and attitudes about collaboration. *Journal of School Counseling, 8*(34), 1–28. https://jsc.montana.edu/articles/v8n34.pdf

Gonzalez, L. M., Borders, L. D., Hines, E. M., Villalba, J. A., & Henderson, A. (2013). Parental involvement in children's education: Considerations for school counselors working with Latino immigrant families. *Professional School Counseling, 16*, 185–193. https://doi.org/10.1177/2156759X1701600303

Griffin, D., & Farris, A. (2010). School counselors and school-family-community collaboration: Finding resources through community asset mapping. *Professional School Counseling, 13(5),* 248–256. https://doi.org/10.1177/2156759X1001300501

Henry, L. M., Bryan, J., & Zalaquett, C. (2017). The effects of a counselor-led, faith-based, school–family–community partnership on student achievement in a high-poverty urban elementary school. *Journal of Multicultural Counseling and Development, 45*, 162–182. https://doi.org/10.1002/jmcd.12072

Hersi, A. A., & Watkinson, J. S. (2012). Supporting immigrant students in a newcomer high school: A case study. *Bilingual Research Journal, 35*(1), 98–111.

Hong, H., Keith, K., & Moran, R. R. (2019). Reflection on and for actions: Probing into English language art teachers' personal and professional experiences with English language learners. *TESL- EJ, 22*(4), 1–16. https://eric.ed.gov/?q=ELL&ft=on&id=EJ1204559

Hoover-Dempsey, K. V., Walker, J. M. T., Sandler, H. M., Whetsel, D., Green, C. L., Wilkins, A. S., & Closson, K. (2005). Why do parents become involved? Research findings and implications. *Elementary School Journal, 106*, 105–130. https://doi.org/10.1086/499194

Johnson, L. V., & Cain, A. (2019). Preparing school-counselors-in-training to implement English-as-a-second language strategies during classroom lessons. *International*

Journal for the Scholarship of Teaching and Learning, 13(1), 1–10. https://doi.org.10.20429/ijsotl.2019.130109

Johnson, L. V., Shell, E. M., Tuttle, M., & Groce, L. (2019). School counselor experiences of response to intervention with English learners. *Professional School Counseling, 22(1)*, 1–11. https://doi.org/10.1177/2156759X19859486

Lashley, C. A., & Stickl, J. (2016). Counselors and principals: Collaborating to improve instructional equity. *Journal of Organizational & Educational Leadership, 2*(1), 1–24. https://digitalcommons.gardner-webb.edu/joel/vol2/iss1/6

Linville, H. A. (2020). A closer look at ESOL teacher advocacy: What we do and why. *TESOL Journal, 11(3)*. https://doi.org/10.1002/tesj.508

Mariani, M., Berger, C., Koerner, K., & Sandlin, C. (2016). Operation occupation: A college and career readiness intervention for elementary students. *Professional School Counseling, 20*(1), 65–76. https://doi.org/10.5330/1096-2409-20.1.65

Mavrogordato, M., & White, R. S. (2020). Leveraging policy implementation for social justice: How school leaders shape educational opportunity when implementing policy for English learners. *Educational Administration Quarterly, 56*(1), 3–45. https://doi.org/10.1177/0013161X18821364

Mitchell, N. A., & Bryan, J. A. (2007). school-family-community partnerships: Strategies for school counselors working with Caribbean immigrant families. *Professional School Counseling, 10(4)*, 399–409. https://doi.org/10.1177/2156759X0701000413

Najarro, N. (2023, March 30). English learners: The debate over English terminology, explained. *Education Week*. https://www.edweek.org/teaching-learning/the-debate-over-english-learner-terminology-explained/2023/03

National Center for Education Statistics (2020, May). *English language learners in public schools*. NCES. https://www.google.com/url?sa=i&source=web&rct=j&url=https://nces.ed.gov/programs/coe/pdf/Indicator_CGF/coe_cgf_2017_05.pdf&opi=89978449&psig=AOvVaw1MriSU_USZSxVRWjXD5qO1&ust=1789645103711000

Nieto, S. (2017). Becoming sociocultural mediators: What all educators can learn from bilingual and ESL teachers. *Issues in Teacher Education, 26*(2), 129–141.

Paone, T. R., & Malott, K. M. (2008). Using interpreters in mental health counseling: A literature review and recommendations. *Journal of Multicultural Counseling and Development, 36*, 130–142. https://doi.org/10.1002/j.2161-1912.2008.tb00077.x

Phillips, A., Barnatt, J., & Viesca, K. (2023). Linguistically responsive leaders: Working with multilingual students and their families. *Journal of Research on Leadership Education, 18*(2). 301–321. https://doi.org/10.1177/19427751221078039

Purgason, L. L., Johnson, G., Vallecillo, O., Covington, C., Parker, R. H., & Airhart-Larraga, S. (2024). English as a second language teachers' perspectives on interprofessional collaboration with school counselors: Supporting emergent bilingual students. *Journal of Educational and Psychological Consultation, 34*(2), 168–197. https://doi.org/10.1080/10474412.2023.2240304

Shi, Q., & Watkinson, J. (2019). English language learners and school belonging: Implications for school counselor practice. *Professional School Counseling, 22*(1b). https://doi.org/10.1177/2156759X19834442

Sugarman, J., & Lazarín, M. (2020). *Educating English learners during the COVID-19 pandemic: Policy ideas for states and school districts*. Migration Policy Institute.

Tuttle, M., Harrison, J., Johnson, L. V., & Mecadon-Mann, M. (2021). What's in a word?: School counselor and ESOL teacher perceptions and attitudes about collaboration. *Journal of School Counseling, 19*(22), 1–35. http:/www.jsc.montana.edu/articles/v19n22.pdf

Tuttle, M., Haskins, N. H., Mecadon-Mann, M., & Windham, H. (2022). RCT: School counselor and Latinx parent partnerships. *Journal of Child and Adolescent Counseling, 8*(3), 115–127. https://doi.org/10.1080/23727810.2022.2102395

Tuttle, M., & Johnson, L. V. (2018). Navigating language brokering in k-12 schools. *Journal of Mental Health Counseling*, *40*(4). 328–340. https://doi.org/10.17744/mehc.40.4.05

Tuttle, M., Yordy, M., Appling, B., & Hanley, E. (2018). School counselor and school nurse collaboration: Partnering for K-12 student success. *Journal of School Counseling*, *16*(4), 1–26. http://www.jsc.montana.edu/articles/v16n4.pdf

Vera, E., Heineke, A., Schultes, A., & Daskalova, P. (2022). Social and emotional needs of emergent bilingual high school students: Perspectives of teachers, school counselors, and school social workers. *Journal of Educational and Psychological Consultation, 32(4)*, 416–453. https://doi.org/10.1080/10474412.2021.2018657

Villegas, A. M., & Lucas, T. (2002). Preparing culturally responsive teachers: Rethinking the curriculum. *Journal of Teacher Education*, *53*(1), 20–32.

Wachter Morris, C. (2025, March 13). Joining forces: Driving change through collaborative practice [Presentation]. *Evidence Based School Counseling Conference. Research Day*, Columbus, OH.

Whitman, M. V., Davis, J. A., & Terry, A. J. (2010). Perceptions of school nurses on the challenges of service provision to ESL students. *Journal of Community Health*, *35*, 208–213. https://doi.org/10.1007/s10900-009-9211-3

Chapter 8

Beyond Departmental Boundaries

A Multi-Campus Collaborative Model for Supporting Multilingual Learners

Isabel Haller-Gryc and Angel Lett

Effective support for high school multilingual learners (MLs) requires integrating expertise in language acquisition, cultural responsiveness, instructional strategies, and counseling practices-knowledge that no single professional typically possesses alone. Collaborative leadership provides the structures and processes for educators to share this knowledge and co-develop strategies that are both culturally and linguistically responsive. This model represents a shift from traditional hierarchical leadership, where a principal or counselor might make critical ML placement decisions in isolation, to a more distributed, team-oriented approach. By leveraging each role's expertise, collaborative leadership breaks down professional silos and involves a broader range of stakeholders, including teachers, counselors, administrators, and families, in shaping priorities and decisions that directly impact student success. We define collaborative leadership as: a school-wide approach in which leadership is shared among a range of individuals, administrators, teachers, counselors, staff, students, and families, who work together toward common goals. Instead of relying solely on top-down decision-making, collaborative leadership involves shared responsibility, open communication, and collective problem-solving to improve student learning. It recognizes that meaningful support for students comes from engaging the diverse perspectives and strengths of the entire school community. This conceptualization aligns with frameworks emphasizing leadership for learning as a collective endeavor, where leadership is viewed as participatory and distributed rather than residing in a single individual (Hallinger & Heck, 2010; Spillane et al., 2001; Supovitz et al., 2010).

This model is especially significant for school counselors working with MLs because it systematically integrates their counseling expertise with the unique expertise of ML educators. Research suggests that counselors are often not fully equipped with the specialized knowledge required to meet the unique needs of MLs, making it difficult for them to provide appropriate support and interventions (Arriero & Griffin, 2018). School counselors often lack the resources or knowledge of resources to support MLs, nor are they always capable of

DOI: 10.4324/9781003711124-10

identifying needs. A collaborative leadership framework addresses this gap by fostering systematic partnerships between counselors and ML educators. These partnerships leverage the counseling expertise in academic planning, social-emotional support, and college/career readiness alongside ML educators' expertise in language acquisition and cultural responsiveness. This ensures that decisions about ML student placement, support, and advocacy are informed by relevant linguistic and cultural expertise rather than made in isolation. In today's complex educational environments, effective ML support depends on this kind of cross-departmental coordination.

This chapter explores how one such collaborative leadership model operates at Plymouth-Canton Educational Park (P-CEP), a unique secondary school complex in Michigan. P-CEP comprises three distinct high schools, Salem, Canton, and Plymouth, unified under a shared leadership structure that actively promotes collaboration across campuses. The chapter analyzes how P-CEP's leadership framework enhances ML academic success through coordinated efforts among counselors, ML educators, and school staff, with particular attention to student placement, ongoing academic progress, and access to appropriate support systems.

This collaborative model at P-CEP is particularly significant given a critical gap in existing research. As the United States becomes more linguistically diverse, school systems face an increasing demand for specialized support for MLs. However, research has predominantly focused on classroom-level interventions rather than examining the broader institutional support systems that influence ML outcomes. While there has been extensive research on secondary language education and MLs' transition to postsecondary education, significantly less attention has been given to understanding how non-classroom educators, particularly high school counselors, impact MLs' academic trajectories (Jiang & Harklau, 2024).

School counselors and ML educators play a crucial role in supporting MLs as they navigate the complexities of their academic journeys. The challenges these students face extend beyond typical academic concerns. The federal designation of "English learner" acknowledges that these students face language barriers that can mask their actual abilities and potential. Allen (2017) aptly described this language barrier as a "wall" that prevents teachers, administrators, and other stakeholders from accurately assessing MLs' genuine academic abilities, and school counselors find themselves in a particularly influential position-one where they can either positively or negatively impact ML academic success (p. 82). This impact occurs through multiple pathways: by providing essential cultural and community support, helping to strengthen student self-efficacy, and actively working to mitigate systemic barriers through targeted advocacy efforts (Johnson et al., 2016).

P-CEP addresses these challenges through an innovative coordinated leadership structure. An ML lead teacher and ML Coordinator work directly with an assistant principal who oversees both counseling and ML programs across all three high schools. This integrated approach requires sophisticated coordination and communication systems that move beyond traditional departmental divisions, reflecting the interconnected nature of students' academic, linguistic, and social development. The leadership model strengthens support systems through streamlined communication channels, integrated oversight of counseling and ML services, and cross-campus coordination that enables resource sharing and standardized protocols across all three schools while creating direct pathways to advocate for ML student needs. This structure also supports integrated opportunities to authentically collaborate and address unique student needs as a comprehensive team.

The Unique Setup of P-CEP

Given these documented challenges in supporting MLs nationwide, examining innovative institutional models becomes critical. P-CEP represents one such innovative approach, where a unique three-campus structure has necessitated the development of collaborative support systems that address many of the coordination challenges identified in the research. P-CEP, also called "the Park," represents a groundbreaking approach to high school education, blending the resources and opportunities of three distinct high schools into one expansive "mini college campus." Located in Canton, Michigan, this educational model emerged organically through strategic land use and community growth rather than from an initial grand vision (Tinsley, 2019).

This evolution began when the school district acquired a large tract of land for multiple high schools. Salem High School was constructed first and opened in 1970, followed by Canton High School in 1972. As the area's student population rapidly increased, Plymouth High School was added in 2002, completing the trio that now forms P-CEP. Today, P-CEP serves over 6,200 students across three geographical areas: Plymouth Township, the City of Plymouth, Salem and Canton Township. The campus operates like a college environment, with students moving between buildings to access specialized programs, creating a dynamic and interconnected educational space that requires significant coordination.

This interconnectedness is enhanced by P-CEP's shared leadership and cross-campus collaboration. Each school functions as a stand-alone high school while offering academy-specific curricular options at each building: Salem High School emphasizes arts education through the Arts Academy; Canton High School focuses on the Business and STEM Academies; and Plymouth High School houses the International Baccalaureate (IB) Academy. This specialization necessitates student movement between campuses to access specific courses, fostering an environment that combines college-style flexibility within a comprehensive traditional high school structure.

The Park's administrative framework supports this complex operation through a carefully coordinated system. Each school operates under a principal supported by three assistant principals who balance dual responsibilities: overseeing specific academic departments while supporting designated student caseloads. For example, at Canton High School, assistant principals divide responsibilities by managing specific departments (Business and CTE, World Language, or English) while simultaneously supporting students grouped alphabetically by surname and by grade level. A similar structure exists at Plymouth and Salem, with assistant principals managing different department/student combinations. This leadership model ensures comprehensive academic oversight and student support across all three schools, maintaining the Park's cohesive educational environment while preserving each school's unique identity.

ML Support in a Complex Educational Setting

Within this intricate organizational framework, the ML Department exemplifies how P-CEP's collaborative structure enables specialized support across all three schools. The department leverages the Park's interconnected nature to provide comprehensive language support services, allowing students to access resources and specialized instruction regardless of their home school assignment. This integration of ML services across the campus demonstrates how P-CEP's unique setup facilitates targeted educational support while maintaining the flexibility needed to serve a diverse student population.

Research has identified a critical challenge in ESL programming that P-CEP's collaborative model directly addresses. As Callahan et al. (2010) note, "ESL placement is a critical component in the education and schooling of language minority ELL students. While Lau mandates that students' linguistic needs be met so that they may take advantage of the full academic curriculum offered in schools, it is also possible that in practice ESL placement functions to exclude them from those very courses" (p. 6). P-CEP's collaborative leadership structure works to prevent this exclusion through intentional coordination between counselors, ML educators, and administrators so that students can access the appropriate services across The Park.

This robust integration of ML services across P-CEP has been made possible through sustained institutional support from the Central Office. The programmatic infrastructure has undergone significant transformation over the last five to seven years, progressing from a limited model comprising only two ML Teachers in a self-contained instructional program to an expansive, integrated framework encompassing six ML teachers. This metamorphosis was launched by the visionary leadership of the ML Director at the Central Office, who implemented a comprehensive equity-centered framework through strategic advocacy and intentional instructional design to ensure that ML students had comprehensive access to a holistic educational experience.

The strategic advocacy anchored access to highly qualified English language development educators as a critical priority which necessitated a collaborative partnership and legacy commitment with district leaders and Human Resources. Access to highly qualified multilingual educators has fostered opportunities for students to be supported across all core content area courses utilizing a multidimensional model of instruction that encompasses elements of co-taught instruction, sheltered courses with push-in support, and expanded department course offerings. This enhanced framework supports school counselors' ability to design educational programming options for students that ensure comprehensive access to critical content pedagogy while simultaneously supporting college and career readiness objectives.

The ML Department supports a remarkably diverse student population speaking more than 40 different languages. To address this linguistic complexity and the varying proficiency levels of its students, P-CEP has developed a sophisticated, multi-tiered support system comprising four distinct instructional modalities.

The foundation of P-CEP's language support framework begins with departmental classes, which primarily serve newcomers and students requiring intensive language acquisition assistance. These classes provide targeted English language instruction through evidence-based curricula designed to accelerate language acquisition while supporting students' socioemotional adjustment. The second modality, sheltered instruction, represents an approach focused on making grade-level content comprehensible to MLs. These classes are led by teachers trained in sheltering techniques, often supported by certified ML specialists who provide push-in support. Teachers utilize strategies, including scaffolding, visual reinforcement, and modified linguistic input, to provide comprehensible input that teaches at a level just beyond students' current language proficiency while offering the scaffolded supports necessary for content understanding.

Co-taught classes constitute the third modality, exemplifying a collaborative model where content specialists and ML experts work in tandem to ensure students receive simultaneous support in both academic content mastery and language development. The fourth modality, mainstream non-supported classes, represents the final tier where MLs demonstrate sufficient linguistic competency to engage independently in general education settings.

The support system is structured across four distinct proficiency levels, each offering progressively advanced academic integration. At the newcomer level (WIDA levels 1–1.9), students are at the entering stages of English development. They typically have limited or no English proficiency and are in the early phases of understanding and using basic social and instructional language. These students, often in their first 12–18 months in U.S. schools, receive intensive language support through departmental EL 1 coursework and language support classes. They participate in sheltered content courses across mathematics, science, and social studies, with substantial scaffolding and native language support where possible.

The emerging level (WIDA levels 2.0–2.9), where learners can understand and produce simple sentences and begin to express basic academic concepts with support, combines departmental EL 2 coursework with continued language support while facilitating transition to more challenging academic content. Students at this level may move between sheltered and non-sheltered courses based on their performance, including co-taught options in subjects like Health.

As students progress to the developing level (WIDA levels 2.9–3.5), where learners can understand and produce more complex language with some specificity and detail in academic contexts, they engage in specialized ML English courses aligned with their grade level while enjoying increased flexibility between sheltered and mainstream options. They maintain access to sheltered social studies and science courses while having the opportunity to transition to mainstream classes based on their progress. The developing/expanding to reaching level (WIDA levels 3.5–6.0), where students demonstrate near-native English proficiency in academic settings with minimal support needs, emphasizes co-taught English classes with grade-appropriate instruction and prioritizes mainstream content course placement. This level primarily serves advanced MLs and long-term MLs, supporting their final transition to independent academic engagement.

Student Demographics and Program Data

To understand how this multi-tiered framework operates in practice and why P-CEP's collaborative model proves essential, it's important to examine the composition and characteristics of the student population these systems serve. P-CEP's ML population is predominantly composed of long-term English Learners (L-TELs)-students who have been in U.S. schools for six or more years without achieving English proficiency. Across all grade levels, L-TELs consistently outnumber newcomers: 9th grade (67 L-TELs vs. 28 newcomers), 10th grade (71 vs. 28), 11th grade (45 vs. 25), and 12th grade (46 vs. 33). This pattern underscores the need for P-CEP's collaborative model between counselors and ML specialists, as L-TELs face complex challenges beyond basic language acquisition.

Exit rates from P-CEP's English Learner program have declined dramatically despite growing populations. From 2021 to 2024, exit rates dropped from 14% (20 of 142 students) to just 3% (9 of 311 students), despite program enrollment more than doubling.

Graduation data reveals persistent achievement gaps. While P-CEP maintains overall graduation rates between 87 and 93%, English Learner graduation rates fluctuate significantly, ranging from 63.2% to 85.7% in recent years. This 20+ percentage point variability demonstrates why systematic, coordinated support structures are essential for consistent student success.

These demographic realities and outcome disparities directly inform P-CEP's collaborative protocols, including quarterly data analysis conducted by counselors, ML educators, and administrators. The substantial L-TEL population and variable outcomes necessitate the sophisticated intervention frameworks that characterize P-CEP's approach.

Academic Performance in Co-Taught Classes: Evidence of Authentic Learning

While these demographic patterns and outcome trends reveal important challenges, they represent only part of the story about student progress at P-CEP. A closer examination of academic performance in specific instructional settings reveals a more complex picture of student achievement. Focused analysis of academic performance in co-taught classes-a key component of the collaborative model-demonstrates strong learning outcomes that contradict what declining exit rates might suggest about student capabilities.

During the 2024–2025 academic year, the ML Curriculum Coordinator focused intensive analysis on three co-taught sections, collecting comprehensive data about course pass/fail rates and grade distributions. In co-taught English 9, 25 ML students achieved an impressive 80% pass rate, with 20 students earning passing grades and only 5 students receiving failing marks. More significantly, the grade distribution reveals substantial academic achievement: 4 students (16%) earned A grades, 11 students (44%) earned B grades, and 5 students (20%) earned C grades, with only 5 students (20%) receiving D or F grades. This means that 60% of ML students in co-taught English 9 achieved B grades or higher, demonstrating mastery that extends well beyond basic proficiency.

The success story becomes even more compelling in co-taught U.S. History, where all 12 ML students (100%) achieved passing grades. The grade distribution in this course is particularly noteworthy: 8 students (67%) earned A grades, 2 students (17%) earned B grades, and 2 students (17%) earned C grades. This means that 83% of ML students in co-taught U.S. History achieved B grades or higher, with the majority demonstrating exceptional academic performance.

The Assessment Paradox: High Academic Achievement Amid Declining Exit Rates

These contrasting datasets create a significant paradox that illuminates critical issues in how student progress is measured and recognized. While formal exit rates suggest declining English proficiency development, classroom-based evidence demonstrates that ML students are achieving substantial academic success when provided with appropriate instructional support through the co-taught model.

This disconnect likely reflects systemic issues with the WIDA assessment process rather than authentic deficiencies in student learning and language development. Multiple factors contribute to this assessment paradox. Many students approach the WIDA test with limited understanding of its significance for their academic trajectory, viewing it as disconnected from their daily classroom experiences and post-secondary goals. This disconnect is particularly pronounced among L-TELs, many of whom have refused ELL services and, in some cases, have declined to take the test in previous years. For these students, the WIDA assessment feels irrelevant to their current school experience, as they have effectively opted out of the support systems and instructional frameworks that the test is designed to inform. This creates a cycle where the very students who might benefit most from targeted language support become increasingly disengaged from the assessment process, viewing it as an imposed requirement rather than a tool for academic advancement. Consequently, their lack of motivation can result in test performances that significantly underrepresent their actual language capabilities as demonstrated through coursework.

The formal testing environment compounds these issues by failing to capture the authentic language use and academic thinking that students demonstrate in supported classroom settings. The co-taught model provides scaffolding, cultural responsiveness, and instructional modifications that enable students to showcase their true academic potential-supportive elements that are entirely absent in standardized testing contexts. This environmental mismatch further widens the gap between students' demonstrated classroom abilities and their assessed language proficiency levels.

Implications for Collaborative Support Systems

These findings have profound implications for P-CEP's collaborative model and the broader field of ML support. The success documented in co-taught classes validates the effectiveness of the collaborative approach between ML specialists and content area teachers, demonstrating that appropriate instructional support enables authentic academic achievement. The 80% pass rate in English 9 and 100% pass rate in U.S. History provide concrete evidence that the collaborative model successfully bridges language development with content mastery.

However, the declining exit rates signal the need for enhanced student education about WIDA's importance and potentially alternative approaches to measuring and recognizing student progress. The collaborative team of counselors, ML coordinators, and administrators must address this assessment engagement issue to ensure that students who are academically ready can formally exit EL status and access the full range of educational opportunities.

Furthermore, these data suggest that academic performance in supported settings may serve as a more authentic indicator of student readiness for mainstream coursework than traditional language proficiency assessments alone. This insight should inform the placement and transition decisions made through the collaborative process, emphasizing classroom-based evidence alongside formal assessment scores.

The contrast between exit trends and academic performance underscores the critical importance of P-CEP's multi-faceted support system. While students demonstrate remarkable success in appropriately supported academic environments, they require enhanced advocacy and preparation to navigate formal assessment processes successfully. This reality reinforces the value of the collaborative model's emphasis on comprehensive student support that extends beyond classroom instruction to include assessment preparation, motivation building, and systematic advocacy for student needs.

These insights about the assessment-achievement gap directly inform how P-CEP's collaborative team implements its multi-tiered support framework. Understanding that students may demonstrate academic readiness that exceeds their formal assessment scores enables more nuanced placement decisions that prioritize classroom-based evidence of student capabilities. This approach requires maintaining essential flexibility to accommodate diverse student needs. For example, long-term MLs typically enroll in mainstream courses unless specific circumstances dictate otherwise, while students with Individualized Education Programs (IEPs) receive placement based on their IEP team recommendations. Movement between tiers is permitted based on individual progress and requirements, ensuring that the system remains responsive to student needs rather than rigid in its implementation.

To protect student privacy, pseudonyms are used for all students discussed in the following case examples. Identifying details have been modified while preserving the educational circumstances and outcomes described.

ML Placement and Success

Collaboration between administrators and counselors plays a vital role in ensuring appropriate class placement for MLs, particularly those who have newly arrived. This partnership combines expertise in language assessment, academic advising, and transcript evaluation to create a foundation for student success. Through examining several cases, we can observe how this collaborative model operates in practice and its impact on student outcomes.

The placement of newly enrolled high school students represents a crucial point of collaboration between the ML Coordinator and school counselors. Upon enrollment, the ML Coordinator administers the WIDA Screener to assess English language proficiency. Based on these results and the district's systematic framework for ML support, the coordinator makes informed placement recommendations across the four instructional modalities: departmental classes, sheltered classes, co-taught classes, and non-supported mainstream classes. School counselors then integrate these recommendations with their comprehensive analysis, which encompasses WIDA Screener scores, prior educational experiences documented in transcripts, and alignment with graduation requirements and elective options.

Throughout this process, the ML Coordinator maintains active oversight by reviewing the student information system to ensure schedule accuracy and completeness. This supervision often reveals opportunities for credit optimization, particularly in applying foreign language credits based on prior schooling experiences.

Ahmed's case demonstrates the model's effectiveness in addressing complex placement situations involving international transcripts and foreign language requirements. Ahmed, a 12th-grade student who relocated to the United States from Egypt, enrolled at P-CEP. As a native Arabic speaker, Ahmed's educational background reflected Egypt's multilingual approach to secondary education: he had received all content area instruction in Arabic while simultaneously taking separate courses in Arabic language arts, French, and English as foreign languages. This linguistic foundation–fluency in Arabic combined with formal instruction in two additional languages–positioned him as an emerging ML navigating a new educational system in his final year of high school.

With a WIDA Screener Overall Score of 2.0, Ahmed was recommended for EL 2 language and content support classes. Initial placement challenges due to unavailable transcripts were resolved through clear communication with parents about grade-level status implications. Once received, collaborative analysis determined Ahmed needed only an elective and U.S. History and Civics courses to graduate.

The complexity of Ahmed's case deepened when addressing P-CEP's foreign language graduation requirements because his multilingual background required careful evaluation of Michigan's alternative pathways for World Language credit. Ahmed's years of formal Arabic instruction throughout his schooling in Egypt, combined with his French language coursework, clearly demonstrated extensive foreign language learning. However, translating this international educational experience into credit recognition required navigating Michigan's specific policies for students educated abroad. According to Michigan guidelines, students who attended school outside the United States may receive foreign language credit based on documentation of their schooling and language experience: one year of instruction in grades 1-12 equals one credit, while two or more years equals two credits.

As McCall-Perez (2000) emphasizes, proactive guidance is essential in helping MLs understand alternative pathways for meeting such requirements. The ML Curriculum Coordinator collaborated with the counselor to assess Ahmed's eligibility, examining his translated transcripts to document his years of Arabic language instruction and his formal French coursework. This collaborative analysis confirmed that Ahmed not only met the foreign language requirement through his Arabic schooling but also qualified for recognition under Michigan's Seal of Biliteracy program. Because Ahmed had moved to the United States after 6th grade and could provide a translated transcript showing at least one year of successful instruction in all subjects in Arabic, he met the eligibility criteria for this prestigious state credential recognizing his bilingual proficiency.

While Ahmed's multilingual background was systematically evaluated and recognized through the Seal of Biliteracy, Maryam's case reveals how even well-established collaborative systems can initially miss eligible students without proactive review. Originally from Afghanistan and fluent in seven languages including Pashto, Farsi, and Urdu, Maryam received world language credit for her Afghan schooling but was initially overlooked for the Seal of Biliteracy. The ML Coordinator's systematic review of student records revealed that Maryam met the same criteria established for Ahmed: arrival after 6th grade and a translated transcript showing successful non-English instruction. This discovery also identified opportunities for additional language recognition through examinations in her other languages.

Another more recent case from the 2024 to 2025 school year involved a student who arrived as a refugee just two months before the end of the academic year, following a four-year interruption in formal education. This student presented unique challenges, especially regarding math placement. With limited time and no recent academic record to reference, the ML team and counseling staff worked together to craft a creative and responsive solution. The student was placed in a small sheltered course that included ML teacher support and was provided an individualized learning plan centered on the online math platform ALEKS. This independent study model allowed the student to work at their own pace, focusing on building foundational math skills in a supportive environment. This was the first time such a placement had been implemented at P-CEP. The goal was to equip the student with the necessary skills and confidence to enter Pre-Algebra in the fall. This approach demonstrated the team's flexibility and dedication to meeting students where they are while using existing resources innovatively.

The collaborative model also demonstrates effectiveness in addressing academic challenges. When a student struggled in a non-supported Multicultural Literature class, the counselor initiated a response involving the Assistant Principal and ML Coordinator. The team's review of WIDA levels and available options identified a more appropriate co-taught section placement. Despite capacity constraints, administrative oversight facilitated quick approval for an override, ensuring necessary academic support.

The cases of Ahmed and Maryam illustrate how P-CEP's collaborative model transforms institutional protocols into actionable student advocacy. Through systematic coordination between ML Coordinators and counselors, the model facilitates nuanced evaluation of international credentials, maximizes credit recognition, and ensures appropriate academic placement. Ahmed's case demonstrates the proactive application of Michigan's alternative pathways for foreign language credit and his qualification for the Seal of Biliteracy, while Maryam's case reveals the importance of ongoing record review to identify students who may have been initially overlooked for the same recognitions. The model's effectiveness extends beyond initial placement, as demonstrated by the rapid intervention in the Multicultural Literature case, where cross-departmental collaboration enabled swift placement adjustments despite capacity constraints.

These examples underscore how the model optimizes existing resources through clear communication channels and defined roles. The ML Coordinator's ongoing oversight of the student information system, combined with counselors' comprehensive schedule analysis, creates multiple checkpoints for student success. This systematic approach proves particularly valuable across P-CEP's three schools, where consistent protocols ensure equitable support for MLs regardless of their school assignment.

Most significantly, these cases demonstrate how structured collaboration can simultaneously address individual student needs while strengthening institutional capacity for serving MLs. The model's success in facilitating timely interventions, maximizing credit recognition, and ensuring appropriate placement suggests its potential as a framework for other multi-campus districts seeking to enhance their support for multilingual students.

Organizational Infrastructure

While these individual success stories demonstrate the effectiveness of P-CEP's collaborative model in practice, they are made possible by a sophisticated underlying infrastructure that strategically bridges departmental boundaries. This system combines carefully structured Professional Learning Communities, systematic data sharing protocols, and strategic administrative oversight to ensure consistent support across all three schools. Understanding these structural elements provides crucial context for how individual cases like Ahmed's and Maryam's can be effectively managed within a large, complex educational environment.

At the foundation of this system is a carefully structured Professional Learning Community (PLC) framework that has evolved to address the unique needs of MLs. Each month, P-CEP dedicates Wednesdays to department-based PLC time, with two Wednesdays serving as PLC days while the remaining two are reserved for department and building-level meetings. Content area departments are allocated bimonthly sessions specifically for professional development, data analysis, and instructional practice evaluation. While this dedicated time promotes valuable intra-departmental cooperation, the Assistant Principal recognized that the complex needs of ML students required more intentional cross-departmental collaboration.

To address this gap, the Assistant Principal pioneered an innovative "crossover PLC" between the ML team and the Park Counseling Department, which includes nearly twenty school counselors. This administrator strategically leverages their supervision of both counseling and ML departments to bridge departmental boundaries, scheduling meetings on alternate Wednesdays to maintain presence with both teams and facilitate rapid intervention coordination for urgent student needs. Research supports this approach, as strong principal-counselor relationships have been shown to correlate with more effective school counseling programs (McConnell et al., 2020).

The crossover PLC's strategic goal centers on creating quarterly opportunities for professional dialogue, learning, and engagement between both teams, establishing a collaborative framework that enhances the ML student experience across academic, socioemotional, and post-secondary contexts. These inter-departmental sessions address critical topics including supporting the social-emotional needs of newly arrived students as they navigate their new community, strategic academic pathway planning, and the development of comprehensive college access pathways tailored to MLs' unique needs and aspirations.

School counselors play a vital role in supporting ML students through social-emotional guidance, academic and post-secondary planning, course placement decisions, graduation eligibility tracking, and campus community integration through clubs and extracurricular activities. Given the complex and nuanced nature of supporting MLs, these crossover PLCs aim to deepen understanding around English language acquisition, appropriate course placement, graduation pathways, and academic credit accounting. Additionally, the PLCs work to identify emerging themes specific to ML student experiences while fostering collaborative opportunities between departments to strengthen student support.

Each quarter, the crossover PLCs examine different aspects of student experience and access through an equity lens. Table 8.1 outlines the themes addressed throughout the academic year, ensuring MLs have equal access to both academic and extracurricular opportunities for their comprehensive high school experience.

While the scale of P-CEP's campus creates inherent challenges for implementing more frequent direct collaboration, these structured quarterly interactions provide valuable opportunities for cross-departmental dialogue and planning

Table 8.1 Crossover PLC Topics

Quarter 1	*Quarter 2*	*Quarter 3*	*Quarter 4*
Academic Course Placement for MLs Targeted Support Strategies for Newcomers Creative Course Substitutions to Support Language Development and Graduation Pathways Helping MLs Find Community at P-CEP	Promoting Student Success Through Academic Interventions Student Centered Conferences	Analyzing Semester 1 Course Success Rates to Inform Future Strategies Course Placement for upcoming Academic Year	Post Secondary Pathways for MLs Graduation Eligibility/Honors Recognition Seal of Biliteracy Eligibility

that directly inform the intervention protocols and placement decisions detailed in the previous cases.

Building upon these collaborative structures, P-CEP has developed a comprehensive Course Placement Guide that serves as a vital bridge between the counseling and ML departments. This guide systematically addresses the diverse academic needs of MLs across proficiency levels by translating assessment data into actionable placement decisions. Organized around key proficiency bands, the guide aligns with P-CEP's multi-tiered language support framework and its four distinct instructional modalities, ensuring consistent implementation across departments.

The Course Placement Guide exemplifies how P-CEP's collaborative systems work in practice. It functions as both a decision-making tool and communication framework, enabling counselors and ML specialists to make informed placement decisions while facilitating transparent discussions about educational pathways. From an administrative perspective, it supports program planning by helping leaders project staffing needs and allocate resources for sheltered and co-taught sections. This standardized approach to placement ensures consistency across all three schools within the educational park, further strengthening the interdepartmental support system (Table 8.2).

In addition to the standardized placement framework, P-CEP has developed structured processes for monitoring student progress and delivering support through consistent data-sharing practices. This data sharing functions as a key tool for collaboration, allowing teams to proactively identify and respond to ML students' needs. Collaboration between the Counseling and ML departments is especially strong during key academic transitions, highlighting how the model enables timely, coordinated interventions.

Each spring, the ML Coordinator and the district ML Instructional Coach, develop comprehensive spreadsheets for incoming ninth-grade students incorporating multiple data points, including Long-term English Learner (L-TEL) status, presence of IEPs or 504 plans, and middle school teacher recommendations for English Language Arts placement. These sheets utilized during the course selection timeframe enable precise student placement across a range of options, from standard English 9 courses to specialized supports including co-taught classes, ML-specific courses (EL 1 or EL 2), and sheltered content courses, demonstrating efficient resource distribution based on student needs.

This system extends beyond 9th-grade placement to current P-CEP students where annual placement recommendations based on teacher evaluations and WIDA assessment scores ensure appropriate academic support while maintaining individualized student advocacy across the P-CEP complex.

P-CEP has also implemented robust intervention protocols that facilitate early identification and response to student concerns. During the first quarter, ML teachers contribute to a comprehensive spreadsheet where they document specific student concerns and identify relevant classes and issues. This

Table 8.2 ML Course Placement Guide

Proficiency Level	*ELD/English*	*Math*	*Science*	*Social Studies*	*Health*
Level 1-1.9	EL 1 EL 1 Content & Language Support * Both courses must be on the student's schedule	Based on placement test or evaluated transcripts • Sheltered Algebra 1 • Sheltered Geometry • Sheltered Algebra 2	Sheltered Physics OR Appropriate sheltered science course if student has met the prerequisites (and needs to take a science to graduate)	Based on grade level requirement • Sheltered World History • Sheltered U.S. History • Sheltered Civics • Sheltered Civics	• Unless necessary do not add Level 1 or first 12–18 months of arrival in US schools into Health
Level 2.0-3.0	EL 2 EL 2 Content & Language Support * Both courses must be on the student's schedule	Based on placement test or evaluated transcripts • Sheltered Algebra 1 • Sheltered Geometry • Sheltered Algebra 2	Based on grade level requirement • Sheltered Physics • Sheltered Science • Sheltered Chemistry	Based on grade level requirement • Sheltered World History • Sheltered U.S. History • Sheltered Econ • Sheltered Civics	Co-taught Health
Level 2.5-3.5	ML English Course • ML English 9 (9th grade) • ML American Literature (10th grade) • EL 3 (11 & 12th)	Based on placement test or evaluated transcripts • Sheltered Algebra 1 • Sheltered Geometry • Sheltered Algebra 2	Based on grade level requirement • Sheltered Physics • Sheltered Science • Sheltered Chemistry	Based on grade level requirement • Sheltered World History • Sheltered U.S. History • Sheltered Econ • Sheltered Civics	Co-taught Health
Level 3.5–6.0	Co-taught English	Non-Sheltered Course	Non-Sheltered Course	Non-Sheltered Course OR Co-taught US History	Co-taught Health

Note. Long-Term English Learners (L-TELs) are enrolled in grade-level courses rather than self-contained EL or sheltered classes, except when a specific circumstance warrants otherwise with approval from the ML Department. For ML students with IEPs, course selections are guided by the recommendations of the IEP team.

collaborative tool provides a holistic view of each student's progress, as multiple ML teachers—from standalone EL 1 or 2 courses to sheltered content classes—can contribute their observations.

The case of Lara illustrates how this intervention system operates in practice. In the first quarter spreadsheet, Lara's EL 2 teacher documented significant concerns about her academic performance and engagement. The teacher noted that Lara consistently struggled with understanding directions and completing assignments, often disengaging when faced with challenges. While some assignments were turned in incomplete or incorrect, others were submitted perfectly completed, raising questions about independent work. The teacher observed that Lara's language proficiency levels across reading, writing, speaking, and listening appeared more aligned with EL 1 than EL 2, despite her WIDA score of 1.9. Additionally, the teacher noted Lara's tendency to rely heavily on L1 peers for translation and communication, along with a noticeable lack of motivation and confidence.

Initially, the teacher recommended moving Lara back to EL 1, citing the benefits of a smaller class setting and new curriculum materials being used with current level 1 students. However, the ML Coordinator and Assistant Principal, noting Lara's success in her sheltered content classes, recognized the need for deeper investigation before making such a significant change—particularly since repeating EL 1 would not earn Lara additional credit toward graduation.

Following the intervention protocol, a comprehensive meeting was convened including the counselor, teacher, parent, translator, ML Coordinator, and Assistant Principal. During this discussion, unexpected factors emerged that shed new light on Lara's struggles. The parent revealed that Lara felt discriminated against by the EL teacher due to certain classroom comments, though the parent herself didn't share this perception. The discussion also uncovered a previously undisclosed medical condition that explained Lara's unauthorized classroom departures, which had been a source of tension with the teacher. This revelation helped contextualize what had been perceived as behavioral issues.

The meeting concluded with a deeper understanding of the root causes behind Lara's academic struggles—namely, her perception of discrimination leading to disengagement—and resulted in a plan for a restorative justice meeting to address these concerns. This case exemplifies how P-CEP's intervention protocols create space for uncovering and addressing complex factors affecting student performance through multiple perspectives and expertise.

Another critical communication protocol involves first semester-end analysis of course failure rates. This collaborative review, conducted by the Counselor, ML Coordinator, Teacher Leader, and Assistant Principal, serves multiple essential purposes. It enables the team to identify patterns of academic struggle that might indicate systemic barriers or needed instructional adjustments, facilitates targeted intervention planning for specific student populations, and helps inform resource allocation and support strategies for the following semester. This data-driven approach ensures that both individual student needs and broader programmatic challenges are identified and addressed proactively.

While more frequent direct collaboration between counselors and ML educators could potentially enhance student support through regular structured meetings focused on student progress, insight sharing, and strategic planning for academic and social-emotional support, P-CEP's alternative approach effectively balances practical constraints with student needs. The institutional complexity of P-CEP's size necessitates alternative collaborative mechanisms. The current solution optimizes resources by leveraging administrative oversight to bridge departmental boundaries and facilitate timely interventions through streamlined communication protocols. The combination of strategic administrative oversight, systematic data management, and coordinated departmental communication creates a responsive framework that enables consistent advocacy while optimizing resource allocation.

The reality of supporting MLs within complex educational systems often requires educators to extend beyond traditional role boundaries—what research describes as "going the extra mile" to ensure comprehensive student support (Farrell et al., 2022). Studies have found that school counselors working with ELL populations consistently report having to operate "beyond the scope of practice" and outside normal work hours to ensure adequate care for students and families (Farrell et al., 2022, p. 5). "Going the extra mile included school counselors having to navigate, decide on, and negotiate the systems of support available to them and their ELL students (Farrell et al., 2022, p. 5). P-CEP's collaborative model acknowledges this reality while working to systematize and distribute these additional efforts. Rather than leaving individual counselors to navigate resources and systems alone, the coordinated oversight structure enables strategic "negotiating systems of support" where the ML Coordinator and Assistant Principal can leverage institutional relationships and administrative authority to secure necessary accommodations and resources. The model's emphasis on systematic data collection, regular cross-departmental meetings, and clear communication protocols helps transform individual advocacy efforts into institutional capacity, reducing the burden on individual staff members while ensuring consistent support for students across all three schools.

This integrated system demonstrates how P-CEP's structural approach effectively translates protocols into tangible student support outcomes. Through this model, timely interventions are facilitated across all three schools, ensuring that ML students receive appropriate academic and social-emotional support regardless of their campus placement. This approach suggests that effective ML support systems must balance ideal practices with practical constraints while maintaining robust communication channels and data-informed decision-making processes.

Overcoming Challenges in the Collaborative Process

While these structural supports have proven effective in cases like Ahmed's, Maryam's, and Lara's, implementing and maintaining such systems across three distinct high schools presents ongoing challenges that require creative solutions and continuous adaptation.

One persistent challenge stems from the physical separation between buildings and the complex scheduling demands of P-CEP's campus structure. With ML students and staff distributed across three buildings, coordinating immediate responses to student needs can be logistically challenging. The district has addressed this through strategic technological integration, implementing a shared digital documentation system that enables real-time communication about student concerns. This system allows counselors and ML educators to flag issues, share observations, and coordinate responses without requiring physical meetings, significantly reducing response times for student support needs.

Resource allocation presents another significant challenge, particularly in balancing the need for specialized ML support with maintaining appropriate class sizes and ensuring equitable access across all three schools. The district has addressed this through careful analysis of enrollment patterns and strategic scheduling of sheltered and co-taught sections. By examining historical data and projected enrollment numbers, administrators can more effectively distribute resources and staff across the campus. This data-driven approach helps ensure that specialized ML support remains accessible to students regardless of their home school assignment.

Professional development time constraints represent another significant challenge, particularly in facilitating cross-departmental training and collaboration. With limited Wednesday meeting slots available, balancing department-specific needs with cross-departmental collaboration can be difficult. The administration has addressed this through a rotating schedule of inter-departmental professional development sessions and the implementation of asynchronous collaboration tools. These tools enable ongoing professional dialogue and resource sharing even when face-to-face meetings aren't possible.

The complexity of transcript evaluation and credit assignment for international students presents ongoing challenges, particularly in ensuring consistent application of district policies across all three schools. To address this, the district hopes to develop detailed guidelines for transcript evaluation and credit assignment, but for now the use of the ML Lead Teacher and the ML Coordinator as extra sets of eyes on student schedules helps to catch any misinterpretations or inaccurate placements. In the future, guidelines could include specific protocols for recognizing international credits and applying them toward graduation requirements, helping to ensure equitable treatment of international students across all three schools.

These challenges and their solutions demonstrate how P-CEP's collaborative model continues to evolve through systematic problem-solving and strategic adaptation. P-CEP's approach to addressing these challenges emphasizes the importance of maintaining clear communication channels, establishing standardized protocols, and remaining flexible in implementation to meet diverse student needs.

Vision for the Future

The vision for the future of the ML program at P-CEP focuses on deepening collaboration with the counseling department while expanding opportunities and support for MLs. Research emphasizes that productive partnerships between principals and counselors lead to better outcomes for students (McConnell et al., 2020). This chapter has highlighted the strong foundation of P-CEP's collaborative model, and looking ahead, we have identified key areas for growth and improvement to further enhance support for ML students across the three-campus complex.

Looking at the data, the documented success in co-taught classes, combined with concerning exit rate trends, creates the first priority for future development: addressing the disconnect between authentic academic achievement and formal language proficiency recognition. However, future initiatives must honestly confront a fundamental challenge: for many L-TELs who have refused services, WIDA results have little practical impact on their academic experience or post-secondary opportunities. This reality suggests the need to explore whether current exit criteria accurately reflect academic readiness and investigate alternative methods for documenting and celebrating the language growth that is clearly occurring in co-taught environments.

Given the demonstrated effectiveness of co-taught classes in supporting authentic academic achievement, the very success that our current assessment system fails to recognize, a key priority for future growth is expanding co-taught course offerings. This model, which pairs content area teachers with ML specialists, has proven highly effective in supporting MLs while upholding rigorous academic standards. At P-CEP, co-taught classes are currently offered primarily in English Language Arts. In the 2023–2024 school year, co-taught health was introduced, and in 2024–2025, a co-taught social studies class was offered for the first time. The vision for the future includes expanding this model to additional subject areas, such as science and mathematics where MLs often face significant language barriers. Research supports the importance of ensuring MLs have access to academically rigorous coursework. As Callahan et al. (2010) found, "Students enrolled in more advanced math and science coursework with greater access to academic content demonstrate greater gains in achievement than students placed in less advanced coursework" (p. 4). This finding reinforces P-CEP's commitment to expanding co-taught offerings.

Complementing the co-taught model, equally important is the expansion of sheltered course offerings, which are designed to make content more accessible while maintaining grade-level expectations. These courses have proven to be highly effective in promoting academic growth. Currently, sheltered courses are offered in foundational subjects like mathematics, science, and history, with each subject having just one section. The goal moving forward is to increase the number of sheltered sections in these foundational areas, providing more students with access to courses that offer language scaffolding, enabling them to engage more effectively with complex concepts. During the 2025–2026 school year, P-CEP will expand sheltered mathematics offerings by introducing Sheltered Pre-Algebra and adding a second section of Sheltered Geometry, ensuring that more MLs have access to language-scaffolded mathematics instruction. By broadening both co-taught and sheltered course offerings, P-CEP aims to provide MLs with greater access to a well-rounded, academically rigorous curriculum while ensuring they receive the necessary language support to thrive. To successfully implement this expanded course offerings vision, teachers across all content areas must be equipped with the skills and strategies for supporting language learners.

Therefore, increasing training in sheltering strategies for additional content and elective teachers represents a crucial component of the future vision. Research has consistently documented the challenges that arise when general education teachers lack the knowledge and strategies necessary to support MLs effectively.

Farrell et al. (2022) found that while some educators demonstrate support for ELL students and collaborative initiatives, the majority of school counselors reported significant difficulties in securing teacher cooperation with necessary accommodations and fostering understanding of student cultural and linguistic contexts. The research revealed that effective ML support requires persistent advocacy and professional dialogue focused on instructional modifications that acknowledge students' ongoing language development while maintaining academic rigor (Farrell et al., 2022). This finding underscores that meaningful progress requires "reframing what success looks like and providing accommodations for students" (Farrell et al., 2022, p. 5) precisely the pedagogical shifts that comprehensive training in Sheltered Instruction facilitates.

Building on this foundation, P-CEP has committed to systematic expansion of training in Sheltered Instruction across departments. During the 2024–2025 school year, all science teachers across the three campuses received this comprehensive training, creating a cohort of educators equipped with research-based strategies for making content accessible to MLs. This initiative will continue with the English Language Arts department in the 2025–2026 school year, ensuring that every ML student has access to language-scaffolded instruction in their core literacy courses. This sequential departmental approach recognizes that sustainable change requires moving beyond individual teacher enthusiasm to institutional commitment. By training entire departments systematically, P-CEP can create cohesive instructional environments where research-based language support strategies become standard practice rather than individual accommodations, directly addressing the teacher preparation gaps documented in current research.

Another innovative approach being considered is the expansion of independent study opportunities specifically tailored to ML student needs and interests. Under the supervision of the ML department administrator, these personalized learning experiences could provide meaningful alternatives to traditional electives. The independent study program could operate flexibly within a ML teacher's teaching schedule, allowing that instructor to meet with students during their preparation period or while simultaneously overseeing other classes. This flexibility enables individualized attention without compromising existing instructional commitments. The recent case of a refugee student, who arrived late in the school year after an extended gap in formal education and was supported through an ALEKS-based independent study model, demonstrates the potential of this approach to meet unique student needs through creative and intentional use of existing resources. When scheduling challenges arise that might otherwise place MLs in unrelated electives, counselors can instead collaborate with the ML department administrator or assistant principal to create targeted independent study options aligned with student needs. Expansion of this model might include:

- Career exploration programs that connect students' linguistic and cultural backgrounds with potential professional paths
- Community engagement initiatives that provide real-world language practice while building leadership skills
- Academic interest projects that bridge gaps between ESL instruction and mainstream content areas

Each independent study would be structured with clear learning objectives, assessment criteria, and regular check-ins, ensuring academic rigor while meeting individual student needs. By implementing these structured independent study opportunities, P-CEP could enhance ML students' educational experiences, fostering both linguistic and academic growth in alignment with their personal and professional aspirations.

These interconnected initiatives, expanding co-taught and sheltered course offerings, systematically implementing training in Sheltered Instruction across departments, and creating flexible independent study opportunities, represent a comprehensive approach to addressing the identified gaps in ML support. Rather than relying solely on formal assessment measures that may not capture authentic student achievement, this vision prioritizes expanding the proven instructional models where MLs demonstrate real academic success. Through these strategic expansions, P-CEP can build upon its existing collaborative foundation to create more equitable and effective educational pathways for all MLs.

Conclusion

P-CEP's innovative collaborative leadership model demonstrates how complex educational institutions can effectively support MLs through strategic coordination and systematic advocacy. The analysis presented in this chapter reveals that successful ML support transcends traditional departmental boundaries, requiring intentional structural design that facilitates seamless communication and coordinated intervention.

The individual cases discussed illustrate how P-CEP's framework transforms institutional protocols into personalized student advocacy. Through systematic coordination between ML specialists and school counselors, supported by strategic administrative oversight, the model successfully navigates complex challenges including international transcript evaluation, appropriate course placement, and timely academic interventions. These individual success stories underscore the model's capacity to address diverse student needs while maintaining consistency across three distinct school campuses.

The analysis of multi-year exit trends alongside co-taught class performance data validates P-CEP's collaborative approach while highlighting critical assessment challenges facing the field. The stark contrast between declining exit rates (from 14% in 2021 to 3% in 2024) and exceptional academic performance in co-taught classes (80% pass rates in English 9, 100% in U.S. History) demonstrates that collaborative instructional models enable authentic learning that may not be captured through traditional assessment measures. This finding reinforces the importance of P-CEP's emphasis on classroom-based evidence and collaborative decision-making, suggesting that effective ML support requires both rigorous academic programming and advocacy for assessment practices that authentically recognize student growth and achievement.

As illustrated in Figure 8.1, the structural elements that enable this success, including the Course Placement Guide, data-sharing protocols, quarterly Crossover PLCs, and comprehensive intervention frameworks, provide a replicable blueprint for other educational institutions serving multilingual populations. Perhaps most significantly, this analysis reveals how P-CEP's three-pillar framework optimizes existing resources through strategic role definition and clear communication channels, all built upon a foundation for equitable access. Rather than requiring extensive additional staffing or resources, the framework leverages collaborative partnerships to maximize impact. The Assistant Principal's dual oversight of counseling and ML departments creates essential bridges between specialized services, while systematic data collection and analysis inform both individual interventions and programmatic improvements.

The challenges identified, including physical separation across campuses, resource allocation complexities, and professional development constraints, highlight the ongoing evolution required in collaborative leadership models. P-CEP's solutions, from digital documentation systems to rotating professional development schedules, demonstrate the importance of continuous adaptation and creative

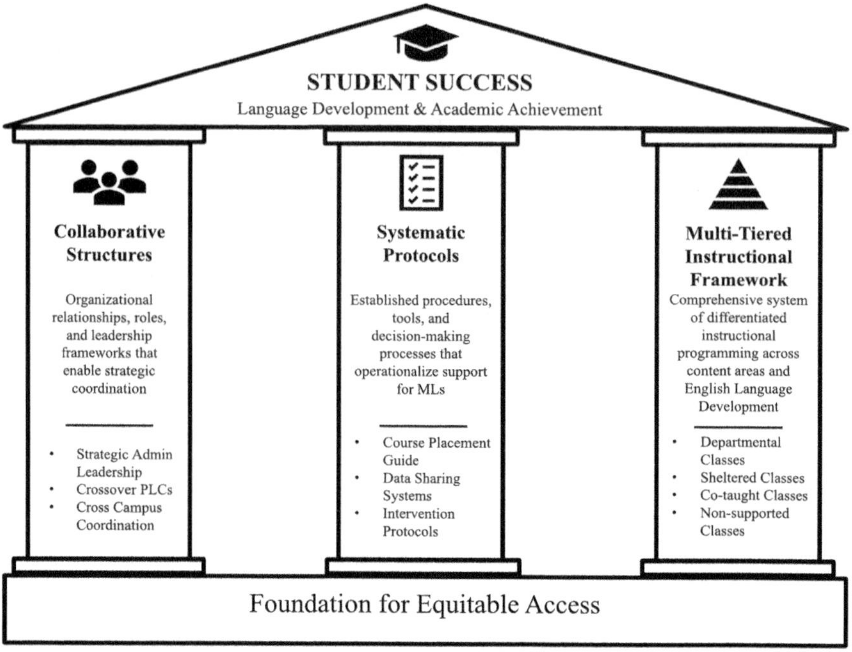

Figure 8.1 Supporting multilingual learners: a three-pillar framework. Graphic by the authors.

Note. The three-pillar framework structures P-CEP's collaborative approach to supporting multilingual learners. This framework integrates collaborative structures, systematic protocols, and a multi-tiered instructional framework-all grounded in equitable access principles-to ensure comprehensive support for multilingual student success.

problem-solving in maintaining effective support structures. Looking toward the future, P-CEP's vision for expanded co-taught and sheltered course offerings, increased training in Sheltered Instruction, and innovative independent study opportunities reflects the model's commitment to continuous improvement built upon years of intentional relationship-building and systematic protocol development.

The implications of P-CEP's model extend beyond the immediate context of ML support, offering valuable insights for any educational institution seeking to enhance cross-departmental collaboration, improve student advocacy systems, and create responsive support structures for diverse student populations. As the United States continues to serve increasingly diverse student populations, with English learners representing over 10% of public school enrollment (National Center for Education Statistics, 2024), the need for effective collaborative support models becomes increasingly critical.

P-CEP's approach aligns with broader research emphasizing the need for comprehensive, collaborative support systems for MLs. Rather than relying solely on English instruction or equal resource distribution, researchers like Jiang and Harklau (2024) advocate for coalition-based approaches that bring together teachers, counselors, families, communities, and colleges in collective action toward equity. P-CEP's collaborative model exemplifies this approach, demonstrating how intentional partnerships between counselors, ML specialists, and administrators can create the systematic support structures necessary for meaningful educational equity.

P-CEP's model demonstrates that sophisticated support systems can be developed and maintained within existing institutional frameworks, provided there is commitment to strategic coordination, systematic communication, and continuous adaptation based on student needs and outcomes. Ultimately, successful support for MLs requires more than individual expertise or isolated interventions-it demands collaborative leadership that transcends traditional boundaries, creating integrated systems where specialized knowledge combines with comprehensive student advocacy.

As educational institutions nationwide grapple with serving increasingly diverse populations, P-CEP's experience offers both practical strategies and theoretical insights for creating more equitable and effective support systems. The model's success lies not in its complexity, but in its intentional simplicity: clear communication, strategic coordination, and unwavering commitment to student success through collaborative action.

The collaborative model developed at P-CEP offers numerous insights for educational leaders seeking to enhance support for MLs. The following reflection questions are designed to help administrators, counselors, and ML specialists consider how these strategies might be adapted and implemented within their own institutional contexts.

1 Examine your institution's course placement procedures for MLs. Who is involved in these decisions, and how consistent are placement practices across different staff members or campuses?
2 P-CEP implemented "crossover PLCs" between counseling and ML departments. What opportunities exist in your setting for cross-departmental professional learning? How could you initiate or enhance such collaboration given your current time and scheduling constraints?
3 Review P-CEP's Course Placement Guide framework. How could you develop or refine placement protocols in your setting to ensure consistency across staff members? What proficiency levels and course options would be most relevant for your student population?
4 The chapter emphasizes that successful ML support requires "more than individual expertise or isolated interventions." How might you shift from individual-focused to systems-focused approaches in your daily practice?
5 Envision your ideal collaborative support system for MLs five years from now. What would it look like, how would it function, and what steps will you take starting today to work toward that vision?

References

Allen, J. K. (2017). Exploring the role teacher perceptions play in the underrepresentation of culturally and linguistically diverse students in gifted programming. *Gifted Child Today*, *40*(2), 77–86. https://doi.org/10.1177/1076217517690188

Arriero, E., & Griffin, D. (2018). ¡Adelante! A community asset mapping approach to increase college and career readiness for rural Latinx high school students. *Professional School Counseling*, *22*(1). https://doi.org/10.1177/2156759x18800279

Callahan, R., Wilkinson, L., & Muller, C. (2010). Academic achievement and course taking among language minority youth in U.S. Schools: Effects of ESL placement. *Educational Evaluation and Policy Analysis*, *32*(1), 84–117. https://doi.org/10.3102/0162373709359805

Farrell, I. C., Binkley, E. E., Garcia, M. A., & Jackson, T. N. (2022). Advocacy of school counselors working with ELL students. *Professional School Counseling*, *26*(1), 1–10. https://doi.org/10.1177/2156759X221134276

Hallinger, P., & Heck, R. H. (2010). Leadership for learning: Does collaborative leadership make a difference in school improvement? *Educational Management Administration & Leadership*, *38*(6), 654–678.

Jiang, L., & Harklau, L. (2024). Multilingual learners' access to college: Students, school counselors, and institutional doxa and hysteresis. *TESOL Quarterly*, *58*(2), 881–908. https://doi.org/10.1002/tesq.3260

Johnson, L., Ziomek-Daigle, J., Haskins, N., & Paisley, P. (2016). An investigation of school counselor self-efficacy with English language learners. *Professional School Counseling*, *20*(1). https://doi.org/10.5330/1096-2409-20.1.44

McCall-Perez, Z. (2000). The counselor as advocate for English language learners: An action research approach. *Professional School Counseling*, *4*(1), 13–22.

McConnell, K. R., Geesa, R. L., Mayes, R. D., & Elam, N. P. (2020). Improving school counselor efficacy through principal-counselor collaboration: A comprehensive literature review. *Mid-Western Educational Researcher*, *32*(2), 133–155.

National Center for Education Statistics. (2024). English learners in public schools. *Condition of Education*. U.S. Department of Education, Institute of Education Sciences. https://nces.ed.gov/programs/coe/indicator/cgf

Spillane, J. P., Halverson, R., & Diamond, J. B. (2001). Investigating school leadership practice: A distributed perspective. *Educational Researcher*, *30*(3), 23–28.

Supovitz, J., Sirinides, P., & May, H. (2010). How principals and peers influence teaching and learning. *Educational Administration Quarterly*, *46*(1), 31–56.

Tinsley, B. (2019, April 29). Three schools, one campus: Plymouth-Canton Community Schools offer a unique high school experience. *WDET 101.9 FM*. https://wdet.org/2019/04/29/three-schools-one-campus-plymouth-canton-community-schools-offer-a-unique-high-school-experience/

Chapter 9

Multilingual Learners' Success

Interdisciplinary Collaboration to Enhance Academic, Career, and Social-Emotional Development

Zachary Pietrantoni, Andy V. Pham, Ryan W. Pontier, Melissa Boyanton, and Emily Martinez

Sofía had only recently immigrated to the United States from México when the school year began. In México, Sofía had always done well in school. She enjoyed subjects such as mathematics and science, often helping her friends with homework. But in her new school, everything felt unfamiliar. Although she took English classes in México, she did not feel confident expressing herself in the language. Oftentimes, even when she understood the concepts, she would keep her ideas to herself, worried that she might not find the words in English to express herself clearly. During group activities, she tended to get lost in the fast-paced conversations, in which students are constantly talking over one another or interrupting each other. She felt unsure how to connect with her peers. After a few weeks, Sofía started to doubt her previous confidence in school and struggled to believe she belonged.

After a few months, Sofía's teachers began noticing her quietness, unsure if she was not grasping the content or was disengaged. During the first quarter progress report, her teachers noted concerns related to her lack of participation, difficulty making friends, and recent low scores on mathematics and science tests. When the school counselor, Mrs. Wright, reviewed Sofía's case following a teacher referral, she recognized a familiar pattern: the monolingual expectations of the school overshadowed Sofía's abilities, making it difficult for her to thrive in the classroom.

A multilingual approach to school counseling is essential in addressing the diverse needs of students in today's increasingly globalized educational environments. As the student population becomes more linguistically diverse, with many students speaking languages other than English at home, a multilingual approach ensures that school counselors can provide equitable support for all students, particularly those from culturally and linguistically diverse (CLD) backgrounds (Suarez-Orozco, 2010).

Research highlights the profound impact of language on student development, academic success, and mental health (Davis et al., 2023; Yeh, 2008). Language is not just a tool for communication but a core aspect of identity and cultural

DOI: 10.4324/9781003711124-11

expression (Garcia & Li, 2014). When students are unable to fully express themselves due to imposed language barriers, it can lead to feelings of isolation, frustration, and disengagement from the school environment, which can negatively affect both their emotional well-being and academic performance (Yeh, 2008). Furthermore, traditional monolingual practices in school counseling may overlook the unique experiences of multilingual learners (MLs), leading to misdiagnoses, inappropriate interventions, or a lack of adequate mental health support (Artiles, 2013).

A multilingual approach facilitates more accurate assessments, particularly when evaluating academic difficulties or mental health concerns. Standardized psychological assessments often fail to account for linguistic and cultural differences, leading to inaccurate diagnoses or interventions (Lopez, 2007). Engaging with students in their home language(s), or understanding their linguistic background, allows school counselors to gain a more holistic understanding of the child's strengths and challenges. It also promotes more effective communication with families, fostering stronger partnerships between schools and homes, which is critical for supporting student success (Klingner & Harry, 2006).

Furthermore, multilingual competencies in school counseling promote inclusivity and respect for diverse cultural backgrounds (Davis et al., 2023). By acknowledging and validating the languages students speak, school counselors not only help reduce stigma but also empower students by honoring their linguistic identities (Davis et al., 2023; Sue & Sue, 2012). This approach contributes to the overall well-being of students, creating a school environment that is supportive, responsive, and culturally competent (Sue & Sue, 2012).

Hence, incorporating a multilingual approach into school counseling is not just a best practice—it is an ethical and practical necessity. It allows school counselors to support the emotional, psychological, and academic needs of MLs more effectively, ensuring that all students, regardless of their linguistic background, receive the individualized support they deserve.

Multilingual Language Development

Multilingual development has historically been constrained by educational policies and cultural attitudes that view linguistic diversity as a deficit rather than an asset (Vera et al., 2022). MLs are a group of students who are engaging, learning, and/or have proficiency in more than one language in their daily lives (Cenoz, 2013). The 20th century saw multiple systematic efforts to suppress MLs in favor of English-only instruction (Schmid, 2000). Subsequently, these challenges have been compounded by limited teacher preparation and bilingual education resources, culturally biased assessments, and socioeconomic barriers that disproportionately affect MLs (Niehaus & Adelson, 2014; Schmid, 2000; Vera et al., 2022). School counselors and other educators might consider the factors that affect multilingual language development from social, cultural, and systemic perspectives.

Historical Context

Bilingual education and native/home language instruction were more common in the 18th and early 19th century United States with schools often designing their curricula around the primary language of the community (Malakoff & Hakuta, 1990). During the 19th century, an "Americanization" movement emerged as a xenophobic response to the drastic influx of newly immigrated people (Schmid, 2000). The movement introduced various public changes to assimilate new immigrants and emphasize so-called American values, including the rise of state laws mandating English-only instruction (Schmid, 2000). The Civil Rights movement in the 1960s aided in the passing of the Bilingual Education Act of 1968, which federally recognized support for bilingual education; however, the law neither defined nor enforced bilingual education or instruction in a language other than English. It was not until 1974 that the landmark decision of *Lau v. Nichols* mandated affirmative efforts to be put in place to support MLs (Schmid, 2000). Today, despite evidence supporting the need for multilingual and multicultural curricula, many schools continue to operate under a monolingual and monocultural framework (Zhu & Camicia, 2012). The March 2025 executive order designating English as the official language of the United States perpetuates a monolingual mindset, conveying the message that multilingualism is seen as a barrier rather than an asset (The White House, 2025). Monolingual pedagogies continue to present myriad obstacles for multilingual and multicultural students, shaping the challenges they encounter in today's classrooms.

Challenges for MLs

MLs are one of the fastest-growing groups of school-aged population in the United States (National Clearinghouse for English Language Acquisition, 2021) representing 10.6% of all K-12 students in 2021 (National Center for Education Statistics [NCES], 2024). Demographic information related to educators and school professionals' multilingual skills is rare, but there have been persistent national shortages of multilingual educators and diverse school professionals to meet the needs of MLs, many of whom identify as non-white. Nearly 80% of public-school teachers are non-Hispanic White (NCES, 2023), and only 2% identify as ESOL or bilingual teachers (NCES, 2019). Similarly, 77% of school counselors are White (American School Counselor Association, 2021). Based on a national survey of school psychologists, approximately 12% of school psychologists reported speaking another language other than English, with little demographic and linguistic change in the workforce in the past two decades (Goforth et al., 2021).

Needs

With the historical context and challenges faced by MLs in mind, the question becomes: how do school systems progress to meet the needs of an increasingly diverse K-12 student population? Two key factors to address in this development are the lack of an inclusive curriculum that reflects students' linguistic identities and the need for increased family engagement. Operationalizing a translanguaging pedagogy within school systems provides a potential solution to a curriculum rooted in monolingualism (García & Li, 2014; García et al., 2017). Translanguaging is a prominent theory of multilingualism that challenges the traditional, narrow view of language by presenting multilingualism as being shaped by social, cultural, and political factors (Donley, 2022). Donley (2022) noted how translanguaging as a theory embraces the dynamic ways MLs use their linguistic repertoire to convey meaning.

Implementing bilingual practices as a pedagogical approach is framed through a social justice lens with a goal of challenging social, cultural, and political influences (Donley, 2022; Pontier & Tian, 2023). Classroom practices shift from solely operating within the confines of the standard curriculum language to facilitating a space that values the experiences of MLs, allowing for creative, intentional use of language (Donley, 2022). García et al. (2017) proposed three characteristics of translanguaging pedagogy: (a) advocates and implements a translanguaging stance, (b) incorporates student-centered multilingual learning resources within classroom design, and (c) allows for flexibility in shifting curriculum to meet the needs of linguistically diverse students. Through the integration of a translanguaging framework, school systems become active participants in the dismantling of exclusionary curricula.

Productive family-school partnerships are also a crucial component in meeting the needs of MLs and supporting their academic achievement. Family engagement is often associated with increased educational equity and overall positive student outcomes (Hine, 2025). Families of MLs may be hesitant to engage with schools that do not facilitate linguistically and culturally sustaining contexts, as well as concerns related to immigration status (Protacio et al., 2021). These concerns may be further aggravated by recent government efforts to carry out mass deportations of immigrants from the United States, including in areas previously considered "sensitive" areas such as schools (National Immigration Law Center, 2025). Given the current political landscape, it is crucial for schools to make a concerted effort to meaningfully engage with families and create a safe, inclusive space for learning (Hine, 2025).

Research suggests that families of MLs may define family engagement differently, viewing actions such as advocacy as engagement rather than participation in school-organized events (Hine, 2025). Additionally, families may be more likely to defer to educators as the experts in their child's education, influencing how their involvement may be perceived within the school system

(Hine, 2025). Thus, schools are better equipped to engage with MLs and families when they adopt a culturally and linguistically sustaining framework to guide family-school partnerships. One such framework, funds of knowledge, encourages schools to build partnerships with families through reciprocal sharing. It values the lived experiences families bring and empowers them to share their cultural knowledge as a way to connect with students and challenge monolithic representations of culture (Protacio et al., 2021). Utilizing this concept of reciprocal sharing, schools are better equipped to offer families meaningful opportunities to bridge cultural and linguistic differences. Overall, it is crucial to adopt a strengths-based framework to combat deficit views of families, authentically engage with families, and enrich students' classroom experiences by affirming their cultural identities.

Systemic Barriers to MLs' Success

Providing students with school support and promoting family-school partnerships aids in addressing critical barriers that impede academic and social-emotional success experienced by MLs (Niehaus & Adelson, 2014). Consider Sofía, who had always done well in school in México, but struggled when she started school in the United States. Her teachers were unsure how to interpret her lack of participation, difficulty building peer relationships, and slowly declining grades. Without meaningful support within the school system and family engagement, her academic performance and sense of belongingness in the classroom erode, impacting her educational and social-emotional experience. These systemic barriers persist across multiple domains and can be examined through the lens of teaching, school counseling, and school psychology—each of which plays a critical role in shaping MLs' educational experiences.

Deficit Mindset and Inappropriate Educational Placement

From a teaching perspective, educators have expressed that their preservice training programs left them underprepared to effectively support the social-emotional needs of MLs in the classroom (Vera et al., 2022). As a result, teachers may hold a "deficit mindset" toward MLs, internalizing misconceptions regarding multilingualism and perceiving students' use of multiple languages as a barrier to English proficiency rather than an asset (Vera et al., 2022). This deficit mindset may contribute to the underrepresentation of MLs in gifted programs, as a beginning level of English proficiency may be seen as an inadequacy in learning (Allen, 2017). Furthermore, school psychologists may lack an understanding of multilingualism and second language acquisition, resulting in improper identification and placement of MLs in special education programs (Becker & Deris, 2019). In addition to limiting academic opportunities, a myopic focus on English proficiency (and not multilingualism) may alienate students from accessing classroom interactions and counseling services, contributing to gaps in social-emotional support (Davis et al., 2023).

Inadequate Social-Emotional Learning (SEL) Support

Research continues to support the prominent influence of SEL skills on academic outcomes (Durlak et al., 2011, 2022). Yet, despite the value of SEL within the classroom, educators are often ill-equipped to provide adequate SEL support to students (Gimbert et al., 2021). This lack of preparedness, likely due to gaps in preservice training and sociopolitical pressures, is exacerbated when MLs are involved (Vera et al., 2022). For example, school counselors report some difficulties building connections with MLs, navigating language differences, and working with interpreters (Vera et al., 2022). The provision of SEL support for MLs is pertinent considering the lack of school belongingness often experienced by these students, which can lead to a decline in academic motivation (Shi & Watkinson, 2019). These micro-level SEL challenges reflect larger-scale sociocultural and systemic barriers that impact MLs' educational experiences.

Intersectional Challenges

MLs are often confronted with compounding sociocultural and systemic challenges that extend beyond unsupportive language and instruction. In fact, their access to academic and social-emotional support has been limited or precluded, and their educational experience impeded due to discrimination, poverty, depression, immigration status, and acculturation difficulties (Talleyrand & Vojtech, 2019). To meet the needs of students, school professionals must be prepared to provide culturally responsible and affirming support and services (Talleyrand & Vojtech, 2019). Without adequate support, MLs may encounter additional barriers that limit access to college preparation and enrollment, hindering long-term academic success (Murillo & Lavadenz, 2020).

Interdisciplinary Collaboration in Supporting MLs

Interdisciplinary collaboration between stakeholders is considered a best practice to support the academic, behavioral, and mental health needs of MLs (Johnson et al., 2019; Tuttle et al., 2021). Each team member offers unique yet complementary knowledge and skills critical for educational decision-making. Within school counseling, interdisciplinary collaboration is described as an interaction between at least two parties voluntarily engaged in shared decision making toward a common goal (Friend & Cook, 2013). The American School Counselor Association (ASCA) Ethical Standards for School Counselors (2022) encourage school counselors to develop and strengthen interdisciplinary relationships to meet clients' needs and interests even when professional views or perspectives may differ. It is essential that respective disciplines share common values and leverage their expertise to maximize system-level efforts, with the aim of providing comprehensive support to MLs and families.

Multi-Tiered Systems of Supports

One systems-level effort that has shown promise for MLs is multi-tiered systems of support (MTSS), a preventative approach that provides a continuum of services to improve students' academic, behavioral, and mental health needs (Gonzalez et al., 2022; Sugai & Horner, 2009). Successful implementation of MTSS requires differentiation of instruction, implementation of evidence-based practices, using high-quality screening and progress monitoring tools, and understanding the learning strengths and needs of all students. Within a culturally and linguistically responsive MTSS, each tier addresses culture and language as part of the instruction, assessment, and intervention processes (Robles et al., 2025). In Tier 1 (universal), all students participate in inclusive curriculum or classroom instruction, which may include translanguaging and/or culturally responsive pedagogy. In Tier 2 (targeted), selected students receive additional support that addresses multiculturalism, multilingualism, and adaptation of evidence-based interventions that address learning or mental health needs. Finally, in Tier 3 (intensive), few students may need additional support beyond large (Tier 1) and small (Tier 2) group interventions using a culturally responsive assessment to inform individualized interventions to meet their multilingual needs (Sugai & Horner, 2009). The frequency and intensity of interventions are based on each student's response to the intervention. In other words, if a student demonstrates insufficient progress, the intervention intensity may increase. Conversely, if a student does show improvement, the intervention may decrease intensity until the student can be successful with Tier 1 universal support. This approach ensures that students receive appropriate levels of support aligned with their individual needs.

MTSS has potential for reducing learning challenges and the over referral of MLs to special education (Hoover et al., 2020). School-based teams also must take an asset-based and ecological approach that considers students' educational, cultural, and linguistic experiences that may differ from their monolingual peers (Hoover & Soltero-Gonzalez, 2018). In MTSS assessment, educational decision-making and instruction should address students' developing linguistic and learning needs. Since issues related to academics, language, and behavior are often intertwined, using culturally and linguistically appropriate screening tools and interventions is important to ensure accurate identification of students' academic and mental health needs. To do so, school-based teams (e.g., educators, school counselors, school social workers, school psychologists, interventions, reading specialists, bilingual consultants, cultural brokers) can collaborate and demonstrate knowledge of language acquisition, acculturation, and ecological variables that affect educational success (Harris & Sullivan, 2017). For students like Sofía, an MTSS framework may have aided in recognizing her quietness and lack of participation not as a sign of disengagement but because of an incompatible learning environment.

Although MTSS provides educators with a framework for accurately identifying and addressing language and learning needs (Multitiered System of Supports for English Learners [MTSS4ELs], 2025), and much of the work has been done primarily with a subset of MLs its effectiveness has garnered mixed results as programs and supports have not addressed students' home language and English development simultaneously (Robles et al., 2025).

Tier 1 Support

Within classrooms, instruction and/or opportunities in multiple languages should be provided and considered throughout the MTSS process. In Tier 1, classrooms that use translanguaging or culturally and linguistically responsive pedagogy can aid in student achievement (Wesley-Nero & Donley, 2024). These instructional practices are student-centered and prioritize MLs' opportunities to use their entire language repertoire to acknowledge their own identities, express ideas, and develop new learning in school (Lucas & Villegas, 2011). For example, students can take notes in their preferred languages or present exit ticket questions in their home languages which is part of a linguistically responsive pedagogy. Other teachers may highlight the importance of linguistic variation and encourage successful meaning-making and communication over mechanics, grammar, and syntax. Alvarez et al. (2023) recommended that educators implement multimodal instruction that includes (1) small-group activities or discussion; (2) hands-on investigations; (3) leveraging resources, such as video, images, text, gestures, and home languages for collaborative activities; and (4) sequence opportunities for students to move between writing for themselves and oral discourse with peers. Culturally and linguistically responsive pedagogy provides MLs with opportunities to make meaningful, real-life connections to the content and curriculum. If these practices are in place, then a majority of the students in the classroom should do well, or an estimated 70–80% of the students would respond to intervention (Sugai & Horner, 2009). To determine if students are making progress in MTSS, teachers and school counselors should collaborate with reading specialists to collect information via formative assessments (e.g., universal screenings, benchmark measures) related to students' language and literacy skills at least three times per year (Landry et al., 2022). These screening assessments should be developed for and validated in multiple languages, and yield data that allow the school team to understand student performance across multiple languages (Wackerle-Holman et al., 2022).

Assessment procedures should also include other tools (e.g., checklists, observations) to gather input from caregivers and teachers that describe social, emotional, and behavioral strengths and difficulties in the context of both home and school (Murietta & Eklund, 2022). Data from universal screening can help to identify school or class needs related to mental health support (e.g., psychoeducation and outreach, classroom behavior management strategies). School counselors can provide resources and strategies for any student who may be adjusting to a new environment.

School-based teams can examine student data on literacy or behavioral measures within grades to identify individuals at risk of difficulties and determine which students may need additional academic or behavioral support. Although there have been emerging screening tools used in Spanish, it is also critical for school-based teams to understand that many assessments used in MTSS have limitations and/or may not be validated with other linguistic groups (Linan-Thompson et al., 2022). Therefore, school counselors should consult with teachers and school psychologists regarding collecting additional information such as work products and observations that capture the student's skills in multiple languages. School-based teams should reduce or mitigate any bias that may occur from using these tools so as not to underestimate the child's ability, misinterpret skills, or inaccurately reflect academic or behavioral needs.

Tier 2 Support

Tier 2 support is typically provided to students who score in the lowest 20% on universal screening (Kearns et al., 2014). When MLs are identified as needing additional instructional or behavioral support, it is important to carefully consider the student's instructional and language context prior to these educational decisions. For example, if a student whose native or dominant language is Spanish scores slightly below benchmark in early literacy, the teacher might consider increasing the intensity of phonological awareness instruction in Spanish. Similarly, the teacher can also implement similar activities in English if the MLs have similar language skills in both English and Spanish (Durán et al., 2016). Moreover, if a student's scores are elevated and they are at risk of internalizing behaviors, then further information gathered from their teacher and peer relationships can provide helpful information about the child's adjustment in their linguistic and social environment. When data are not as clear on recommending the student for Tier 2, other sources of information such as grades, teacher-administered assessment data, and input from caregivers can provide useful information in the decision-making process.

Within MTSS, the student's cultural and linguistic background should be considered when assessing their growth and selecting interventions is essential for determining their progress and goals (Linan-Thompson et al., 2022). Research has shown that providing native/home (e.g., Spanish) language instruction does not hinder growth in English (Dixon et al., 2025). Understanding what MLs can do in each target language AND across languages helps differentiate academic challenges from typical bilingual/second language development (Sánchez et al., 2018). When benchmark assessments are not available for MLs, state or district policies should provide guidance for identifying students who do not meet grade-level expectations or for determining which students will receive additional intervention (Linan-Thompson et al., 2022). Thus, collaboration between bilingual/ESOL teachers and reading specialists is essential for monitoring progress related to language and literacy, while collaboration with school counselors, school social workers, and school psychologists can aid in monitoring mental health or behavior progress over time. School team members should also focus on identifying students' strengths and needs relative to the presenting problem instead of focusing on their characteristics as the cause of the problems. A strength-based approach will help to minimize deficit-based approaches to intervention. School team members want to review data to determine the number of MLs that do not meet benchmarks to determine if there are system-level factors that influence academic and behavior outcomes. Data may include school climate, classroom support, or instructional materials, which can be compared across grade levels, special education categories, or language programs (e.g., English immersion, bilingual). School team members can analyze these data by classrooms and schools to determine those who need support and to identify tiered interventions that can help MLs be successful academically, socially, and emotionally.

Limited evidence-based interventions exist for MLs (Klingner & Edwards, 2006); however, they should be tailored to individual student needs. Tier 2 interventions can involve a small group of students (e.g., four to six) experiencing similar difficulties. Strategic grouping can assist students at their instructional level, address specific academic or social skills explicitly, and facilitate appropriate pacing of instruction. Monitoring student progress should be done weekly or bimonthly to determine individual student growth, any necessary intervention or goal changes, and whether to discontinue Tier 2 intervention. The school-based team may also discuss the rationale and goals for group counseling sessions or potentially adapting existing interventions with students' cultural experiences in mind. This requires thorough understanding and knowledge of the elements of the intervention, cultural and linguistic backgrounds of the target audience, and school resources needed to make changes or adaptations. The school team can also work collaboratively to ensure procedures that determine intervention fidelity (i.e., steps in delivering or adapting the intervention as intended). Adaptations to interventions can occur at the surface level, which can include translation of instructions and activities or providing images of people and places that are familiar to the target audience (Bernal et al., 2009). They can also occur at the deep structural levels which may involve adding cultural, social, and historical elements that influence core values, attitudes, beliefs, feelings, and behavior in the proposed target audience (Bernal et al., 2009). School counselors should gather input from cultural brokers or families when adapting interventions or counseling strategies that align with the student's cultural values and language skills. School counselors can collaborate with school psychologists to identify targeted culturally responsive and affirming approaches to support the cultural and linguistic needs of MLs. Moreover, school counselors can collaborate with teachers to create a classroom environment that addresses the targeted needs of MLs.

Tier 3 Support

MLs who struggle to progress despite Tier 2 interventions may be provided with more individualized or intensive support in Tier 3. In addition to facilitating or adapting evidence-based interventions (e.g., linguistically and culturally sustaining practices), school-based teams should carefully develop, review, and update protocols to ensure appropriate evaluation procedures are in place pertaining to referrals and special education processes. School-based teams should use a comprehensive ecological approach to assessment, considering the language strengths, repertoire, and resources of the student, while continuing to gather information from families in the process (Artzi et al., 2022). The goal of ecological assessment is to gain information about the interplay between students and environments rather than making comparisons with other students. This can be challenging since results from standardized norm-referenced assessment often conducted by school psychologists and speech-language pathologists compare student performance to a norm (often monolingual) group which may not yield fair or accurate comparison (Woodruff et al., 2025). Therefore, school-based teams must be reflective and inquisitive in their practice of interpreting and using standardized test scores for educational decision-making.

Strategies for Success: Dismantling Barriers and Providing Recommendations

Given the systemic challenges of schools to adequately address the needs of MLs, schools with a high proportion of MLs might encounter significant challenges with academic achievement and social-emotional learning (SEL; Goldsmith, 2013; Mouboua & Akintayo, 2024; Niehaus & Adelson, 2014). Interdisciplinary collaboration provides an opportunity for school counselors to work with other educators to create effective support systems for MLs by dismantling institutional barriers that impede their academic, career, and social-emotional development. Successful strategies must involve coordinated efforts between school counselors, teachers, administrators, and community stakeholders to address MLs' comprehensive needs.

Academic Strategies

School counselors can use academic strategies that emphasize language awareness and provide ample opportunities for language practice to foster academic success for MLs (Palmer et al., 2014). Academic strategies require intentional language awareness and practice integration across all subject areas (Calafato, 2019). School counselors can collaborate with teachers to implement cross-curricular language development strategies that honor students' linguistic assets while building academic English proficiency. School counselors can promote and advocate for programs like dual language, the Department of Defense Education Activity Multilingual Learner Program as strategies to support the academic development of MLs. School counselors can advocate for appropriate resource allocation to ensure access to bilingual materials and technology to support teachers with culturally responsive pedagogical practices. For example, school counselors can collaborate with bilingual/ESOL teachers and reading specialists to identify academic and social-emotional interventions and technologies such as tablets equipped with translation software and books translated in multiple languages. Finally, school counselors can also work with school psychologists to ensure multilingual assessments are effectively implemented and interpreted.

Career Strategies

Multilingualism presents a number of benefits, one of which is access to great economic opportunities as speaking multiple languages can be advantageous to employers. School counselors can collaborate with teachers to target career development lessons that highlight the value of multilingual skills in the workforce. Moreover, school counselors can collaborate with career and technical education teachers to create pathways that leverage students' linguistic abilities in all career fields. School counselors can also facilitate connections with multilingual professionals in the community who can serve as mentors and provide insights about various career fields that value linguistic diversity.

SEL Strategies

School counselors want to consider the social-emotional development of MLs as it relates to their identity formation and rich cultural experiences (Rutgers et al., 2021). School counselors can collaborate with teachers and administrators to create inclusive environments that validate students' multicultural identities while helping them navigate adjustment to new academic and cultural contexts (Niehaus & Adelson, 2014). Effective SEL programs such as Student Success Skills or peer support programs might work to address the unique stressors of living between multiple cultures and languages. These approaches can help students learn skills to balance their academic and social expectations at school, while navigating the complexities of different cultural and linguistic expectations at home. School counselors can also work with teachers to integrate multicultural perspectives into the curriculum that leverage linguistic diversity and inclusivity (Niehaus & Adelson, 2014). Given Sofía's lack of confidence in sharing ideas in English, creating a learning environment that reflected and validated her experience may have helped her feel understood. Additionally, participating in a peer support program may have allowed her to form connections with peers through cultural and linguistic validation.

Mental Health Strategies

A MLs' attitude, motivation, anxiety, and willingness to communicate can play a role in their mental health (Liu, 2018; Paradis & Jia, 2017). School counselors and other educators should implement culturally sustaining approaches that counter the complex psychological impacts of language learning, cultural adaptation, and potential trauma histories for MLs in U.S. schools. School counselors can collaborate with teachers, administrators, and school psychologists to create safe spaces for students to process their experiences, provide crisis intervention services that consider cultural contexts, and establish referral networks with community mental health providers who specialize in working with multilingual populations. Additionally, school counselors can advocate for and work with administrators to create a trauma-informed school by providing professional development to help all faculty and staff recognize signs of mental health concerns in MLs so they can report those to school counselors, school psychologists, and school social workers to address and prevent the concerns from becoming more of an issue.

Family and Community Strategies

School counselors can utilize MLs support systems outside of school, such as families and community networks to enhance their school experience. School counselors can collaborate with families by engaging interpretation services, conducting outreach in community settings, and creating multiple pathways for family involvement that respect diverse cultural values and communication styles. As previously stated, many families may defer to teachers as having authority over their child's educational experience—coupled with inexperience in the U.S. public schooling system, families such as Sofía's may feel unsure how to approach and resolve concerns. Thus, creating accessible communication channels and reinforcing family collaboration becomes key to supporting MLs.

Moreover, collaboration with community organizations, religious institutions, and cultural centers can provide additional support networks and resources for students and families. School counselors can collaborate with administrators to create policies that welcome and support multilingual families. School counselors can also collaborate with school social workers to bridge communication between schools and families and help connect families with community resources.

Conclusion

Simply having more programs for MLs does not equate to better outcomes; rather, what matters is having high-quality support that respects and leverages students' multilingual, multicultural knowledge and experiences (Niehaus & Adelson, 2014). Supporting MLs requires schools to view their languages as strengths rather than a deficit (Vera et al., 2022). Educators need to work with families and communities to help MLs succeed academically, socially, and emotionally.

School counselors play a key role in connecting all these groups and making sure everyone has the attitudes, knowledge, and skills to support the needs of MLs. Schools need better training for staff, culturally and linguistically sustaining resources, and policies that foster welcoming environments where MLs can succeed while keeping their cultural identities and developing their bi/multilingualism. The goal is to prepare all students for a world where speaking multiple languages is valued.

Reflection Questions

1. What information and resources do you and other professionals have in supporting MLs' academic and mental health needs at your school?
2. Describe the collaboration that exists between you and other professionals and families. What are some areas to improve on? How would you seek professional development in these areas?
3. What are the strengths and challenges associated with using best practices discussed in this chapter (e.g., translanguaging, MTSS, family school partnerships) for your school? How would these challenges be overcome?

References

Allen, J. K. (2017). Exploring the role teacher perceptions play in the underrepresentation of culturally and linguistically diverse students in gifted programming. *Gifted Child Today*, *40*(2), 77–86. https://doi.org/10.1177/1076217517690188

Alvarez, L., Capitelli, S., & Valdés, G. (2023). Beyond sentence frames: Scaffolding emergent multilingual students' participation in science discourse. *TESOL Journal*, *14*, e*720*. https://doi.org/10.1002/tesj.720

American School Counselor Association (2021). ASCA research report: State of the profession 2020. https://www.schoolcounselor.org/getmedia/bb23299b678d-4bce-8863-cfcb55f7df87/2020-State-of-theProfession.pdf

American School Counselor Association (2022). ASCA ethical standards for school counselors. https://www.schoolcounselor.org/getmedia/44f30280-ffe8-4b41-9ad8-f15909c3d164/EthicalStandards.pdf

Artiles, A. J. (2013). Cultural diversity and the special education system: An overview of issues and policy perspectives. *Journal of Special Education, 47*(3), 135–145.

Artzi, L., Hsin, L. B., Sanford, A. K., Brown, J. E. & Guin, S. (2022). Meeting the language needs of emergent multilingual students at risk for learning disabilities through multitiered systems of support. *Learning Disabilities Research & Practice, 37*, 189–203. https://doi.org/10.1111/ldrp.12288

Becker, G. I., & Deris, A. R. (2019). Identification of Hispanic English language learners in special education. *Education Research International, 1*, 1–9. https://doi.org/10.1155/2019/2967943

Bernal, G., Jiménez-Chafey, M. I., & Domenech Rodríguez, M. M. (2009). Cultural adaptation of treatments: A resource for considering culture in evidence-based practice. *Professional Psychology: Research and Practice, 40*(4), 361–368. https://doi.org/10.1037/a0016401

Calafato, R. (2019). The non-native speaker teacher as proficient multilingual: A critical review of research from 2009-2018. *Lingua, 227*. https://doi.org/10.1016/j.lingua.2019.06.001

Cenoz, J. (2013). Defining multilingualism. *Annual Review of Applied Linguistics, 33*, 3–18. https://doi.org/10.1017/S026719051300007X

Davis, L., Harward, K., & Yazzie, A. (2023). Counselor-teacher collaboration in multilingual learner contexts: A qualitative case study investigating counselor-teacher partnership. *Professional School Counseling, 27*(1), 1–10. https://doi.org/10.1177/2156759X231177624

Dixon, L. Q., Kim, H., Dayani, A., Guo, W., Kuo, L. J., Eslami, Z., & Chen, Z. (2025). The relationship of home language and literacy practices to biliteracy development among immigrant bilingual children: A review of studies from 2014 to 2023. *Literacy, 59*(2), 151–164. https://doi.org/10.1111/lit.12393

Donley, K. (2022). Translanguaging as a theory, pedagogy, and qualitative research methodology. *NABE Journal of Research and Practice, 12*(3-4), 105–120. https://doi.org/10.1080/26390043.2022.2079391

Durán, L. K., Hartzheim, D., Lund, E. M., Simonsmeier, V., & Kohlmeier, T. L. (2016). Bilingual and home language interventions with young dual language learners: A research synthesis. *Language, Speech, and Hearing Services in Schools, 47*(4), 347–371. https://doi.org/10.1044/2016_LSHSS-15-0030

Durlak, J. A., Mahoney, J. L., & Boyle, A. E. (2022). What we know, and what we need to find out about universal, school-based social and emotional learning programs for children and adolescents: A review of meta-analyses and directions for future research. *Psychological Bulletin, 148*(11-12), 765–782. https://doi.org/10.1037/bul0000383

Durlak, J. A., Weissberg, R. P., Dymnicki, A. B., Taylor, R. D., & Schellinger, K. B. (2011). The impact of enhancing students' social and emotional learning: A meta-analysis of school-based universal interventions. *Child Development, 82*(1), 405–432. https://doi.org/10.1111/j.1467-8624.2010.01564.x

Friend, M., & Cook, L. (2013). *Interactions: Collaboration skills for school professionals* (7th ed.). Allyn & Bacon.

Garcia, O., & Li, W. L. (2014). *Translanguaging: Language, bilingualism and education*. Palgrave Macmillan.

García, O., Johnson, S., & Seltzer, K. (2017). *The translanguaging classroom: Leveraging student bilingualism for learning*. Caslon.

Gimbert, B., Miller, D., Herman, E., Breedlove, M., & Molina, C. (2021). Social emotional learning in schools: The importance of educator competence. *Journal of Research on Leadership Education. 18*. 194277512110149. https://doi.org/10.1177/19427751211014920.

Goforth, A. N., Farmer, R. L., Kim, S. Y., Naser, S. C., Lockwood, A. B., & Affrunti, N. W. (2021). Status of school psychology in 2020: Part 1, demographics of the NASP membership survey. *NASP Research Reports*, *5*(2), 1–17.

Goldsmith, W. (2013). Enhancing classroom conversation for all students. *Phi Delta Kappan*, *94*(7), 48–52. https://doi.org/10.1177/003172171309400716

Gonzalez, J. E., Durán, L, Linan-Thompson, S., & Jimerson, S. R. (2022). Unlocking the promise of multitiered systems of support (MTSS) for linguistically diverse students: Advancing science, practice, and equity. *School Psychology Review,* 51(4), 387–391. https://doi.org/10.1080/2372966X.2022.2105612

Harris, B., & Sullivan, A. L. (2017). A framework for bilingual school consultation to facilitate multitier systems of support for English language learners. *Journal of Educational and Psychological Consultation, 27*, 367–392. doi:10.1080/10474412.2017.1307758

Hine, M. G. (2025). Where are the families?: Examining family engagement inequities using nationally representative data and path analysis. *Educational Review*, 1–28. https://doi.org/10.1080/00131911.2025.2470708

Hoover, J. J., and L. Soltero-González. (2018). "Educator Preparation for Developing Culturally and Linguistically Responsive MTSS in Rural Community Elementary Schools." *Teacher Education and Special Education* 41, no. 3: 188–202. https://doi.org/10.1177/0888406417753689

Hoover, J. J., Soltero-González, L., Wang, C., & Herron, S. (2020). Sustaining a multitiered system of supports for English learners in rural community elementary schools. *Rural Special Education Quarterly, 39*(1), 4–16. https://doi.org/10.1177/8756870519847466

Johnson, L. V., Shell, E. M., Tuttle, M., & Groce, L. (2019). School counselor experiences of response to intervention with English learners. *Professional School Counseling*, *22*(1), 1–11. https://doi.org/10.1177/2156759X19859486

Kearns, D. M., Lemons, C. J., Fuchs, D., & Fuchs, L. S. (2014). Essentials of a tiered intervention system to support unique learners: Recommendations from research and practice. In J. Mascolo, V. Alfonso & D. Flanagan (Eds.), *Essentials of planning, selecting, and tailoring interventions for unique learners* (pp. 56–91). John Wiley & Sons.

Klingner, J. K., & Edwards, P. A. (2006). Cultural considerations with response to intervention models. *Reading Research Quarterly*, *41*(1), 108–117. https://doi.org/10.1598/RRQ.41.1.6

Klingner, J. K., & Harry, B. (2006). The role of culture in assessing the academic and behavioral needs of English language learners. *Theory Into Practice*, *45*(1), 41–47. https://doi.org/10.1177/002221940603900201 01

Landry, L. N., Keller-Margulis, M., Matta, M., Kim, H., Gonzalez, J. E., & Thomas Schanding, G. (2022). Long-term validity and diagnostic accuracy of kindergarten acadience reading with English learners. *School Psychology Review*, *51*(4), 454–467. https://doi.org/10.1080/2372966X.2021.1984170

Linan-Thompson, S., Ortiz, A., & Cavazos, L. (2022). An examination of MTSS assessment and decision making practices for English learners. *School Psychology Review*, *51*(4), 484–497. https://doi.org/10.1080/2372966X.2021.2001690

Liu, M. (2018). Bilingual/multilingual learners' willingness to communicate in and anxiety on speaking Chinese and their associations with self-rated proficiency in Chinese. *International Journal of Bilingual Education and Bilingualism*, *21*(1), 54–69. https://doi.org/10.1080/13670050.2015.1127889

Lopez, F. L. (2007). Bilingualism and bilingual education: A critical perspective. *Educational Policy*, *41*(2), 287–302.

Lucas, T., & Villegas, A. M. (2011). A framework for preparing linguistically responsive teachers. In T. Lucas (Ed.), *Teacher preparation for linguistically diverse classrooms: A resource for teacher educators* (pp. 55–72). Routledge.

Malakoff, M., & Hakuta, K. (1990). History of language minority education in the United States. In A. Padilla, H. Fairchild & C. Valadez (Eds.), *Bilingual education: Issues and strategies* (pp. 27–42). Sage Publications. https://files.eric.ed.gov/fulltext/ED329635.pdf

Mouboua, P., & Akintayo, O. (2024). Multilingualism and socioeconomic mobility: Analyzing the correlation in immigrant populations. *World Journal of Advanced Research and Reviews*, *22*(2), 144–156. https://doi.org/10.30574/wjarr.2024.22.2.1314

Murillo, M. A., & Lavadenz, M. (2020). *Examining English learners' college readiness and postsecondary enrollment in California* (Policy Brief No. 8). Center for Equity for English Learners, Loyola Marymount University. https://doi.org/10.15365/ceel.policy.8

Murrieta, I., & Eklund, K. (2022). Universal screening to detect emotional and behavioral risk among English language learners. *School Psychology Review*, *51*(4), 441–453. https://doi.org/10.1080/2372966X.2021.1984169

National Center for Educational Statistics (2019). Table 209.42. Percentage of public school teachers who teach English Language Learner (ELL) students and students with disabilities and percentage with selected qualifications or coursework, by selected teacher and school characteristics: 2017–18. https://nces.ed.gov/programs/digest/d20/tables/dt20_209.42.asp

National Center for Educational Statistics (2023). Characteristics of Public School Teachers https://nces.ed.gov/programs/coe/indicator/clr/public-school-teachers

National Center for Educational Statistics (2024). English Learners in Public Schools https://nces.ed.gov/programs/coe/indicator/cgf/english-learners-in-public-schools

National Clearinghouse for English Language Acquisition (2021). Profile of English learners in the United States. https://ncela.ed.gov/sites/default/files/legacy/fast_facts/DEL4.4_ELProfile_508_1.4.2021_OELA.pdf

National Immigration Law Center (2025). Trump's rescission of protected areas policies undermines safety for all. https://www.nilc.org/resources/factsheet-trumps-rescission-of-protected-areas-policies-undermines-safety-for-all/

Niehaus, K., & Adelson, J. L. (2014). School support, parental involvement, and academic and social-emotional outcomes for English language learners. *American Educational Research Journal*, *51*(4), 810–844. https://doi.org/10.3102/0002831214531323

Palmer, D. K., Martínez, R. A., Mateus, S. G., & Henderson, K. (2014). Reframing the debate on language separation: Toward a vision for translanguaging pedagogies in the dual language classroom. *The Modern Language Journal*, *98*, 757–772. https://doi.org/10.1111/modl.12121

Paradis, J., & Jia, R. (2017). Bilingual children's long-term outcomes in English as a second language: Language environment factors shape individual differences in catching up with monolinguals. *Developmental Science*, *20*(1), e12433. https://doi.org/10.1111/desc.12433

Pontier, R. W., & Tian, Z. (2023). "If you want to be taken seriously, you have to speak like a white person": TESOL graduate students' grappling with translanguaging as social justice. In Z. Tian & N. King (Eds.), Developing translanguaging repertoires in critical teacher education. DeGruyter Mouton.

Protacio, M. S., Piazza, S. V., & David, V. (2021). Family engagement in the middle: Reaching out to families of English learners. *Middle School Journal*, *52*(1), 30–39. https://doi.org/10.1080/00940771.2020.1840268

Robles, A. R., Quirk, M., Paul, M., Perez, E., McGuinness, J., Dowdy, E., Gonzalez, E. G., Lara, C. Z., & Draper-Rodriguez, C. (2025). Culturally and linguistically responsive MTSS: Ethical and actionable strategies for supporting multilingual learners in multi-tiered frameworks. *Psychology in the Schools*. https://doi.org/10.1002/pits.23533

Sánchez, M. T., García, O., & Solorza, C. (2018). Reframing language allocation policy in dual language bilingual education. *Bilingual Research Journal*, *41*(1), 37–51. https://doi.org/10.1080/15235882.2017.1405098

Schmid, C. (2000). The politics of English only in the United States: Historical, social, and legal aspects. In R. Dueñas González & I. Melis (Eds.), *Language ideologies: Critical perspectives on the official English movement* (vol. 1,pp. 64–86). Lawrence Erlbaum Associates.

Shi, Q., & Watkinson, J. (2019). ELL students and school belonging: Implications for school counseling practice. *Professional School Counseling, 22*(1a), 54–62. https://doi.org/10.1177/2156759X19834442

Suarez-Orozco, C. (2010). Challenges for immigrant youth: The importance of considering educational and psychological outcomes. *American Psychologist, 65*(2), 122–134.

Sue, S., & Sue, D. W. (2012). *Counseling the culturally diverse: Theory and practice* (6th ed.). Wiley.

Sugai, G., & Horner, R. H. (2009). Defining and describing schoolwide positive behavior support. In W. Sailor, G. Dunlop, G. Sugai, & R. Horner (Eds.), *Handbook of positive behavior support* (pp. 307–326). Springer Publishing Company. https://doi.org/10.1007/978-0-387-09632-2_13

Talleyrand, R. M., & Vojtech, J. T.-G. (2019). Potential stressors of undocumented Latinx youth: Implications and recommendations for school counselors. *Professional School Counseling,* 22(1), Article 2156759X19847168. https://doi.org/10.1177/2156759X19847168

The White House. (2025). *Designating English as the official language of the United States.* https://www.whitehouse.gov/presidential-actions/2025/03/designating-english-as-the-official-language-of-the-united-states/

Tuttle, M., Harrison, J., Johnson, L. V., & Mecadon-Mann, M. (2021). What's in a word?: School counselor and ESOL teacher perceptions and attitudes about collaboration. *Journal of School Counseling, 19*(22), n22. http://www.jsc.montana.edu/articles/v19n22.pdf

Vera, E., Heineke, A., Schultes, A., & Daskalova, P. (2022). Social and emotional needs of emergent bilingual high school students: Perspectives of teachers, school counselors, and school social workers. *Journal of Educational and Psychological Consultation, 32*(4), 416–453. https://doi.org/10.1080/10474412.2021.2018657

Wackerle-Hollman, A., Durán, L., Miranda, A., Chávez, C., Rodriguez, M., & Medina Morales, N. (2022). Understanding how language of instruction impacts early literacy growth for Spanish-speaking children. *School Psychology Review, 51*(4), 406–426. https://doi.org/10.1080/2372966X.2021.1906620

Wesley-Nero, S. & Donley, K. (2024). Culturally and linguistically responsive pedagogy: Examining teachers' conceptualizations of affirmative instructional practices for multilingual learners. *TESOL Journal, 15*, e881. https://doi.org/10.1002/tesj.881

Woodruff, M. C., Weiss, R. A., & Tamura, K. (2025). Multilingualism and psychological assessment: Understanding the impact of language and promoting equity. *Professional Psychology: Research and Practice.* Advance online publication. https://doi.org/10.1037/pro0000611

Yeh, C. J. (2008). *Acculturation and mental health of immigrant children and adolescents.* In M. M. Suárez-Orozco & D. B. Qin-Hilliard (Eds.), *Globalization: Culture and education in the new millennium* (pp. 135–151). University of California Press.

Zhu, J., & Camicia, S. P. (2012). The curriculum as cultures in conflict: Exploring monocultural and multicultural ideologies through the case of bilingual education. *International Journal of Literacy, Culture, and Language Education, 1*(0). https://doi.org/10.14434/ijlcle.v1i0.26828

Chapter 10

Launching a Multilingual Learner Immigrant-Based School Counseling Program

An Interdisciplinary Partnership Venture

Drew S. Fagan and Jessica Diaz McKechnie

Introduction

Ms. Chen is a ten-year veteran professional school counselor (PSC) at a local high school in Capital Region Public Schools (CRPS). She checks her email: *Request for an immediate parent meeting regarding Sofia M.,* Sent by the 11th-grade ELD (English Language Development) teacher.

Ms. Chen has been monitoring Sofia. Since arriving in CRPS six months ago, Sofia has quietly navigated her classes, making slow but steady progress in English. However, her attendance has recently become sporadic, and she has missed several appointments for her college-readiness curriculum check-ins. When Ms. Chen finally pulled her aside, Sofia was withdrawn and only offered, "I am tired, and my mother is busy."

Ms. Chen recalls the initial intake paperwork. Sofia lives with her single mother and younger brother. Her mother works two low-wage jobs, and the family is financially strained. The intake forms, which Ms. Chen is legally required to collect, were completed with the help of a school-provided interpreter and seemed to cause Sofia's mother significant anxiety.

The teacher's email explains that Sofia has started sleeping during class. When the teacher tried to call Sofia's mother, the number was disconnected. The teacher suspects Sofia is struggling with more than language acquisition—perhaps financial hardship or a lack of acculturation support—but feels ill-equipped to probe deeper into family or immigration status issues.

Ms. Chen sighs. Her current caseload is 292:1, already higher than the recommended ratio. She feels the ethical obligation of her professional standards to be an advocate for all students, particularly those from marginalized groups. Yet, she is paralyzed by questions her training never answered:

- How do I sensitively address the potential trauma and displacement that Sofia or her mother may have experienced without re-traumatizing them?

DOI: 10.4324/9781003711124-12

- How do I build the necessary trust with Sofia's mother, who may fear disclosing family dynamics or unofficial status to a school administrator?
- My master's program did not cover the specific intersection of immigration policy, English language acquisition, and mental health—I only know general counseling principles.
- How do I adapt my evidence-based practices for a student facing these unique, systemic barriers?

Ms. Chen's experiences in this vignette exemplify a change in U.S. public school education that is characteristic nation-wide: multilingual learner (ML) and immigrant populations growing faster than professional development opportunities for educators to address these students' academic, language, and socio-emotional needs. The profession of school counseling in the United States has evolved to include academic, career, and personal/social development, with a focus on access for all students (American School Counselor Association, 2022). PSCs are, in general, well-positioned to help students succeed in that they provide links between social-emotional and academic achievement. Despite this, there is a concerning disparity in PSCs' preparedness to effectively address the needs of ML and immigrant populations specifically (Shi & Watkinson, 2019). These students often face a complex array of challenges, including navigating new cultural norms, overcoming language barriers, experiencing trauma related to displacement or conflict, and dealing with the stress of family separation or financial hardship (Enriquez, 2015; Suárez-Orozco et al., 2011). In addition to addressing factors attributed to these students' individual lived experiences, many of their obstacles are due to an educational system not designed to meet their needs (Davis et al., 2023). Simultaneously, there is a lack of both empirical scholarship on school counselors working with MLs and comprehensive training for pre- and in-service school counselors in this area (Hilliard, 2024). These findings underscore the need for specialized training to equip PSCs with the necessary knowledge, skills, and dispositions to effectively serve all culturally and linguistically diverse students.

While each individual state's K-12 system has witnessed its own unique demographic changes, the state of Maryland has been named an exemplar for paralleling nationwide trends in (1) overall increases in students designated as MLs, coinciding with increases in recently arrived immigrant populations (11.2% of the total state K-12 student population compared to the U.S. national average of 10.6%.), (2) majority of language backgrounds represented among K-12 ML populations (i.e., Spanish, French, Chinese, and Arabic), and (3) program availability at the state-level (traditional English for Speakers of Other Languages, or ESOL, and dual language immersion programs) (American Immigration Council, 2024; Archibald, 2024; National Center for Education Statistics, 2024). It is important to address two points: not all immigrants in the United States are MLs, nor are all MLs immigrants. While immigration data from Maryland align with national trends, where just under half of the state's immigrant population are considered MLs (Moslimani & Passel, 2024), where the data diverge is with the number of MLs eligible for ELD services in public schools: approximately 42% of the state's ML student population are not born in the United States as opposed to only 25% nationally. Put simply, more school-aged MLs in Maryland are immigrants compared to the national average (Sugarman & Geary, 2018). Given this, there is a stronger association in this state connecting the general increase in immigrants and the overall doubling, in less than a decade, of MLs eligible for ELD services in the state's public school system (Maryland State Department of Education, 2024).

As states across the country have done since 2015 with implementations of their Every Student Succeeds Act (ESSA) state plans, the Maryland State Department of Education (MSDE) and its individual school districts have enacted changes in their accountability and certification policies to address diversifying student populations' needs. Following the directives of Maryland's ESSA State Plan, which stipulates that all students should have opportunities for academic achievement and language proficiency through educational programming, MSDE convened a workgroup in 2021 whose charge was to investigate "the availability of and access to resources for [multilingual] learners and their families and make recommendations that will accelerate their academic achievement" (Maryland State Department of Education, 2022, p. 4). Consisting of members from within and outside of MSDE with expertise in multilingual learning and programming, multiple recommendations were put forth to drive change in the public school system. These included, but were not limited to, supporting and sustaining multilingualism by promoting an asset-based approach for language development, enhancing engagement with multilingual families and communities, implementing instructional programs to support MLs' needs, and requiring all educator preparation programs to provide training in ML-related competencies.

Considering these recommendations, more school district-sponsored and university-based programs within the last several years have developed to prepare in- and pre-service classroom teachers and specialists to work successfully with MLs (Fagan, 2024). Not as focused state-wide has been the preparation of Maryland's PSCs. This is surprising given that these educators are tasked by the American School Counselor Association (ASCA) to be leaders and advocates for all students, particularly those from marginalized groups such as MLs and immigrant populations (American School Counselor Association, 2022). In reality, many PSCs lack specialized training and cultural competency to effectively address the unique needs of these students. Those not equipped to understand these experiences and provide culturally responsive services may inadvertently contribute to further marginalization and academic struggles for these students. With this in mind, the current chapter explores the grassroots development process of the state's first post-master's certificate program to equip in-service PSCs with the specialized knowledge and skills necessary to effectively serve this growing student population. Here, we lay out a roadmap of the process involved in creating and implementing the program, from the initial collaboration and administrative logistics to the curriculum development and delivery stages. We also shed light on the impact and lessons learned from the first cohort of participants (currently in progress as of this writing). Finally, we offer insights and recommendations for future improvements and adaptations to the program, as well as describe how this program exemplifies the need for more interdisciplinary collaborations in meeting the evolving needs of immigrant and ML student populations.

The Context

The CRPS[1] currently ranks as the district with the largest ML population in Maryland at 39,639/125,747 students, or ~32% of all students in the district (CRPS ELD Supervisor Personal Communication, September 16, 2024). It is also sixth in the nation when it comes to unaccompanied minors. Simultaneously, in 2024, CRPS's International Student Admissions and Enrollment Office (ISAEO) provided registration and counseling services to 6,949 international students, a 30% increase over the previous year and the largest number of students ever served in the district, representing 148 countries. The cultural and linguistic diversity of the district's students is exemplified by it being in the county with the highest number of immigrants nationally from Cameroon and Sierra Leone, the second highest from Nigeria, and the fifth highest from El Salvador, Guatemala, and Honduras, respectively (CRPS ISAEO Director Personal Communication, October 21, 2024). These statistics underscore the significant role that CRPS plays in serving diverse student populations, highlighting the unique challenges and opportunities faced by the district. This, however, leaves the school system vulnerable to unmet needs, particularly when it comes to preparing its school counselors.

It is important to note that ASCA's recommended caseload for students per PSC is 250:1; with 446 total PSCs in CRPS currently, the counselor-student ratio is 282:1, which is higher than ASCA's recommended load but slightly lower than the state average of 310:1 (American School Counselor Association, n.d.; U.S. Department of Education, 2024). Even with this slightly lower state-wide ratio, what separates CRPS from other Maryland school districts is the sheer number of culturally and linguistically diverse students they serve and their unique needs which are not readily addressed by standard PSC preparation programs (Dogan, 2017).

According to the MSDE, there are several pathways to becoming a PSC. Most of these paths include holding a master's degree in school counseling or a related field and completing three credits of special education. While these programs' content is not dictated by MSDE, they must be approved by an accrediting body such as the Council for Accreditation of Counseling and Related Educational Programs (CACREP) or the Association for Advancing Quality in Educator

Preparation (AAQEP). Upon reviewing the standards for each of these accrediting bodies, though, no specific guidelines are provided to programs requiring coverage of topics on immigration and/or ML needs. The ASCA Standards do emphasize core principles of supporting all students, which include culturally responsive practices, understanding cultural and social context, high expectations for all, using cultural knowledge, and advocating for systemic change. These standards are meant to be the basis for which school counseling programs, but gaps continue to exist between what is taught in preparation programs and the realities in the field.

Given the demographic shifts and current shortcomings of PSC preparation, CRPS' ISAEO initially approached the University of Maryland's (UMD) School Counseling Program to discuss the development of a graduate-level program to provide their in-service PSCs with the necessary tools to adequately address all the district's students' needs. Choosing to collaborate with UMD, specifically its College of Education (COE), as opposed to other institutions of higher education was purposeful. First, the COE's mission states that it is an "action-oriented and equity-minded community transforming the fields of education, counseling, human development, and quantitative methodology through impactful research, innovative teaching, and mutually beneficial partnerships with schools and communities. We co-create knowledge and advance the public good as we prepare educators, counselors, administrators, researchers, and policymakers for leadership in schools and society."

Second, UMD is local to CRPS and has had a history of effective partnerships which demonstrate the university's commitment to and expertise in addressing district needs. UMD's long-standing presence within CRPS, including teacher education, school counseling internship programs, and administrative leadership training, has fostered familiarity with the district. Existing long-term partnership programs focusing on the needs of MLs had already been established prior to these initial talks. These have included post-baccalaureate certificate and master's programs in Teaching English to Speakers of Other Languages (TESOL) to prepare non-ESOL certified CRPS teachers to work with MLs across general classroom settings. Additionally, the state's first-ever Ed.D. program in School System Leadership with a Specialization in TESOL and Dual Language Education was developed specifically as a partnership program to prepare CRPS's administrators, teacher leaders, and superintendent central office staff to effect change at the system-level to better meet MLs' needs. These already established partnership programs have prepared to date several hundred CRPS staff to work with MLs, thus proving that UMD not only can prepare CRPS to address diverse learners' needs but also that the university's programs can do so in a way that contextualizes the field to meet the specific needs of the school district.

Program Development

Once it was established that CRPS wanted to partner with UMD to provide a program that would equip its in-service PSCs with tools to best address the district's ever-increasing immigrant student populations' needs, and when it was deduced that currently existing program routes would not lead to this goal, proceeding with developing a program took place over multiple stages. What would eventually become the Post-Master's Certificate Program in Supporting Immigrant Students for PSCs emerged from collaborative discussions both within and between UMD and CRPS, driven by a shared recognition of the growing need for specialized support for immigrant students. Initial conversations among UMD colleagues across two departments yielded enthusiastic support, with faculty recognizing from a teaching perspective the significant need for these students and their families. These two departments, one housing the Counseling Program and one housing TESOL Programs, demonstrated their commitment by reworking existing courses to align with the needs of this new program. This inter-organizational (UMD and CRPS) and inter-departmental collaboration, while not entirely unique, presented its own set of challenges. Coordinating across different institutions and academic departments required careful planning, communication, and a shared commitment to the program's goals.

The first discussions were about what type of program to provide. The two authors played key roles in this early stage. Jessica, the field placement director for the pre-service School Counseling program, was chosen by the university to oversee the coordination of this new program. Drew had already developed and was currently directing the previously mentioned TESOL Programs with CRPS. Initial discussions focused on the practicality of offering such a program to full-time in-service PSCs. Anecdotal evidence from PSCs in CRPS confirmed that a degree-bearing program would not suffice given that, in Maryland, all PSCs must already have completed a full 60-credit master's graduate degree in School Counseling to be hired. Simultaneously, non-degree credentialing programs have consistently been on the rise for already well-established educators wanting to add to their repertoire of knowledge. Certificate, certification, apprenticeship, and licensure programs not associated with an undergraduate or graduate degree enable experienced employees to more easily add to their content and pedagogical knowledge while not being burdened with degree oversight regulations or extensive exit criteria (e.g., theses or dissertations) that go beyond their employment needs (Albert, 2019). At the same time, educators value expanding their knowledge through official post-secondary programs, i.e., programs that lead to an official certificate from a post-secondary institution as opposed to solely taking random coursework as a non-degree student that does not lead to anything official other than transcript confirmation of courses taken (Albert, 2019). Given these factors, it was decided to create a 12-credit Post-Master's Certificate Program in Supporting Immigrant Students for PSCs.

To ensure this program would meet the needs of the students and the counselors serving them, the program developers recognized the importance of seeking input from various stakeholders. Consequently, the decision was made to establish an advisory board that included PSCs, ELD program representatives, UMD alumni, high school students, and parents. Board meetings took place virtually via Zoom during the COVID-19 pandemic. Importantly, the shift to virtual meetings facilitated broader participation from a range of stakeholders who might not have been able to attend in-person meetings. This virtual format also allowed for valuable feedback on the proposed curriculum and the overall program concept. Additionally, gathering data for UMD leadership was essential. Separate intra-university meetings were held with department chairs, the dean, program directors, and faculty to secure buy-in and align the program with UMD's mission and vision. This internal alignment process was interwoven with the development of program learning outcomes drafted from the advisory board, ultimately serving as the driving force behind all subsequent decisions that laid the groundwork for a program designed to meet the CRPS student needs.

In collaboration with CRPS stakeholders, a clear mission and vision were created. The program envisions PSCs who are well-equipped to protect the welfare, promote the growth and development, and recognize the unique challenges students from immigrant and refugee families face. This includes helping students and families manage trauma, post-traumatic stress, culture shock, and poverty, as well as promoting students' health, well-being, English language acquisition, academic achievement, and socioemotional growth and development.

This mission directly informs the program's learning outcomes, which are designed to translate the broad goals into specific, measurable skills and knowledge:

- Enhanced Knowledge and Skills: The program aims to enhance PSCs' knowledge of English language acquisition and cross-cultural teaching approaches, and to help them grasp how differences between the United States and other nations' educational counseling systems require modification of evidence-based counseling practices. This directly aligns with the mission of providing specialized training to address the complex needs of this population.
- Promotion of Student Success: Learning outcomes focus on accelerating immigrant students' educational, career, social, emotional, and personal skills development through individual counselor-student meetings. This reflects the program's mission to promote students' health, well-being, and overall growth.
- Understanding Systemic Influences: PSCs will gain insight into how CRPS's recent and historical immigration policies have influenced immigrant students and families. This knowledge will enable them to advocate for policies that enhance equity of access to and benefit from school services, aligning with the program's vision of protecting the welfare of these students.

- Culturally Competent Practices: The program emphasizes the importance of understanding diverse immigrant family cultural and family dynamics, building trust and partnerships with families, and delivering culturally appropriate counseling interventions. This directly supports the mission of providing PSCs with the skills to address the unique challenges faced by immigrant families.
- Sensitivity to Diversity: Learning outcomes include increasing sensitivity to how the diversity of immigrant students—especially intersecting identities of race, gender, religion, ethnicity, ability/disability, culture, sexual orientation, and immigration status—must be considered in crafting counseling strategies that maximize health, mental health, acculturation, and achievement. This aligns with the program's vision of promoting the growth and development of all students, with an understanding of the varied factors that affect this population.

To develop the certificate program that would achieve these outcomes, Jessica and the School Counseling Program collaborated with Drew and his colleagues in the TESOL Program. This interdisciplinary approach offered several key advantages: aligning with potential student population growth in both fields, facilitating discussions about adapting courses, and fostering collaboration within the broader school counseling field extending to in-service professional development. This collaboration is supported by scholarship in both the School Counseling and English language teaching (ELT) fields. Oehrtman (2022) found that collaboration among education professionals and a shared vision are vital for school counselors to maximize their impact, and Lashley and Stickl (2016) found that unified school stakeholders—counselors, principals, and teachers—enhance student achievement and equity. The ELT field, with a particular focus on newly arrived immigrant students in primary and secondary education settings, has begun to move toward more interdisciplinary research and practice recognizing that language and academic learning do not occur in an English language classroom vacuum but rather in all components of schooling, including in classrooms across disciplines (e.g., de Oliveira, 2022; Horn et al., 2008) and with administrators (e.g., Fagan & Kanney, 2023). Recognizing that traditional school counseling programs often lack specific focus and resources for addressing the policy issues affecting immigrant students, the program strategically adapted already existing courses. Leveraging established curricula and expertise allowed for a more efficient development process than creating entirely new courses. Following the identification of suitable courses that directly related to the program's intended learning outcomes, the next step involved presenting a draft proposal to the department chairs for their support. Ultimately, the four chosen courses directly address the unique needs of immigrant students who are also MLs and their families:

- Foundations of Educating Multilingual Learners: Introduces the research, practice, trends, and public policy issues affecting MLs in the USA, and specifically in Maryland's primary and secondary education settings; supports

the program's mission to enhance PSCs' knowledge of acquiring English as an additional language and cross-cultural teaching approaches.
- Cross-Cultural Communication and Multilingual Learners: Provides participants with opportunities to research and critically reflect upon aspects of culture as a basis to understand students and to develop principles to guide culturally inclusive teaching decisions. Participants better understand the role of culture and language in schooling to create academic settings where culturally and linguistically diverse students can succeed.
- Family and Social Support Systems: Focuses on understanding the role of family support systems and specialized methods for counseling immigrant and refugee families; aligns with the program's goal of describing diverse immigrant family cultural and family dynamics and delivering culturally appropriate counseling interventions.
- Immigrant Child Counseling and Consultation: Covers the theory, research, and experiential learning of child therapy for immigrant families; supports the program's learning outcome of accelerating immigrant students' educational, career, social, emotional, and personal skills development through individual counselor-student meetings.

To launch the program efficiently and with maximum flexibility, UMD established key program criteria in collaboration with faculty, staff, and CRPS. Recognizing the demanding schedules of practicing school counselors, the two courses offered during the academic year were designed to be online, alternating between asynchronous and synchronous sessions held in the evenings after PSCs were done with their workday. This format ensured accessibility for participants while accommodating their work commitments. For the summer sessions, a blended or hybrid model was adopted, offering a balance of online flexibility and in-person interaction at a centralized location within CRPS, further enhancing accessibility and convenience for participants. It was also important to CRPS that the program be completed by participants within a 12-month period and in consecutive semesters. Based on prior programming experience with higher education institutions, better retention and completion experiences occurred with programs that had highly structured scheduling parameters. Specifically, students had to take courses when they were offered to their specific cohort, and they had to complete the program when their cohort did. This was easy to accommodate given the relative flexibility of the chosen faculty's teaching schedules. The program now runs from summer to summer, allowing participants to meet and engage with each other in person during the first and last courses.

Program approval required going through numerous levels of committee review. The approval process was initiated at the department level, where the proposed program would be housed, the same department where the Master's in School Counseling already resided. As this was an interdisciplinary venture, the use of TESOL Program-specific courses and faculty also required a separate approval from the department housing that program. Following the department was college-level review, where the focus was on how the program aligned with and would lend to the college's vision where "[the college's] impact and expertise will lead to collaborations that influence policies, inform practice and advance broader social, civic and democratic goals for a healthy and equitable society for all." At the university level of review, the focus was on whether the program exemplified the university as the state's flagship institution, where it is expected that program innovativeness helps varied state entities, including its school districts, address problems of practice and move the state as a whole forward. Additionally, as this would be a partnership outreach program with a school district, the university wanted to ascertain whether it would be financially self-sustaining, i.e., not using resources from the university itself but rather from the profits of the program. The final level of approval resided outside of the university with the state's higher education commission, whose goal is to establish statewide higher education policies and administrative regulations as they relate to programming. The commission concluded that the proposed program did, indeed, meet these regulations and, given that it was the first of its kind in the state, had the potential to advance these regulations in the future, pending program outcomes. In all, program approval took 1.5 years.

Program Implementation

Working with in-service PSCs presents unique challenges, particularly when developing graduate-level coursework (Damianidou, 2024; Emstad & Sandvik, 2020; Huhtala & Vesalainen, 2017). These professionals often bring decades of practical experience to the program, which can create a sense of apprehension about returning to a traditional classroom setting. Recognizing the demanding schedules and professional responsibilities of these experienced counselors, the program prioritizes flexibility in its delivery, offering varied scheduling options and adaptable learning activities to accommodate their ongoing commitments. However, this flexibility must be carefully balanced with the critical need to maintain the quality and rigor expected of graduate-level work. These experienced counselors possess a wealth of knowledge and expertise, and understandably, therefore, want their time to be valued and their contributions recognized. They do not want to be treated as if they lack understanding, nor do they want to feel as though their time is being wasted. The program's goal is to create a learning environment that respects their experience and builds upon it. Therefore, the program design integrates their practical insights while challenging them with advanced academic content and expectations appropriate for graduate study. Ultimately, the core purpose of this Post-Master's Certificate program is to equip these dedicated professionals with the specialized knowledge and skills necessary to bridge the identified gap in effectively serving immigrant students, including MLs, and their families.

Drawing on principles of adult learning theory (Knowles et al., 2025), we fully anticipate that program participants, given their extensive experience in the field, will actively engage with and hold faculty accountable for demonstrating real-world expertise relevant to the lived experiences of the students and families they serve. This aligns with the tenets of experiential learning (Kolb, 2015), where professionals seek knowledge that directly informs and refines their practice, particularly when addressing the complex dynamics of realities and challenges faced by MLs, immigrants, and refugee communities. This expectation underscores the importance of selecting faculty with demonstrable experience and expertise in these specific areas who can deliver course content in a way that truly resonates with our PSCs.

Collaboration and trust between departments are also vital for the program's success. When departments work together, they can combine resources and find instructors who have a genuine understanding of cultural contexts and who recognize the challenges faced by students. This teamwork not only enhances the faculty roster but also elevates the educational experience for everyone involved. Additionally, fostering trust between departments creates a welcoming environment for open communication and shared decision-making in the faculty selection process. This collaborative spirit is essential for ensuring that all instructors meet the program's standards and objectives, ultimately providing impactful training that aligns with the needs of our PSCs. Thus, selecting faculty is not just an administrative task; it's a significant step in fulfilling our commitment to educational excellence.

For the initial start-up of the program, we prioritized selecting faculty with a diverse range of relevant experiences. These include full-time faculty and adjunct professors who have worked as school counselors, are seasoned counselor educators, have dedicated years to working closely with these student populations, have personally lived the immigrant experience within CRPS, and/or have committed themselves to the study of relevant policy and effective teaching practices. This combination of lived experience, practical expertise, and academic knowledge ensures that our participants will learn from instructors who truly understand the complexities of the issues at hand and can provide them with the most effective tools and strategies for supporting their students.

As had been the case throughout the entire program development process, the university and CRPS partnered in admissions. It was quickly determined that the program needed to follow a cohort-based learning model, one that enabled a group of students of similar professional backgrounds to jointly collaborate on practical applications and the adaptability of the learned ideas to settings that they had shared knowledge of and experience working in. Additionally, cohort-based models of learning allow students more opportunities for peer collaboration and community building both inside the classroom and in the shared workspace (Fenning, 2004). As such, admissions followed a regular decision model as opposed to rolling admissions, thus keeping all potential cohort members together even at the initial steps in the program process. The university and CRPS jointly held information sessions hosted at a school district location following work hours to allow more attendees the option to partake. CRPS' ISAEO led the recruitment advertising as this office had the inside know-how of where to reach the district's PSCs with such information.

CRPS conducted an initial round of application vetting. This included having applicants submit a district-internal application form documenting their demographic information, three letters of professional recommendation (one from the immediate supervisor or principal), three essay questions, and an unofficial transcript showing completion of a Master's degree. While keeping in mind university admissions requirements, CRPS performed this initial round of admissions vetting due to their in-depth knowledge of directly linking district needs and expertise with the PSCs who would most benefit from the program and, in turn, benefit the school district most with this certificate experience.

Applicants who passed the initial CRPS vetting were then invited to apply directly to the university. Since they had already prepared their materials for CRPS with many of the same university-required admissions materials, the university's application process was relatively straightforward. If Jessica, as program director, found any concerns with an application, she would request a Zoom interview with the applicant for further review. This might be because she needed more information on a student's experience, may request another writing sample, or may need to gauge an applicant's readiness for graduate-level work. University faculty made the final recommendations for who would eventually be in the program. In the end, the first cohort had 25 PSCs admitted to the university; four ultimately chose to defer to a subsequent cohort and two opted not to complete the registration process, leaving 19 students for cohort one.

Cohort One's Experiences

The first cohort of the Post-Master's Certificate Program in Supporting Immigrant Students for PSCs commenced with an in-person orientation event providing an opportunity for the cohort members to convene, meet the instructing faculty, and begin building community. While many participants were already acquainted from within the same school district, several met in person for the first time. It was also gratifying for university faculty and staff to connect with familiar faces from other long-standing partnerships with CRPS. Significant excitement and discussion revolved around the program's necessity and the individual motivations for applying. However, as icebreakers concluded and the community began to form, a significant challenge emerged: the program schedule. For some, emerging scheduling issues posed a potential deal-breaker which was not the case when they had originally applied.

PSCs operate on diverse schedules, varying by school district. Some are employed for 9, 10, or 11 months, with schedules either fixed or adjusted according to district needs. CRPS has consistently adapted to student and staffing requirements. Notably, between program development and cohort one's orientation, CRPS transitioned their PSCs from 9-month to 11-month employment. This change rendered the initial plan for daytime, in-person summer courses unfeasible for participants. Quick adaptation was imperative. Principals would not permit participants to miss a potential 45 hours of work time across four to five weeks, repeated over two summer sessions. Consequently, we regrouped and revised our curriculum to accommodate a new hybrid schedule, allowing for virtual and in-person classes after work hours. Upon sharing the revised schedule, participants expressed that their concerns had been heard and that the accommodations made would enable their continuation in the program.

The successful implementation of this new schedule was only possible due to the dedication and flexibility of course instructors. Jessica, as program director, meets regularly with the instructors to discuss progress in curriculum development and student advancement, instructors' own continued progress within the program, celebrate wins, and address challenges. It was important to receive updates on how each instructor infuses their personal experiences working with culturally and linguistically diverse students and the program's overarching mission and learning objectives into their course. If the course instructor of the first course in the sequence successfully fosters a strong sense of community within the cohort, this needs to be communicated and sustained throughout subsequent courses. Conversely, if group cohesion is lacking, subsequent instructors are tasked with strengthening it. These regular instructor meetings also allow Jessica as program director to do student check-ins as needed given that she is also program advisor to each cohort member. Periodic class visits provide Jessica with opportunities to solicit student feedback, disseminate important information promptly, and directly assess student needs, with the goal of intervening before disengagement escalates into more serious issues. Cohort one has exhibited a varying degree of engagement. While many students are highly engaged, prepared for the program's rigor, and enthusiastic about sharing their learning with their school teams, a few have expressed surprise at the workload, felt overwhelmed by participation requirements and assignments, and occasionally missed class.

At the time of this writing, all members of the first cohort have successfully completed their first program course, Family and Social Support Systems, which provided them with valuable opportunities for self-reflection and a deeper understanding of the family systems of immigrant students within their own school communities. One key lesson learned from this initial experience was the importance of not overloading participants with large projects toward the beginning and end of the semesters, which often corresponds with significant work responsibilities. Moving forward, projects are to be more evenly distributed throughout the semester to balance workload effectively particularly during academic year courses. Additionally, to better accommodate PSCs' evolving work schedules, we shifted to a primarily hybrid format, with virtual and in-person evening sessions. Recognizing the importance of transparency and planning, we also finalized and published the full four-semester course schedule before the admission deadline, allowing prospective students to make more informed decisions.

The insights gleaned from cohort one's initial academic experience underscore our commitment to both pedagogical excellence and sustainable growth. The program's financial sustainability is largely dependent on tuition revenue generated by each cohort. The university's strong partnership with CRPS, bolstered by the high demand for this specialized program, positions us well for continued enrollment, supporting both instructional needs and administrative overhead. This successful model offers a promising foundation for future expansion to other districts, even as we adapt to current admissions trends. As we prepare to welcome cohort two, we are applying key insights gained from our inaugural group while preserving the program elements that proved most effective. Our goal remains clear: to support PSCs in serving culturally and linguistically diverse students through a responsive, rigorous, and community-centered learning environment. Changes to improve the experience have been made, but core program values and structures remain in place.

Conclusion

The rapid demographic shifts in Maryland's student population reflect broader national trends, underscoring the urgent need for PSCs to receive specialized interdisciplinary training in support of immigrant and multilingual students. These students face a constellation of challenges that go beyond academics, including trauma, cultural displacement, language acquisition obstacles, and institutional barriers (de Oliveira & Wachter Morris, 2015). PSCs are uniquely positioned to be advocates, connectors, and culturally responsive guides through those challenges. Yet, until now, few professional development opportunities have existed that comprehensively address this critical need at the certificate level. The curriculum is tailored to real-world demands faced by practicing PSCs. It has honored the expertise counselors bring to the table while broadening their ability to work effectively at the intersection of culture, language, immigration policy, and mental health.

Engaging with the larger state and national calls for preparing educators to address the needs of a more culturally and linguistically diverse student population, the experiences and lessons learned from this first-of-its-kind program in Maryland highlight two points. First is the importance of having professional development addressing the needs of immigrant students, and particularly MLs, that are inclusive of school-wide personnel beyond traditional classroom settings, i.e., professionals without the title "teacher." PSCs work in a very specific niche within the larger primary and secondary school systems, hovering between and beyond academics and students' social and emotional needs and well-being inside and outside of classrooms. As states' public-school systems revise and update their policies and procedures to better meet the needs of a diversified learner population, much of their focus, not surprisingly, is on classroom teacher professional development over other school personnel. Simultaneously, the ASCA Standards explicitly state that PSCs are to be leaders and advocates for all students, particularly those from marginalized groups such as MLs and immigrant populations, yet they do not provide detail of what knowledge is needed to execute counseling practices. More preparatory programs are required to address these professional populations who fall within the cracks of greater state-wide educational foci and organization standards' generalities.

Second is the importance of interdisciplinary collaborations in program development, implementation, and continuation. Traditionally, work focusing on MLs and immigrant students fell to the purview of TESOL programs. However, the acronym TESOL starts with the word "teaching," thus historically defaulting to preparing teachers and other specialists to address these students' academic and language needs within the classroom. Conversely, PSCs whose workloads now include increasing numbers of MLs and immigrant students continue to lack education that specializes in these student populations. It was only through interdisciplinary collaboration between these two traditionally siloed fields that this specific program was able to be the state-wide model that it is today.

This program was created with the hope that every school counselor will feel prepared to meet the needs of their student population with knowledge, compassion, and advocacy. As demand continues to grow, this program can serve as a model for how collaboration and professional development can bring about real momentum toward educator professional development not only for PSCs but for educators addressing these culturally and linguistically diverse students' needs in all aspects of their educational experiences leading toward future academic, professional, and personal achievement.

Reflection Questions

1 **Interdisciplinary Collaboration:** How might your school counseling program proactively seek to cultivate interdisciplinary partnerships with other departments (e.g., teacher preparation, social work, public health) within your institution or with community organizations to better address the complex needs of diverse student populations, particularly immigrant and MLs?

2 **Balancing Core Programs with Specialized Initiatives:** How can school counseling program directors balance the resource allocation, faculty workload, and administrative oversight needed to launch and sustain specialized certificate programs for in-service professionals while also ensuring the continued quality and integrity of their core, degree-bearing school counseling preparation programs?

3 **Program Design for Practicing Professionals:** Considering the insights into adult learning theory and the demanding schedules of in-service professionals, how can your program create flexible yet rigorous graduate-level professional development opportunities (e.g., post-master's certificates, hybrid formats, cohort models) that address the realities of practicing school counselors and effectively integrate their prior experience?
4 **Curriculum Responsiveness and Gaps:** In what ways does your current school counseling curriculum prepare pre-service and in-service counselors to tackle the unique challenges faced by immigrant students and MLs, including issues of trauma, acculturation, family dynamics, and policy influences? What gaps exist, and how could your program modify existing courses or develop new ones to meet these evolving demographic needs?

Note

1 Pseudonym.

References

Albert, K. (2019). *What we know about non-degree credentials: A literature scan.* Non-Degree Credentials Research Network, George Washington University. https://gwipp.gwu.edu/sites/g/files/zaxdzs6111/files/downloads/06.23.19%20NCRN%20Literature%20Scan.pdf

American Immigration Council (2024). *New Americans in Maryland.* https://map.americanimmigrationcouncil.org/locations/maryland/#.

American School Counselor Association (n.d.). The role of the school counselor. https://www.schoolcounselor.org/About-School-Counseling/School-Counselor-Roles-Ratios

American School Counselor Association (2022). ASCA ethical standards for school counselors. https://www.schoolcounselor.org/About-School-Counseling/Ethical-Responsibilities/ASCA-Ethical-Standards-for-School-Counselors-(1)

Archibald, R. (2024, May 2). Unaccompanied migrant children come to Maryland at a higher rate than any other state. *The Baltimore Banner*. https://www.thebaltimorebanner.com/maryland/maryland-leads-nation-migrant-children-rate-XQYSJPKJQJCKHB7W564OSIZOEA/.

Damianidou, E. (2024). Obligatory professional training for in-service teachers: Worthy time or a waste of time? *European Journal of Teacher Education, 47*, 23–40. https://doi.org/10.1080/02619768.2021.1961734

Davis, L., Harward, K., & Yazzie, A. (2023). Counselor–teacher collaboration in multilingual learner contexts: A qualitative case study investigating counselor–teacher partnerships. *Professional School Counseling, 27*(1). https://doi.org/10.1177/2156759X231177624

de Oliveira, L. C. (Ed.) (2022). *The handbook of TESOL in K-12.* Wiley Blackwell.

de Oliveira, L. C., & Wachter Morris, C. (2015). *Preparing school counselors for English language learners.* TESOL Press.

Dogan, S. (2017). *School counselors' work with immigrants : a phenomenological study of competence, social justice, and family language policy.* [Doctoral dissertation, Ohio State University]. https://etd.ohiolink.edu/acprod/odb_etd/ws/send_file/send?accession=osu1468418221&disposition=inline

Emstad, A. B., & Sandvik, L. V. (2020). School-university collaboration for facilitating in-service teacher training as a part of school-based professional development. *Acta Didactica Norden, 14*, 1–20. http://dx.doi.org/10.5617/adno.7934

Enriquez, L. E. (2015). Multigenerational punishment: Shared experiences of undocumented immigration status within mixed-status families. *Journal of Marriage and Family, 77*(4), 939–953. http://www.jstor.org/stable/24582819

Fagan, D. S. (2024, Spring). An era of rapid educational change for Maryland's multilingual learners: 2018-2024 and beyond. *Maryland TESOL Quarterly*. https://marylandtesol.com

Fagan, D. S., & Kanney, M. (2023, March). *Educating K-12 administrators in TESOL: The why's and how's*. Portland, OR: TESOL International Association Convention.

Fenning, K. (2004). Cohort based learning: Application to learning organizations and student academic success. *College Quarterly, 7*(1). https://collegequarterly.ca/2004-vol07-num01-winter/fenning.html

Hilliard, C. J. (2024). *The experiences of multilingual learning-focused school counselors: A phenomenological investigation.* [Doctoral dissertation, Old Dominion University]. https://digitalcommons.odu.edu/cgi/viewcontent.cgi?article=1156&context=chs_etds

Horn, B., Stoller, F., & Robinson, M. S. (2008). Interdisciplinary collaborations: Two heads are better than one. *English Teaching Forum, 46*(2), 2–13.

Huhtala, A., & Vesalainen, M. (2017). Challenges in developing in-service teacher training: Lessons learnt from two projects for teachers of Swedish in Finland. *Apples – Journal of Applied Language Studies, 11*(3), 55–79. https://dx.doi.org/10.17011/apples/urn.201712104584

Knowles, M. S., Holton, E. F. III, Robinson, P. A., & Caraccioli, C. (2025). *The adult learner: A definitive classic in adult education and human resource development* (10th ed.). Routledge.

Kolb, D. A. (2015). *Experiential learning: Experience as the source of learning and development* (2nd ed.). Pearson.

Lashley, C. A., & Stickl, J. (2016). Counselors and principals: Collaborating to improve instructional equity. *Journal of Organizational and Educational Leadership, 2*(1). http://digitalcommons.gardner-webb.edu/joel/vol2/iss1/6?utm_source=digitalcommons.gardner-webb.edu%2Fjoel%2Fvol2%2Fiss1%2F6&utm_medium=PDF&utm_campaign=PDFCoverPages

Maryland State Department of Education (2022). *Blueprint for Maryland's Future: Workgroup on English learners in public schools- Final report.* https://blueprint.marylandpublicschools.org/wp-content/uploads/sites/20/2022/11/Workgroup-on-English-Learners-in-Public-Schools_Final-Report_2022.pdf

Maryland State Department of Education (2024). *English learners in Maryland: EL data for the 2023-24 school year.* https://marylandpublicschools.org/programs/Documents/English-Learners/2023-2024-EL-Data-A.pdf

Moslimani, M., & Passel, J. S. (2024, September 7). What the data says about immigrants in the US. *Pew Research Center*. https://www.pewresearch.org/short-reads/2024/09/27/key-findings-about-us-immigrants/#:~:text=How%20well%20do%20immigrants%20speak,English%20at%20home%20(17%25)

National Center for Education Statistics. (2024). English learners in public schools. *Condition of Education.* U.S. Department of Education, Institute of Education Sciences. https://nces.ed.gov/programs/coe/indicator/cgf/english-learners-in-public-schools

Oehrtman, J. P. (2022). Developing and maintaining intra/interprofessional collaborative relationships for student success: A grounded theory study on school counselor collaboration. *Professional School Counseling*, *26*(1), 1–12. https://doi.org/10.1177/2156759X221134263

Shi, Q., & Watkinson, J. (2019). English Language learners and school belonging: Implications for school counselor practice. *Professional School Counseling*, *22*(1b). https://doi.org/10.1177/2156759X19834442

Suárez-Orozco, C., Yoshikawa, H., Teranishi, R. T., & Suárez-Orozco, M. M. (2011). Growing up in the shadows: The developmental implications of unauthorized status. *Harvard Educational Review*, *81*(3), 438–473. https://doi/10.17763/haer.81.3.g23x203763783m75

Sugarman, J., & Geary, C. (2018). English learners in Maryland: Demographics, outcomes, and state accountability policies. *Migration Policy Institute*. https://www.migrationpolicy.org/sites/default/files/publications/EL-factsheet2018-Maryland_Final.pdf

U.S. Department of Education, National Center for Education Statistics, Common Core of Data (CCD). (2024). *State Nonfiscal Public Elementary/Secondary Education Survey, 2023-24 v.1a*. https://nces.ed.gov/ccd/

Section III

Systemic Shifts and Targeted Support

Chapter 11

A Needs Assessment Tool to Determine Program Strengths, Priorities, and Resources for Counseling Multilingual Learners

Tom Salsbury, Jihee Im, and Eugenie Mainake

Introduction

Needs assessment is a systematic, evidence-based process for identifying the gap between current performance and desired outcomes, and for prioritizing the actions and resources required to close that gap (Appalachian Regional Advisory Committee, 2005; Redding, 1997). In K-12 contexts, high-quality needs assessments triangulate multiple data sources (achievement, attendance/behavior, stakeholder perceptions) and explicitly involve the people who will act on the findings (educators, families, students, community partners) (Bear, 2020). Needs assessment is the foundation of effective school improvement, providing a rigorous, data-driven process to identify priority gaps, allocate resources strategically, and engage stakeholders in continuous improvement. Exemplars from Pittsburgh's districtwide reform (Davis & Denton, 1987), the Appalachia RAC (Appalachian Regional Advisory Committee, 2005), Delaware's School Climate Surveys (Bear et al., 2021), and Kentucky's Migrant Education Program (Kentucky Department of Education, 1992) illustrate how comprehensive, mixed-method assessments reveal academic, social, and equity challenges. These assessments guide aligned interventions—from instructional coherence and family engagement to culturally responsive practices and social-emotional learning.

Rather than beginning with programs or solutions, a needs assessment asks: what problems of practice are we actually trying to solve, and what evidence shows they are urgent, actionable, and within our capacity to change? Mintrop's (2016) framework is instructive: leaders should select problems that are urgent for the organization, actionable within their sphere of influence, feasible in a short timeframe, strategically aligned, and tied to concrete practices that can be improved through iterative cycles of work (e.g., 30-60-90-day plans) and evidence (e.g., low-inference observations of what adults do and say).

For middle and high schools in particular, a coherent needs assessment must account for the broader system in which any single initiative sits. The National High School Center's (Fryer & Johnson, 2010) tool operationalizes eight elements that often determine whether improvement persists: rigorous curriculum

DOI: 10.4324/9781003711124-14

and instruction; assessment and accountability; teacher effectiveness and professional development; student and family supports; stakeholder engagement; leadership and governance; organization and structure; and resources for sustainability. By rating evidence for each element and converting gaps into next-step actions, the tool allows school teams to see strengths and weaknesses holistically and align their plans with state priorities and funding streams. This emphasis on *system coherence* matters because sustainable change rarely comes from single programs; it comes from aligning leadership, data systems, schedules, staffing, professional learning, and family/community supports to the problems of practice that a needs assessment surfaces (Garbers et al., 2018).

Counseling and student support services illustrate the point. Dahir et al.'s (2009) statewide study in Alabama found grade-band differences in counselors' priorities and readiness to implement comprehensive counseling aligned to the ASCA National Model, as well as lower ratings for collaboration on school improvement, diversity, and increasing underrepresented participation in advanced coursework. Their conclusion: needs assessments must also diagnose staff beliefs, priorities, and professional development needs, so that counseling work aligns with academic goals and equity commitments across levels (elementary, middle, high school). Similarly, Garbers et al. (2018) assessment of school-based health centers (SBHCs) identified structural, systemic, and interpersonal components of culturally competent care and documented notable gaps (e.g., limited training for frontline staff; uneven inclusion of preferred pronouns and gender identity on intake forms; regional differences in materials review). The lesson for schools is practical: when needs assessments include visible environments, forms/policies, and staff training, they yield specific, fixable targets that improve student experience and access to supports—and they draw attention to the district policies that enable or hinder implementation across campuses (Allred & Foster, 2021; Garbers et al., 2018).

The message for needs assessment scholarship and practice is clear: diagnosis must be coupled with structures that make the work possible every day (schedules, professional learning communities, monitoring routines, resource lines), and with district policies that align people, time, and tools to the priorities the assessment names (Allred & Foster, 2021). These essentials frame the chapter that follows and anchor the application to school improvement.

Needs Assessment Tool

In this chapter, we present a needs assessment tool for school administrators, teachers, staff, and other stakeholders to use for school-wide program improvement of counseling services for multilingual learners (MLs). We wanted to answer the big question about needs and services for MLs. How do schools identify student needs for counseling services, and how are those services delivered? This is important because MLs are a vulnerable student population whose cultural and linguistic backgrounds vary enormously. We wanted to study how schools approach counseling needs and services for MLs by focusing on what teachers and counselors actually report doing and how these actions are received by students and their care givers. Thus, the needs assessment tool emerged from this project exploring counseling needs and services for MLs. We conducted structured interviews with general education teachers, teachers of MLs, school counselors, parents, and small focus groups of middle school MLs at four middle schools in the same geographical region in the Inland Northwest of the United States. The percentages of students served in a Transitional Bilingual Instructional Program (TBIP) at one of the four participating schools varied at the time from about 6% to as high as 20% (OSPI, 2025). However, given the nature of school reporting, many more multilingual students were enrolled in the schools. Those students had either tested out of a TBIP program or were exempted from a program entirely. Interview data from the participants was transcribed and analyzed. From this analysis, we identified five major themes which we aligned to the literature in the field.

The chapter is organized as follows: First, we present the background literature to support the five major themes to emerge from the interview data. As we summarize the literature, we also provide excerpts from the data that illustrate key elements of that theme. This interpretive synecdoche (Richards-Tutor et al., 2013) provides fine detail and is intended to illustrate the significance to the theme as a whole. Second, we briefly summarize how to use the needs assessment tool. We illustrate its use as a vignette with excerpts from a pilot of the tool conducted with a participating middle school. Finally, we present the needs assessment tool in its entirety in the Appendix.

Services for Counseling Multilingual Learners: Five Major Themes

Our analysis of the data revealed five major themes along with several sub-themes. The first major theme described *Connections*. We divided this theme into three sub-themes: *connections between and across programs and schools*, *connections to youth*, and *connections to families and communities*. The Connections theme is the first and arguably the most important theme in the data based on the number of times this theme was referenced by participants. The second theme in the data is *Assessment and Student Data*. The third theme in the data is *Awareness of Language and Culture*. We divide this theme into two sub-themes: *awareness of language*, and *awareness of culture*. The fourth theme we call *Leadership, Social Justice, and Efficacy*. The fifth and final theme in the data is *Roles, Responsibilities and Workplace Satisfaction*. In the following sections, we explain each of these themes, but at the same time, recognize that these are interrelated constructs, as illustrated in Figure 11.1.

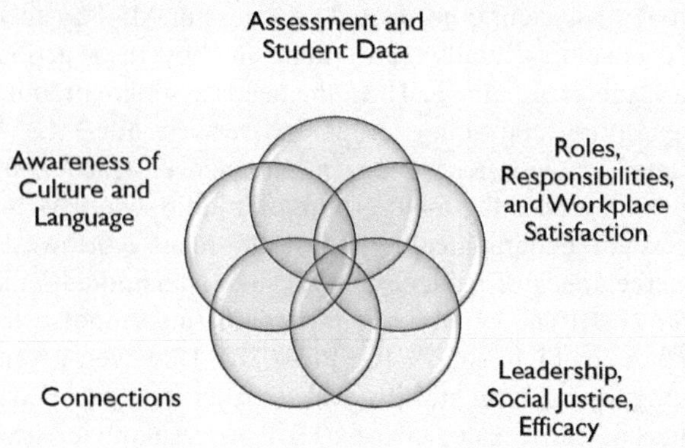

Figure 11.1 Five interrelated themes on counseling needs and services for multilingual learners.

Connections

Connections Between and Across Programs and Schools

Faculty collaborations within specific school programs and across those programs figure prominently in the literature on support services for MLs. These collaborations involve (1) communication and coordination, (2) wraparound services, (3) teacher access to information, (4) time to collaborate with other professionals in the school, and (5) transcollaboration.

Effective multicultural school counseling requires communication and coordination with strong partnerships within the school community (Goh et al., 2007). Research indicates that these partnerships enhance counselors' preparation to work with MLs and lead to improved student outcomes, including increased English literacy, academic mastery, and smoother transitions (McCall-Perez, 2000). Thus, schools should establish cross-disciplinary teams, including ML specialists, counselors, teachers, and administrators, to align curriculum, integrate support services, and ensure access to school resources (Rance-Roney, 2009). This level of communication is illustrated from one of the structured interviews:

> With the counselor, it's constant, constant communication. Starting at the beginning well, starting now, for example for next year, once I find out who is, what teachers are teaching what subjects, then we start looking at student lists for next year, and kind of grouping them together, saying, when we look at training, okay these teachers have been trained for beginning kids. You know,

> they have had experience with them, and, and then so we will work on getting them kind of blocked so that either I can, so I kind of minimize the number of teachers that necessarily, that kind of need that support throughout the year.

School counselors build support systems for students, particularly those from diverse backgrounds. They facilitate activities that help students establish connections before graduating, ensuring a smoother transition to college (Ashley, 2012). To do this, school counselors collaborate with various stakeholders—including courts, legislators, law enforcement, educators, and parents—to create community-based support programs. These school-wide and community efforts, which focus on developing students' cultural, linguistic, and emotional resilience are referred to as wraparound services (Park-Taylor et al., 2007). They require long-term planning and collaboration from a multilingual, multicultural, and collective approach involving administrators, mentors, family, and community allies. The goal is to minimize service duplication and strengthen wraparound support for students and their families (Francis, 2012; Park-Taylor et al., 2007).

Student mobility across schools and districts, particularly with migrant students, creates challenges in coordinating academic records and making that information available to teachers and counselors (McCall-Perez, 2000; Nevárez-La Torre, 2012; Rance-Roney, 2009). Improving the retrieval and transmission of ML student data is thus essential for both effective advising and course placement. By systematically collecting information on students' linguistic and academic backgrounds—including years in an English-medium environment, literacy levels, prior schooling, and English proficiency—counselors can make more informed decisions. Researchers advocate for improved training for school staff on managing student records, a standardized system for credit transfers, and the use of technology to track and share student data (Nevárez-La Torre, 2012). Additionally, schools should collect comprehensive academic histories, conduct intake interviews with translators, and maintain individual ML student profiles to better guide instruction and support student success (Rance-Roney, 2009). In doing so, schools promote timely access to ML student information for general education teachers for instructional support.

School counselors trained to support MLs can significantly impact academic achievement by collaborating with teachers and engaging in responsive services (Aydin, 2011; Cleveland, 2008; Heineke et al., 2012; Nevárez-La Torre, 2012; Park-Taylor et al., 2007). Partnering with teachers in curriculum planning and system support activities improves ML student success while strengthening counselors' roles. This professional collaboration is vital for supporting multilingual and transient students. Thus, counselors need time to collaborate with their colleagues. This includes common planning periods, professional development through study groups, co-teaching, practitioner inquiry, and the creation of learning communities where teachers and administrators share strategies and resources. Collaboration fosters teacher professional growth, reduces isolation, and enhances educational outcomes for bilingual students. Sustained collaboration among educators, counselors, and administrators is essential in creating equitable learning environments that support the diverse needs of MLs and other students (Heineke et al., 2012).

Transcollaboration refers to moving beyond traditional culturally responsive teaching to create a third space, allowing students to navigate multiple cultural identities rather than assimilating into a singular one (García et al., 2012). Transcollaboration is a strategy where schools, communities, and institutions work together to support students academically, socially, and emotionally. This strategy involves (1) mentorship and collaboration or *compadrazgo* to build strong learning communities by promoting group work and partnerships beyond school walls; (2) linguistically responsive practices that value and utilize linguistic diversity, ensuring bilingual students receive targeted support; (3) collaborative learning communities that implement looping, where teachers and counselors stay with the same group of students for multiple years, fostering deeper relationships and better academic and social outcomes; and (4) engagement of diverse stakeholders to actively involve families, teachers, administrators, and specialists in decision-making, ensuring instructional interventions are culturally and linguistically appropriate. Ultimately, these approaches highlight the importance of cross-sector partnerships, shared responsibility, and culturally inclusive practices in improving educational outcomes for bilingual and immigrant students (García et al., 2012; Ortiz et al., 2011; Smith, 2012).

Connections to Youth

Building strong teacher-student relationships is fundamental to students' success, not only in academic achievement but also in overall personal development. When these consistent relationships and solid connections that students build with teachers are positive, they help students to eventually feel more engaged and have a sense of belonging with school, be resilient, and be active participants in the learning process (Gehlbach et al., 2012; Sointu et al., 2017). Positive connections go beyond surface-level interactions as they incorporate trust, mutual respect, and meaningful engagement, which if done collectively, promotes an encouraging and collaborative atmosphere for learning. Hence, these bonds enhance motivation, improve academic outcomes, and support emotional well-being (Bernstein-Yamashiro & Noam, 2013; Gutierrez & Buckley, 2019).

Teachers and counselors play a critical role in cultivating these relationships by demonstrating genuine personal regard for students and facilitating meaningful peer interactions. Through their efforts, they create a nurturing and inclusive environment where students are not only empowered to thrive academically but also develop the social and emotional skills needed for their long-term success

(Gutierrez & Buckley, 2019). Empirical studies have consistently supported these claims. For instance, Wang et al. (2024) found that teacher-student relationships in Chinese schools significantly impacted both academic outcomes and psychological well-being. Similarly, Majumder and Beri (2025) emphasized the role of positive relationships in fostering a supportive classroom climate, particularly for MLs. These findings align with observations by Feryok (2024), who highlighted the transformative impact of teacher care on MLs' motivation and identity.

MLs in particular benefit greatly from educators who can establish trust and rapport, lessening barriers such as cultural and linguistic differences (Flores & Smith, 2009). Students are more likely to feel connected to school when they perceive it as a safe and welcoming environment, which is critical for fostering a sense of inclusion and belonging. Research by Fatimah et al. (2024) revealed that culturally responsive teaching significantly enhanced MLs' sense of belonging, leading to improved academic performance and engagement. Furthermore, during critical transitions such as moving from middle to high school or adapting to a new school in a different country, supportive relationships with teachers and counselors can significantly enhance students' academic performance and reduce behavioral challenges (Longobardi et al., 2016; Martin & Collie, 2019). These transitions can be particularly overwhelming for MLs and other minority students, making it even more important for educators to provide consistent encouragement and culturally responsive support. Positive teacher-student relationships during these times not only mitigate the negative effects of adjustment but also foster long-term academic and social success (Buka, 2013). Communication between teachers and counselors is important, illustrated in the following excerpt from a participating general education teacher:

> I work with creating that relationship, so I can go and say, hey okay so I had somebody come and talk to me because they notice that you are not acting the same. What's going on? And then you know kind of basing it from there, if it seems like something that's a little more for counseling need as opposed to a middle school student typical behavior, then working with the counselor and saying hey this is what I've seen. This is what is going on. And then working with her to kind of find resources.

The cumulative effects of positive relationships with teachers and counselors are profound. A greater number of positive interactions correlates with increased student engagement and sustained academic and social benefits (Martin & Collie, 2019). Conversely, negative or neglectful relationships can exacerbate school-related and personal challenges, highlighting the need for intentional and ongoing efforts to build strong, supportive connections with all students, especially those from marginalized or vulnerable populations.

Connections to Families and Communities

Family and community engagement play an essential role in MLs' academic and emotional well-being. Schools that promote meaningful connections with parents and caregivers help create a supportive ecosystem where families feel welcomed and valued (Arias & Morillo-Campbell, 2008; Kelty & Wakabayashi, 2020). Orientation programs and multilingual communication channels allow parents to navigate the school system and actively participate in their children's education (Gonzalez-DeHass et al., 2022). Studies have shown that when schools acknowledge parents' linguistic and cultural backgrounds, they strengthen home-school partnerships and improve student outcomes (Baquedano-López et al., 2013; Kelty & Wakabayashi, 2020). Collaborative efforts, such as parent workshops and bilingual liaisons, facilitate this engagement and empower both parents and caregivers to advocate for their children's needs (Mapp & Kuttner, 2013). One of our participating school counselors shared the following:

> Some parents I'm able to reach and get a hold of them. We've had student study team meetings, and we've gotten parents to come in. Other ones it's hard to get a hold of them or they don't speak English, so I'll have work with the ELD teacher to see if we need to get a hold of them and if we need a translator or things like that. And then we've got a district advocate too. She'll come if we have any meetings with those students. There's an elementary representative and a secondary representative.

Partnerships between schools and communities are also instrumental in addressing MLs' socio-emotional and academic challenges. Research suggests that schools should collaborate with community organizations to provide culturally appropriate counseling and special education services (Gaitan, 2012). With this approach, schools can ensure that families receive necessary support while maintaining their cultural values and practices (Gaitan, 2012; Olivos et al., 2011). Culturally responsive approaches to family engagement recognize that ML families contribute valuable knowledge and perspectives, enriching the educational experience for all students (Epstein, 2011). By creating inclusive family-school partnerships, educators can promote equitable access to learning opportunities and nurture a sense of belonging for MLs.

Assessment and Student Data

Dynamic assessment practices are a significant contributor to effectively educating emergent bilinguals (García et al., 2012). These assessments are ongoing and adaptable rather than a one-time evaluation (Park-Taylor et al., 2007; Rance-Roney, 2009). They emphasize differentiation to meet individual student needs and challenge traditional, static assessment models (García et al., 2012). Concerns about the inequitable reliance on English-language standardized tests have led to the development of new, culturally and linguistically responsive assessment tools (Gottlieb, 2021; Lalas, 2007). The literature also supports alternative assessment methods that include verbal and nonverbal communication to accommodate MLs with low literacy in their first and second languages (Nevárez-La Torre, 2012). Specific language assessments serve multiple roles, including identifying student strengths, guiding language instruction, and informing decisions about transitioning students from bilingual to English-only programs (Ortiz et al., 2011). In terms of record keeping, schools maintain detailed English language learning records, tracking progress and guiding individualized instruction (Rance-Roney, 2009).

Data-driven decision-making plays a key role in setting academic and counseling goals, with factors like state assessments, attendance, discipline records, and classroom performance guiding program development. The literature discusses encouraging students to reflect on their strengths, weaknesses, and sense of belonging which can foster a stronger sense of identity and purpose in their academic journey (Maldonado et al., 2009). As mentioned earlier, learning communities and looping, where students stay with the same teachers for multiple years, fosters strong relationships, especially benefiting bilingual and immigrant students (Heineke et al., 2012). A single year's assessment may not accurately reflect ML progress. Thus, language assessment data should track student performance over time to guide instruction, prevent misidentification of learning disabilities, and inform program placement.

One concern raised in the literature is on academic tracking, where students are grouped based on ability, motivation, or past academic achievement. This system is intended to create a more effective learning environment by placing students with peers of similar ability. However, tracking can significantly impact students' postsecondary opportunities, as those in vocational tracks often have fewer academic challenges and limited career options compared to students in advanced tracks (Akos et al., 2007; Coulter & Smith, 2006; Ohrt et al., 2009). The literature highlights issues faced by MLs and minority students in academic tracking. MLs often receive low-quality instruction that limits their interaction with native speakers and academic content. Many are placed in remedial classes with lower expectations, which negatively impacts their academic achievement (Coulter & Smith, 2006; Rance-Roney, 2009).

The literature emphasizes the importance of systematizing the retrieval and transmission of ML student data to enhance student advising and course placement. Participants in the current study expressed some frustrations with how assessment data is managed and made available to them at their school, mostly because assessment data is not systematized:

> I don't recall having a lot of data on them [multilingual learners]. I do know if I am struggling with where a student is at and what I should be doing, I can go and talk to the, our ELD gal, and she gives feedback and we talk. And we work out

> a plan for the student, and she'll give more background and more information, and she is very good about that. But it's not easily available to me otherwise.

This is felt most acutely with migrant students who face challenges to schooling due to high mobility, lack of consistent academic standards, and inadequate tracking of student records (Ashley, 2012; Nevárez-La Torre, 2012). By ensuring counselors have access to accurate student profiles—including English proficiency levels, literacy in their native language, prior schooling, and ESL experience—MLs see increased enrollments in subjects like science and mathematics (McCall-Perez, 2000). Researchers suggest that states and schools adopt standardized credit transfer systems, improved documentation practices, and technological solutions for tracking student records (Nevárez-La Torre, 2012). Additionally, general education teachers should be better informed about their MLs early in the school year to provide appropriate instructional support. Schools should implement intake procedures that document each student's academic history, language background, and personal goals to guide instruction effectively (Rance-Roney, 2009).

Awareness of Culture and Language

Student populations are becoming increasingly diverse, and there is a growing need for educators to develop multicultural competencies to accommodate the needs of these learners (Holcomb-McCoy, 2004). Hence, school districts play important roles in promoting cultural awareness by offering on-the-job training and professional development programs designed to improve multicultural competencies among teachers and counselors. The effectiveness of multicultural training in improving educators' ability to engage with diverse student populations is highlighted by Castro-Atwater (2024). Furthermore, programs that incorporate implicit bias training, cultural competency workshops, and real-world applications have been shown to increase self-awareness among educators and lead to more inclusive teaching and counseling practices (Wallace & Jacoby, 2025). These initiatives ensure that teachers and counselors gain the skills that they need to understand and support students from different cultural backgrounds in the school.

Cultural identity and acculturation are key components of every student's educational experience. Students from diverse cultural and linguistic backgrounds bring unique perspectives, values, and linguistic identities to the learning environment, shaping their educational experiences (August-Mowers & Maarman, 2024). Research suggests that when educators acknowledge and integrate these experiences into their instructional methods, students demonstrate higher engagement and academic achievement (Chiu et al., 2025). Additionally, fostering an environment that respects cultural identity enhances students' psychological well-being and sense of belonging in the school community (Dawson, 2025).

Therefore, it is essential for teachers and counselors to connect with students' cultural experiences and use them as a foundation for educational and counseling strategies. A participating counselor in the current study shared the following:

> I think different cultures, different things are more acceptable, so some cultures may be very open with feelings where as others are more introverted and introspective and so I think, if like, I work with students who are more wanting to talk about their feelings, but their culture is not as acceptable, so they don't have that outlet, and they think that's not okay—a conflict within themselves. And so when they get to the United States, it can be really hard for that acculturation piece, trying to still hold on to their old culture while accepting the American culture, that's huge. There's a whole different counseling piece that could address that.

Furthermore, awareness of language and cultural nuances allows teachers and counselors to develop culturally appropriate interventions in collaboration with parents, guardians, and stakeholders. Studies indicate that culturally sensitive approaches improve communication between educators and families, leading to more effective support systems for students (Haggerty-Basurto, 2024). Focusing on language, culture, and identity in professional development can support educators in adopting culturally responsive practices and reducing disparities in student outcomes (Fickel et al., 2017). For instance, school counselors who undergo multicultural competency training are better equipped to address race-based incidents and promote equity within their institutions (Moon, 2024). While training programs have effectively enhanced educators' and practitioners' understanding of culturally responsive strategies, challenges persist when it comes to practical implementation (Zeleke et al., 2021). Hence, this highlights the need for ongoing professional development that emphasizes culturally responsive practices in both teaching and counseling settings.

Multicultural competency is crucial for educators and school counselors to effectively support diverse student populations. It involves developing cultural awareness, knowledge, and skills to create an inclusive and supportive learning environment (Pang et al., 2011). School districts must prioritize well-designed professional development in multicultural education to equip educators with the skills needed to foster inclusive, equitable classrooms, and implement effective, culturally responsive interventions (Parkhouse et al., 2019). At the same time, school counselors need to maintain and assess their own multicultural competence to meet ethical mandates and support diverse students effectively (Mayorga et al., 2013). By fostering a culture of awareness and inclusiveness, educators can ensure that all students, regardless of their background, receive equitable access to educational opportunities and emotional support. Continuing emphasis on multicultural training will help bridge cultural gaps, promote understanding, and create a more cohesive and supportive educational system.

Leadership, Social Justice, and Efficacy

Educators must adopt a culturally responsive and socially just approach, recognizing students' diverse backgrounds and addressing issues of power and marginalization (; Hansuvadha & Slater, 2012; Lalas, 2007; Nelson & Bustamante, 2007; Owens et al., 2010). This includes fostering cultural pride, supporting bilingualism, and encouraging parental involvement in education. School counselors can help students navigate culture shock, identity conflicts, and emotional struggles through individual counseling and group support. To do this effectively, counselors should understand the challenges immigrant students face, including lack of family and social support, trauma from war or poverty, and health concerns (Goh et al., 2007; Nevárez-La Torre, 2012). These factors contribute to behavioral issues, poor school attendance, and difficulties in making friends (Goh et al., 2007; Park-Taylor et al., 2007). Increased scrutiny and political debate have altered the acculturation experience for immigrants, making integration more challenging due to racial profiling and discrimination. Migrant and immigrant students face unique challenges in education due to their transient lifestyle, language barriers, and cultural adjustments (Goh et al., 2007; Jasis & Marriot, 2010; Lalas, 2007; Nevárez-La Torre, 2012). Many experience stress, isolation, and emotional struggles due to family separation, stereotypes, and socioeconomic hardships (Aydin, 2011; Maldonado et al., 2009). The constant movement of migrant families affects student attendance, academic performance, and peer relationships (Goh et al., 2007).

Educators should understand the human and material resources available (federal, state, and community) to support educating MLs (Nevárez-La Torre, 2012). Schools partner with community organizations, clinics, and higher education institutions to support mental health and educational development. For example, schools have targeted programs for students dealing with depression, offering counseling and mental health services through collaborations with local hospitals and agencies (García et al., 2012). University enrichment programs provide opportunities for K-12 students to explore higher education, with direct involvement from college staff, interns, and visits to campuses.

School counselors working with diverse students often face challenges such as large caseloads, limited bilingual staff, and insufficient resources for MLs (Aydin, 2011; McCall-Perez, 2000). When there is a significant shortage of bilingual teachers and counselors, this impacts the quality of support available to MLs and immigrant students. Additionally, schools with large ML populations often struggle with overcrowded classrooms, inadequate instructional materials, and lack of training for teachers.

Research emphasizes the importance of teachers collaborating with colleagues, parents, and the community to improve bilingual education. Teachers are urged to understand language policies and use them to advocate for their bilingual students, ensuring that educational practices align with students' needs

(Aydin, 2011; Coulter & Smith, 2006; García, 2008; García et al., 2012; Heineke et al., 2012; Nevárez-La Torre, 2012; Olivares-Cuhat, 2011; Sharp-Ross, 2011). Teachers can use their knowledge of policies to drive change and improve bilingual education. Studies show that MLs often lag behind their English-speaking peers due to policies that segregate them, and many teachers express concern about the negative impact of these policies on student achievement (Nevárez-La Torre, 2012).

Students from disadvantaged backgrounds, including those with beginning levels of English proficiency and low socioeconomic status (SES), often face significant barriers to academic achievement because of limited access to resources as well as discriminatory practices (Akos et al., 2007; Aydin, 2011; Bryan et al., 2009; Goh et al., 2007; Jasis & Marriot, 2010; Lalas, 2007; Nevárez-La Torre, 2012; Ohrt et al., 2009; Olivares-Cuhat, 2011; Park-Taylor et al., 2007; Sawyer et al., 2013; Smith, 2012). Research shows that out-of-school time (OST) investments to support students' development, especially those from underserved communities, are highly impactful (Bryan et al., 2009). School counselors can help mitigate some of these issues, particularly for English learners (ELs) and migrant children, who often face additional difficulties such as trauma, language barriers, and instability due to migration. One of the participating school counselors shared the following during the structured interview:

> Our kids do come with, you know, poverty issues, and you know other counseling issues, like most of our students. I think one of the needs for our kids is really kind of getting to let go and really be a kid. We have a lot of our kids that, you know, kind of have to be the adults and they have to, you know, help Mom and Dad. And they do the translating and things like that. So I know that's, that's one of the areas that we have worked on – is students, you know, letting go and not micromanaging everything. You know, it's okay to be a kid.

Research suggests that school principals' expectations and involvement significantly influence school-family partnerships, community collaboration, and overall support for MLs (Aydin, 2011; Coulter & Smith, 2006; Goh et al., 2007; Hansuvadha & Slater, 2012; Heineke et al., 2012; Nevárez-La Torre, 2012; Ortiz et al., 2011). Thus, school administrators play a key role in either empowering or hindering efforts toward multicultural education. Administrators have the authority to influence the success of multicultural programs by providing resources, modeling attitudes promoting diversity, and organizing events that support multicultural understanding (Ortiz et al., 2011). They also lead professional development initiatives that help staff understand the needs of immigrant students. Administrators can leverage education policies to promote inclusive reforms, such as encouraging bilingual education and community engagement, to better support MLs. The literature frequently calls for improved teacher training to better address the diverse needs of MLs. Administrative leadership is considered a key factor in the success of programs for MLs, with some advocating for administrators to view linguistic and cultural diversity as resources rather than obstacles (Goh et al., 2007; Heineke et al., 2012; Nevárez-La Torre, 2012). Effective leadership, both at the central administration level and on individual campuses, is critical for ensuring that MLs receive quality instruction, appropriate early intervention, and the necessary resources for their academic success (Ortiz et al., 2011). Administrators must have or gain expertise in cultural and linguistic differences, effective instruction for MLs, and research-based interventions for struggling learners.

Roles, Responsibilities, and Workplace Satisfaction

Educators' roles and responsibilities in supporting MLs have expanded significantly, requiring them to balance multiple instructional and emotional support tasks. Studies highlighted that teachers and counselors often serve as mentors and trusted adults for MLs, providing guidance beyond academic instruction (Harper & de Jong, 2009). Long-term relationships with educators enhance MLs' confidence and academic persistence, particularly for those navigating linguistic and cultural transitions (Cummins, 2000; Destin & Williams, 2020). However, a body of research has also indicated that the increasing demands on teachers and counselors—such as managing large caseloads and addressing diverse student needs—can lead to burnout and job dissatisfaction (Souto-Manning, 2013). To maintain high-quality instruction and student support, schools must ensure manageable workloads and provide adequate professional development (García & Kleifgen, 2018). One of the participating counselors shared the following about increasing demands on her limited time and the impact it has on her ability to follow the American School Counselor Association (ASCA) model:

> Even though those needs are there and even though you recognize it – and probably most of us in this building do – it's really hard trying to find the time and the models or the ways to go about doing that. Because I know that most of my first part of the year was spent, first building the master schedule scheduling students in and getting them all settled in their classes, getting settled for the year. Like April or beginning of May was all testing for the state tests. And so there is a lot of time that is lost. And I think if I was able to get some of those needs met, but like I said we're not able to entirely follow the ASCA national model. I think we have a lot of needs that either a second counselor or something would help.

Workplace satisfaction among teachers and counselors is closely linked to the availability of institutional support and resources. Research suggests that smaller class sizes and reasonable caseloads enable educators to provide institutionalized support to MLs (García & Kleifgen, 2018; Harper & de Jong, 2009;

Valdés, 2001). Schools that offer traditional classroom support based on student demographics and language development needs create more equitable learning environments (Ruiz de Velasco & Fix, 2000). Furthermore, professional learning communities and mentorship programs for educators enhance job satisfaction and retention, particularly in schools serving high numbers of MLs (Darling-Hammond, 2010). Ensuring that teachers and counselors feel supported in their roles is crucial for sustaining effective education for MLs and improving positive student outcomes.

Development of the Needs Assessment Tool

The needs assessment tool was developed through an analysis of key informant and focus group interviews supported by the research literature in the field. In our analysis of these structured interviews, we identified patterns in the data, developed categories, and refined our understanding of counseling needs and services for MLs. Our research process was closely aligned with the constant comparative method in qualitative research (Saldaña, 2021). The needs assessment tool that we present in the Appendix at the end of the chapter is the culmination of onsite school visits to conduct structured interviews, analysis of the data aligned to the literature reviewed for the project, the development of the tool itself, and finally a pilot of the tool conducted with one of the participating schools. We intended the needs assessment tool to be one part of a school's comprehensive needs assessment, specifically focusing on stakeholder engagement and collaborative identification of improvement (Cuiccio & Husby-Slater, 2018). We wanted a tool that was both easy to use and closely aligned to current realities and research on counseling needs and services for MLs. We adapted our needs assessment tool from templates found on the Washington Office of Superintendent of Public Instruction (OSPI) and the U.S. Department of Education. The columns in our tool apply across all of the themes from the interview data. For each theme, focus groups are asked three questions: (1) How well do we already do this? (2) How important is this to us? (3) How available are resources (human and financial) under the current budget? Work groups respond on a scale of 1-3, and there is a fourth column for notes on interpretation of the prompt and next steps. Our rationale for developing the needs assessment tool in this way was to produce a versatile tool, and as much as possible, one that was also self-explanatory.

Using a template, the next step was to craft statements under each theme or sub-theme to which users of the tool could respond. The statements aligned to the themes from the interview data and are supported by the research literature. The full needs assessment tool is available in the Appendix. We developed statements that lend themselves to open-ended responses and might reveal varying perspectives from different stakeholders. For example, the first statement under the sub-theme Connections between/across schools and program is *Wraparound services involve enough players (school and community) to fully support MLs' social and academic needs.* It is our hope that a school counselor, principal, ELD teacher, general education teacher, and a participating parent, for example, might each experience wraparound services in different ways, thus deepening the conversation around this critical service. We believe this to be the case for each of the 30 statements in the needs assessment tool. To illustrate how stakeholders might use the needs assessment tool, we present a vignette consisting of excerpts and narrative description of a participating school's use of the tool in a pilot session.

Vignette—A Practical Use of the Needs Assessment Tool

To pilot the needs assessment tool with one participating middle school, we invited the middle school principal, the ML teacher, the school counselor, an ELA teacher, and a math teacher all from the same school to participate in work session with the tool. The work session lasted for just under three hours total. When participants arrived, they were each given a printed copy of the tool to review. An electronic copy of the tool was projected onto a screen for all participants to see. As participants spoke, the research team took notes and projected those notes onto the screen so that participants could see how their responses were being recorded in real time.

The tool contains 30 statements to which participants responded. They worked through the tool often combining and discussing more than one statement at a time. They read the statement out loud, unpacked the language in the statement itself and then entered into discussion, coming to consensus on a numerical score for each guiding question and ultimately to actionable items.

Excerpts from the pilot session illustrate the process. For example, the first statement for discussion was *Wraparound services involve enough players (school and community) to fully support MLs' social and academic needs*. The guiding question asked participants to respond with a numerical score from 1 to 3 to *How well do we do this already?* The Principal first established some norms for communicating.

Principal: Maybe just start with the first one and go, and if we all kind of agree and say we're not there, or we are there, and this is what we do, and so on. We can go from there. So what do you say?

After reading the first statement, the Counselor asked for clarification about what is meant by "wraparound service."

Counselor: Let's define some things first. Let's define wraparound services. So, do you guys have a thought in mind about what is meant by the term wraparound services?

Math Teacher: It's school-wide, correct?

Principal: So, school-wide wraparound service. School and community.

Counselor: So, so examples of school services would be, of course, counselors, teachers, parents, coaches, I mean, I don't know. Is that, is that what we're, you know, kind of where we're going? Coaches, and then for community members, that would be maybe outside counselors, outside agencies,

Principal: Who else? Who else in community?

Counselor: I think that Interpreters, maybe? Well, interpreters play a role, too. Yeah.

Participants in the pilot study discussed this item as a group, bringing up concerns about the lack of physical space, the need for a list of community resources, and concerns about levels of academic English for true beginning-level MLs. Illustrated in the excerpt below, the conversation among participants was not linear; in other words, the group moved between statements and guiding questions. To structure the conversation, the Principal assumed the role of facilitator. There was a natural flow to the conversation as each individual shared experiences and asked others in the group for their input, illustrated in the following excerpt when the Principal asked the ML Teacher a question related to resource availability.

Principal: So, a question for you. What would your ideal program include?

ML Teacher: One teacher at school, minimum. Okay, yeah, more ideally [*laughs*]. Maybe a para-pro or two at each school. I mean, right now, it's me, and we just have two para-pros that were hired last March that continued over, and so that's great, so there's three of us now, we have a department! And there's Rebecca at the high school, but she and I don't really coordinate very much because she's at the high school, and I was always at my buildings.

Principal: You know, I look under the right column where it says, you know, how available are resources such as human and financial under the current budget, and I'd say it's all over the place. I put "1" [*not readily available*]. Where do our resources go? Our resources are you, and like you said, Rebecca. Last year, we had Rebecca for one, one period.

Counselor: Just the itinerant nature of it. It's hard, you know, I think about any of our itinerant teachers. They have a difficult time. They pop in, they pop out, and I think it's hard for that communication and wraparound piece. I mean, I think about the times that you [*to ML teacher*] and I talk. It's around scheduling. And then once the schedules are settled, everybody just kind of goes about their own business, you know, so it's, that's difficult, and it is difficult because, like, there are many days when I start off and I think, oh, you know, [*ML teacher*] will be here 6th and 7th today. I need to run down and ask her, and then by the time that actually hits, it's whatever it was is, like, gone, you know. And so the day just by 6th and 7th period, the day just gets away from me anyway. You know, certainly not through anybody's fault.

ML Teacher: Right? It's just the way the whole system is built.

Principal: Right, and I think we're probably gonna see maybe a lot of this, kind of a 1-3-1 [*referring to the numerical score on the needs assessment tool*]. I think it's important to us, but then you kind of get into that idea of how important is it if we don't put resources towards it?

For the guiding question, *How well do we already do this?* The group came to a consensus around a numerical score of *1—Not well at all.* The group continued their discussion about this first item, and they agreed that in terms of importance (respond to *How important is this to us?*), in fact, wraparound services to support MLs were *very important* to them, which they scored as *3* on the tool. As illustrated in the excerpt above, they talked about available resources to improve wraparound services (responding to *How available are resources (human and financial) under current budget?*). They scored resource availability with a *1*, meaning current resources were limited. As participants talked, the research team typed notes under the column heading *What does this mean? What are the next steps? Where do we go from here?* Participants were able to check the accuracy of the notes because they were projected on the screen as they talked. The work session continued in this way, with participants working through all 30 statements. Following the work session, the research team summarized the notes under the column *Action Items.* The completed tool was then sent to the school counselor to share with the whole work team. Figure 11.2 shows the completed tool for this first item.

Discussion and Conclusion

This needs assessment tool offers schools a systematic and structured way to evaluate how they are meeting the counseling needs of MLs. It is context sensitive and school specific rather than adhering to a one-size-fits-all approach. Because it combines input from stakeholders (teachers, counselors, students, families) and evidence from previous literature, it ensures that stakeholder decisions are community focused and research driven. Our goal in developing the tool was to encourage a grounded, inclusive, and relevant improvement process that serves those for whom it was meant to support. The use of a needs assessment tool is also timely and relevant because the number of MLs across the United States continues to increase.

The needs assessment tool promotes equity by encouraging meaningful collaboration among the people who work in, and are directly impacted by,

Themes and Guiding Questions for Discussion	3 = Very well	2 = Pretty well	1 = Not well at all	3 = Very important	2 = Somewhat important	1 = Not very important	3 = Readily available	2 = Possibly available	1 = Not readily available		
Theme 1: Connections	**How well do we already do this?**			**Importance?**			**Resource availability?**			**What does this mean? What are the next steps? Where do we go from here?**	**Action Items**
Sub-Theme: Connections between/across schools and programs											
Wrap-around services involve enough players (school and community) to fully support ML students' social and academic needs.	1			3			1			Physical space is an issue we should address. We have our community, but we need more staff and faculty. Of the resources we have, they are mostly human resources. Most of the communication is around scheduling. It would be great to have a list of community resources available to us. Let's focus on both social and academic language needs. We are concerned we don't have enough services for MLs who are absolute beginners (newcomers)? We need to know what services are out there.	1. List of community resources 2. Focus on social as well as academic language needs 3. Find out more about Newcomer programs

Figure 11.2 Completed tool for one statement.

school-based counseling: teachers, counselors, students, and families. We developed the tool to be adaptable to different school settings, grade levels, and stakeholder groups, offering a flexible yet structured way to support MLs' success across varied contexts. The combination of the rating scales and open-ended prompts allows for both quantitative clarity and qualitative depth, enabling schools to move from discussions to actionable planning and protocols.

We welcome future research with this needs assessment tool to further explore counseling MLs. We believe the tool can be used to foster productive discussion and dynamic changes around equity-driven school change and reflection on the evolving needs of MLs. We envision the tool can be used as a springboard to inform professional development learning communities, district plannings, and school accommodations to better support MLs' social and academic growth. Further validation studies could explore the role this tool plays in advocating for MLs' needs across different school settings, providing useful information for both in-service teachers and counselors as well as candidates entering the profession during internships and teacher education courses at the university.

Reflection Questions

1 How can school teams move from understanding the counseling needs of MLs to implementing sustainable, equity-driven change across their school systems?
2 What enabling conditions, such as leadership support, structural alignment, or shifts in mindset, are necessary for a tool like this to produce lasting, meaningful change?
3 In reflecting on your own professional context, what assumptions about MLs and school counseling might need to be challenged or reexamined after reading this chapter?
4 In what ways can needs assessments be reframed as tools of empowerment, not just for schools, but for MLs and their families?

Author Note

The authors would like to thank Dr. Susan Jensen for her work in data collection and analysis for this project. We also thank the Nichols Mitchell Fellowship from the Washington State University College of Education, Sport, and Human Sciences for their financial support of this project.

References

Akos, P., Lambie, G. W., Milsom, A., & Gilbert, K. (2007). Early adolescents' aspirations and academic tracking: An exploratory investigation. *Professional School Counseling*, *11*(1), 57–64. https://doi.org/10.1177/2156759X0701100108

Allred, S. G., & Foster, K. A. (2021). *Without trumpets: Focus on sustainability to continue educational improvement*. Bloomsbury Publishing USA.
Appalachian Regional Advisory Committee (AP RAC) (2005). *Report of the Appalachian Regional Advisory Committee for educational needs assessment*. U.S. Department of Education, Office of Educational Research and Improvement. Contract No. ED04CO0043/0001.
Arias, M. B., & Morillo-Campbell, M. (2008). *Promoting ELL parental involvement: Challenges in contested times*. Education Policy Research Unit, Arizona State University.
Ashley, F. B. III (2012). A journey of faith. Transforming the educational experience of young men of color. *School Counseling Series*, *2*, 12–14.
August-Mowers, C. M., & Maarman, R. (2024). Using change laboratory workshop to enhance capabilities for multilingual learners in the Western Cape. *Southern African Review of Education*, *29*(2), 69–85.
Aydin, N. C. (2011). A national study: School counselor involvement in school, family and community partnerships with linguistically diverse families [Unpublished doctoral dissertation]. University of Iowa.
Baquedano-López, P., Alexander, R. A., & Hernández, S. J. (2013). Equity issues in parental and community involvement in schools: What teacher educators need to know. *Review of Research in Education*, *37*(1), 149–182. https://doi.org/10.3102/0091732X12459718
Bear, G. G. (2020). *Improving school climate: Practical strategies to reduce behavior problems and promote social and emotional learning*. Taylor & Francis Group.
Bear, G. G., Yang, C., Harris, A., Mantz, L., Hearn, S., & Boyer, D. (2021). *Technical manual for the Delaware School Survey: Scales of School climate; bullying victimization; student engagement; positive, punitive, and social–emotional learning techniques; and social and emotional competencies*. Center for Disabilities Studies, University of Delaware.
Bernstein-Yamashiro, B., & Noam, G. G. (2013). Teacher-student relationships: A growing field of study. *New Directions for Youth Development*, *2013*(137), 15–26. https://doi.org/10.1002/yd.20045
Bryan, J., Moore-Thomas, C., Day-Vines, N. L., Holcomb-McCoy, C., & Mitchell, N. (2009). Characteristics of students who receive school counseling services: Implications for practice and research. *Journal of School Counseling*, *7*(21), 1–29.
Buka, P. (2013). Promoting academic achievement through positive relationships. *Journal of Educational and Social Research*, *3*(3), 323. https://www.richtmann.org/journal/index.php/jesr/article/view/572
Castro-Atwater, S. A. (2024). Teaching implicit bias in multicultural counseling courses: Framework, tools, and limitations. *Journal of Counselor Practice*, *15*(2), 52–82. https://doi.org/10.22229/aws6739306
Chiu, Y. J., Lee, H., Lu, J., Ntinda, K., Chen, R. K., & Castillo, Y. A. (2025). Integrating technology to support learning and accessibility in counselor education and supervision. In D. Bates & C. Ortega (Eds.), *Innovative approaches in counselor education for students with disabilities* (pp. 105–140). IGI Global Scientific Publishing. https://doi.org/10.4018/979-8-3693-3342-6.ch005
Cleveland, R. (2008). Serving English language learners. *WSCA School Counselor Insights*.
Coulter, C., & Smith, M. L. (2006). English language learners in a comprehensive high school. *Bilingual Research Journal*, *30*(2), 309–335. https://doi.org/10.1080/15235882.2006.10162879.
Cuiccio, C., & Husby-Slater, M. (2018). *Needs assessment guidebook: Supporting the development of district and school needs assessments*. State Support Network, U.S. Department of Education. https://eric.ed.gov/?id=ED606124
Cummins, J. (2000). *Language, power and pedagogy: Bilingual children in the crossfire*. Multilingual Matters. https://doi.org/10.21832/9781853596773

Dahir, C. A., Burnham, J. J., & Stone, C. B. (2009). Listen to the voices: School counselors and comprehensive school counseling programs. *Professional School Counseling, 12*(3), 182–192. https://doi.org/10.1177/2156759X0901200302

Darling-Hammond, L. (2010). *The flat world and education: How America's commitment to equity will determine our future*. Teachers College Press.

Davis, L. E., & Denton, S. E. (1987, March). *Strategies for improving the educational outcomes of low achieving and ethnic minority students: The Pittsburgh experience, 1980–86* (Rev.). Paper presented at the Annual Conference of the Association for Supervision and Curriculum Development, New Orleans, LA.

Dawson, C. B. (2025). *Licensed Professional Counselors' Competency and Preparedness Treating Race-Based Incidents for Black Americans in the Southern Region of the United States* (Doctoral dissertation, Capella University). Available from ProQuest Dissertations & Theses A&I. (3160740538). https://www.proquest.com/dissertations-theses/licensed-professional-counselors-competency/docview/3160740538/se-2

Destin, M., & Williams, J. L. (2020). The connection between student identities and outcomes related to academic persistence. *Annual Review of Developmental Psychology, 2*, 437–460. https://doi.org/10.1146/annurev-devpsych-040920-042107

Epstein, J. L. (2011). *School, family, and community partnerships: Preparing educators and improving schools* (2nd ed.). Routledge.

Fatimah, F., Dewi, I. S., Amrullah, Y. F., & Talenta, P. I. (2024). Investigating the impact of barriers on perceptions of online learning for maritime English cadets. *Journal of Maritime Research, 21*(3), 235–243.

Feryok, A. (2024). *Language teacher identity and wellbeing*. Cambridge University Press.

Fickel, L. H., Henderson, C., & Price, G. (2017). Language, culture and identity at the nexus of professional learning. *Educational Research, 59*(4), 391–407. https://doi.org/10.1080/00131881.2017.1373029

Flores, B. B., & Smith, H. L. (2009). Teachers' characteristics and attitudinal beliefs about linguistic and cultural diversity. *Bilingual Research Journal, 31*(1-2), 323–358. https://doi.org/10.1080/15235880802640789

Francis, R. M. (2012). An asset approach to supporting young men of color. Transforming the educational experience of young men of color. *School Counseling Series, 2*, 22–23.

Fryer, L., & Johnson, A. (2010). *A coherent approach to high school improvement: A school and district needs assessment tool* (ED511822). American Institutes for Research, National High School Center.

Gaitan, C. D. (2012). Culture, literacy, and power in family–community–school–relationships. *Theory Into Practice, 51*(4), 305–311. https://doi.org/10.1080/00405841.2012.726060

Gándara, P., & Escamilla, K. (2017). Bilingual education in the United States. In O. García, A. M. Y. Lin & S. May (Eds.), *Bilingual and multilingual education* (pp. 439–452). Springer International Publishing.

Garbers, S., Heck, C. J., Gold, M. A., Santelli, J. S., & Bersamin, M. (2018). Providing culturally competent care for LGBTQ youth in school-based health centers: A needs assessment to guide quality of care improvements. *The Journal of School Nursing, 34*(6), 424–429. https://doi.org/10.1177/1059840517727335

García, O. (2008). Multilingual language awareness and teacher education. In Hornberger, N. H. (Eds.), *Encyclopedia of language and education*. Springer, Boston, MA. https://doi.org/10.1007/978-0-387-30424-3_163

García, O., Homonoff Woodley, H., Flores, N., & Chu, H. (2012). Latino emergent bilingual youth in high schools: Transcaring strategies for academic success. *Urban Education*, 48(6), 798–827. https://doi.org/10.1177/0042085912462708

García, O., & Kleifgen, J. (2018). *Educating emergent bilinguals: Policies, programs, and practices for English learners* (2nd ed.). Teachers College Press.

Gehlbach, H., Brinkworth, M. E., & Harris, A. D. (2012). Changes in teacher–student relationships. *British Journal of Educational Psychology*, *82*(4), 690–704. https://doi.org/10.1111/j.2044-8279.2011.02058.x

Goh, M., Herting Wahl, K., Koch McDonald, J., Brissett, A. A., & Yoon, E. (2007). Working with immigrant students in schools: The role of school counselors in building cross-cultural bridges. *Journal of Multicultural Counseling and Development*, *35*, 66–79.

Gonzalez-DeHass, A. R., Willems, P. P., Powers, J. R., & Musgrove, A. T. (2022). Parental involvement in supporting students' digital learning. *Educational Psychologist*, *57*(4), 281–294. https://doi.org/10.1080/00461520.2022.2129647

Gottlieb, M. (2021). *Classroom assessment in multiple languages: A handbook for teachers*. Corwin.

Gutierrez, A. S., & Buckley, K. H. (2019). Stories from the field: Building strong teacher-student relationships in the classroom. *Transforming Education.*

Haggerty-Basurto, M. (2024). *School counselors' needs in northeast Texas to serve rural emergent bilingual students* (Doctoral dissertation, University of the Southwest). Available from ProQuest Dissertations & Theses A&I. (3142494916). https://www.proquest.com/dissertations-theses/school-counselors-needs-northeast-texas-serve/docview/3142494916/se-2

Hansuvadha, N., & Slater, C. L. (2012). Culturally competent school leaders: The individual and the system. *The Educational Forum*, *76*(2), 174–189. https://doi.org/10.1080/00131725.2011.653094

Harper, C. A., & de Jong, E. J. (2009). English language teacher expertise: The elephant in the room. *Language and Education*, *23*(2), 137–151. https://doi.org/10.1080/09500780802152788

Heineke, A. J., Coleman, E., Ferrell, E., & Kersemeier, C. (2012). Opening doors for bilingual students: Recommendations for building linguistically responsive schools. *Improving Schools*, *15*(2), 130–147.

Holcomb-McCoy, C. (2004). Assessing the multicultural competence of school counselors: A checklist. *Professional School Counseling*, *7*(3), 178–186.

Jasis, P., & Marriot, D. (2010). All for our children: Migrant families and parent participation in an alternative education program. *Journal of Latinos and Education*, *9*(2), 126–140. https://doi.org/10.1080/15348431003617814.

Kelty, N. E., & Wakabayashi, T. (2020). Family engagement in schools: Parent, educator, and community perspectives. *Sage Open*, *10*(4). https://doi.org/10.1177/2158244020973024

Kentucky Department of Education (1992). *State plan for migrant education program — Kentucky: FY 1992–1995* (ED 354 125). U.S. Department of Education.

Lalas, J. (2007). Teaching for social justice in multicultural urban schools: Conceptualization and classroom implication. *Multicultural Education*, *14*(3), 17–21.

Longobardi, C., Prino, L. E., Marengo, D., & Settanni, M. (2016). Student-teacher relationships as a protective factor for school adjustment during the transition from middle to high school. *Frontiers in Psychology*, *7*, 1988. https://doi.org/10.3389/fpsyg.2016.01988

Lucas, T., & Villegas, A. M. (2013). Preparing linguistically responsive teachers: Laying the foundation in preservice teacher education. *Theory Into Practice*, *52*(2), 98–109. https://doi.org/10.1080/00405841.2013.770327

Majumder, P., & Beri, N. (2025). Systematic review of classroom climate and its influence on English language achievement. *Multidisciplinary Reviews*, *8*(5), 2025134. https://doi.org/10.31893/multirev.2025134

Maldonado, J., Kushner, J. D., Barr, J., & Korz, K. (2009). Ethnic identity and acculturation of English as second language learners: Implications for school counselors. *Michigan Journal of Counseling: Research, Theory and Practice*, *36*(1), 13–23.

Mapp, K. L., & Kuttner, P. J. (2013). *Partners in education: A dual capacity-building framework for family-school partnerships*. U.S. Department of Education.
Martin, A. J., & Collie, R. J. (2019). Teacher–student relationships and students' engagement in high school: Does the number of negative and positive relationships with teachers matter? *Journal of Educational Psychology, 111*(5), 861–876. https://doi.org/10.1037/edu0000317
Mayorga, M. G., Furgerson, K., Cook, K., & Wardle, E. A. (2013). School counselor's perception of their multicultural competency. *Journal on Educational Psychology, 6*(3), 41–49. https://doi.org/10.26634/jpsy.6.3.2092
McCall-Perez, Z. (2000). The counselor as advocate for English language learners: An action research approach. *Professional School Counseling.*
Mintrop, R. (2016). *Design-based school improvement: A practical guide for education leaders*. Harvard Education Press.
Moon, J. (2024). Fostering diversity: The role of intergroup contact in counselor education. *International Journal for the Advancement of Counselling*, 1–20. https://doi.org/10.1007/s10447-024-09588-7
Nelson, J. A., & Bustamante, R. M. (2007). The school-wide cultural competence observation checklist for professional school counselors: An assessment tool for leading culturally and linguistically diverse schools. In G. R. Walz, J. C. Bleuer, & R. K. Yep (Eds.), *Compelling counseling interventions: Celebrating VISTAS' fifth anniversary* (pp. 211–220). Ann Arbor, MI: Counseling Outfitters.
Nevárez-La Torre, A. A. (2012). Transiency in urban schools: Challenges and opportunities in educating ELLs with a migrant background. *Education and Urban Society, 44*(1), 3–34.
Ohrt, J., Lambie, G. W., & Ieva, K. P. (2009, October). Supporting Latina and African-American students in advanced placement courses: A school counseling program's approach. *Professional School Counseling, 13*(1).
Olivares-Cuhat, G. (2011). Learner factors in a high-poverty urban middle school. *PennGSE Perspectives on Urban Education, 9*(1), 1–11. http://www.urbanedjournal.org/archive/volume-9-issue-1-fall-2011/learner-factors-high-poverty-urban-middle-school.
Olivos, E. M., Jiménez-Castellanos, O., & Ochoa, A. M. (2011). *Bicultural parent engagement: Advocacy and equity for Latino students*. Teachers College Press.
Ortiz, A. A., Robertson, P. M., Wilkinson, C. Y., Liu, Y.-J., McGhee, B. D., & Kushner, K. I. (2011). The role of bilingual education teachers in preventing inappropriate referrals of ELLs to special education: Implications for response to intervention. *Bilingual Research Journal: The Journal of the National Association for Bilingual Education, 34*(3), 316–333. https://doi.org/10.1080/15235882.2011.628608
Owens, D., Bodenhorn, N., & Bryant, R. M. (2010). Self-efficacy and multicultural competence of school counselors. *Journal of School Counseling, 8*(17).
Pang, V. O., Stein, R., Gomez, M., Matas, A., & Shimogori, Y. (2011). Cultural competencies: Essential elements of caring-centered multicultural education. *Action in Teacher Education, 33*(5-6), 560–574. https://doi.org/10.1080/01626620.2011.627050
Parkhouse, H., Lu, C. Y., & Massaro, V. R. (2019). Multicultural education professional development: A review of the literature. *Review of Educational Research, 89*(3), 416–458.
Park-Taylor, J., Walsh, M. E., & Ventura, A. B. (2007, October). Creating healthy acculturation pathways: Integrating theory and research to inform counselor's work with immigrant children. *ASCA Professional School Counseling, 11*(1), 25–34.
Rance-Roney, J. (2009). Best practices for adolescent ELLs. *Educational Leadership (ASCD): Supporting English Language Learners, 66*(7), 32–37.

Redding, S. (1997). *Quantifying the components of school community* (Publication Series No. 8; ED 419066). Mid-Atlantic Laboratory for Student Success, Temple University & National Research Center on Education in the Inner Cities. U.S. Department of Education, Office of Educational Research and Improvement.

Richards-Tutor, C., Solari, E. J., Leafstedt, J. M., Gerber, M. M., Filippini, A., & Aceves, T. C. (2013). Response to intervention for English learners: Examining models for determining response and nonresponse. *Assessment for Effective Intervention, 38*(3), 172–184. https://doi.org/10.1177/1534508412461522

Ruiz de Velasco, J., & Fix, M. (2000). *Overlooked and underserved: Immigrant students in U.S. secondary schools*. The Urban Institute.

Saldaña, J. (2021). *The coding manual for qualitative researchers* (4th ed.). Los Angeles: SAGE Publications.

Sawyer, C. B., Nelson, J. A., Marquez, J. A., & Weaver, L. (2013). Elements of a bilingual school counselor training program for Spanish speakers. *Ideas and Research you can Use: VISTAS 2013*. https://www.counseling.org/docs/default-source/vistas/elements-of-a-bilingual-school-counselor-training-program-for-spanish-speakers.pdf?sfvrsn=8

Sharp-Ross, M. (2011). *The role of ESL teacher support in facilitating school adjustment in English language learners* [Unpublished doctoral dissertation]. Philadelphia College of Osteopathic Medicine.

Smith, H. (2012). Beyond schools: Learning outside the classroom. Transforming the educational experience of young men of color. *School Counseling Series, 2*, 18–21.

Sointu, E. T., Savolainen, H., Lappalainen, K., & Lambert, M. C. (2017). Longitudinal associations of student–teacher relationships and behavioural and emotional strengths on academic achievement. *Educational Psychology, 37*(4), 457–467. https://doi.org/10.1080/01443410.2016.1165796

Souto-Manning, M. (2013). *Multicultural teaching in the early childhood classroom: Approaches, strategies, and tools*. Teachers College Press.

Suárez-Orozco, C., Suárez-Orozco, M. M., & Todorova, I. (2018). *Learning a new land: Immigrant students in American society*. Harvard University Press.

Tomlinson, C. A. (2017). *How to differentiate instruction in academically diverse classrooms* (3rd ed.). edition.). ASCD.

Valdés, G. (2001). *Learning and not learning English: Latino students in American schools*. Teachers College Press.

Wallace, D. D., & Jacoby, R. (2025). Increasing self-awareness in online students in counselor education. In A. Harrison & S. Golden (Eds.), *Culturally sustainable counseling curricula in online higher education* (pp. 31–50). IGI Global Scientific Publishing. https://doi.org/10.4018/979-8-3693-5431-5.ch002

Wang, X., Yao, C., Su, S., Yu, X., Bai, N., & Gao, S. (2024). Teacher–student relationships and coping styles in Chinese children: The chain mediating role of peer relationships and psychological Suzhi. *Behavioral Sciences, 14*(9), 797. https://doi.org/10.3390/bs14090797

Washington Office Superintendent of Public Instruction (2025). https://ospi.k12.wa.us/.

Zeleke, W. A., Hughes, T. L., & Kanyongo, G. (2021). Assessing the effectiveness of professional development training on autism and culturally responsive practice for educators and practitioners in Ethiopia. *Frontiers in Psychiatry, 11*, 583674. https://doi.org/10.3389/fpsyt.2020.583674

Appendix: Needs Assessment Tool

Themes and Guiding Questions for Discussion	3 = Very well	2 = Pretty well	1 = Not well at all	3 = Very important	2 = Somewhat important	1 = Not very important	3 = Readily available	2 = Possibly available	1 = Not readily available	
Theme 1: Connections	**How well do we already do this?**			**How important is this to us?**			**How available are resources (human and financial) under current budget?**			**What does this mean? What are the next steps? Where do we go from here?**
Sub-Theme: Connections between/across schools and programs										
Wraparound services involve enough players (school and community) to fully support MLs' social and academic needs.										
Communication and coordination between the ML program, counseling program and other programs are goal oriented and intentional.										
Teachers and counselors have adequate time to communicate and collaborate on behalf of MLs at school.										

(*Continued*)

Sub-Theme: Connections to youth				
Students find trusting relationships with counselors/teachers who are able to connect with them regardless of language and culture differences.				
Students have access to grade appropriate content regardless of their level of English language proficiency.				
MLs are able to connect to school because they perceive this space as safe and welcoming for them.				
Sub-Theme: Connections to families and communities				
Parents/Caregivers of MLs are oriented to their children's school and feel welcome in that space.				
Parents/Caregivers feel they can collaborate in their children's schooling regardless of language and cultural differences.				
Parents/Caregivers are partners in the process of exploring culturally appropriate counseling services and special education services for their children.				

(Continued)

Theme 2: Assessment and Student Data	**How well do we already do this?**	**How important is this to us?**	**How available are resources (human and financial) under current budget?**	**What does this mean? What are the next steps? Where do we go from here?**
Academic and cultural background data on MLs within the school district is accurate and readily available to teachers and counselors.				
Information on MLs is standardized within the district to facilitate interpretation across schools.				
Assessments for MLs are ongoing and differentiated for English language proficiency.				
A process or model is in place (such as RTI) to identify special education supports for MLs that also consider the cultural appropriateness of these supports				
Theme 3: Awareness of Culture and Language	**How well do we already do this?**	**How important is this to us?**	**How available are resources (human and financial) under current budget?**	**What does this mean? What are the next steps? Where do we go from here?**
Sub-Theme: Awareness of Culture				
The school district assists with on-the-job training and professional development that aims to develop multi-cultural competency among teachers and counselors.				

(Continued)

Cultural identity and acculturation are components of all students' experiences. Teachers and counselors understand, connect with, and build upon these experiences.				
Teachers' and counselors' awareness of language and culture allow them to develop culturally appropriate interventions in consultation with parents/guardians and other stakeholders.				
Sub-Theme: Awareness of Language				
Teachers and counselors use their knowledge of literacy (in English and other home languages) to promote the development of academic language for all students, especially MLs.				
Teachers and counselors use their knowledge of second (additional) language development and English language proficiency standards to differentiate content instruction and make it accessible to all learners.				

(*Continued*)

Teachers and counselors understand the social, political, and economic contexts of the languages spoken within their community and are able to advocate for students with this knowledge.				
Teachers, counselors, students and their families have ready access to translation and interpretation services and/or electronic tools when needed.				
Theme 4: Leadership, Social Justice and Efficacy	**How well do we already do this?**	**How important is this to us?**	**How available are resources (human and financial) under current budget?**	**What does this mean? What are the next steps? Where do we go from here?**
Teachers and counselors demonstrate knowledge of the immigration and/or migration experience and its impact on the lives of their students, families and communities.				
Teachers and counselors understand the allocation of resources and funding available to support MLs, and they have a voice in this process.				

(*Continued*)

Teachers' and counselors' knowledge of language policy and programs as well as their students' language needs puts them in a strong position to advocate, lead and promote equitable education.				
Programs and services are in place to adequately address, in culturally appropriate ways, the learning needs of MLs from low socio-economic households.				
The school district provides sufficient time and resources to respond to changes in curriculum and standards, demographic changes, and changes to Federal/State law, particularly related to educating Multilingual Learners.				
Administrators demonstrate a deep knowledge of language programs and policies, and they support efforts in these areas that directly benefit Multilingual Learners.				

(Continued)

Theme 5: Roles, Responsibilities and Workplace Satisfaction	**How well do we already do this?**	**How important is this to us?**	**How available are resources (human and financial) under current budget?**	**What does this mean? What are the next steps? Where do we go from here?**
MLs find mentors and connections to trusted adults in the school that are durable, lasting beyond a single school year.				
Even though counselors take on multiple responsibilities beyond counseling, their connection to MLs is intentional and balanced relative to their services for all students.				
Class sizes and caseloads are manageable to allow teachers and counselors time to connect with their MLs.				
Additional classroom support is available for teachers based on student demographics and language development needs.				

Chapter 12

AI-Powered Postsecondary Guidance for Multilingual Learners

Norma Feriz-Gordon and Andy Szeto**

Introduction

The rapid proliferation of AI in education is redefining postsecondary guidance, reshaping how students navigate transitions from high school to college and career pathways. AI-enabled systems—such as predictive analytics, personalized recommendation engines, and advising chatbots—now supplement traditional counseling by providing continuous access to information and support (Greenberg, 2025; Legatt, 2024; Najarro, 2024). For students facing linguistic or structural barriers, these technologies present both opportunities and risks. While delivering timely, personalized, and culturally responsive guidance, it also raises concerns regarding bias, data privacy, cultural sensitivity, and the potential weakening of human connections that make counseling effective.

This chapter explores how AI systems can support multilingual learners while examining the ethical and practical challenges they introduce. It considers how technology can expand access and personalize advice without replacing the trust, human judgment, and relationships central to effective postsecondary guidance. Emphasis will be placed on ethical guardrails and implementation practices that can help ensure AI inclusion and readiness for all learners. Although public discourse surrounding the use of AI in education is rapidly expanding, empirical research on its use in postsecondary guidance for multilingual learners remains limited. This chapter aims to help fill this gap and provide educators, policymakers, and researchers with insights into how AI can be leveraged responsibly for equitable postsecondary success.

Systemic Gaps in Student Access to Counseling and Postsecondary Guidance

The responsibilities of school counselors have expanded significantly, particularly since the COVID-19 pandemic. Counselors are now expected to manage annual student conferences, deliver guidance lessons focused on social-emotional

* The authors contributed equally to the development and writing of this chapter.

DOI: 10.4324/9781003711124-15

well-being, support academic and postsecondary planning, oversee attendance outreach, and provide mandated counseling for individuals and small groups. In many states, these expectations are embedded within formal mandates and educator evaluation systems, making school counseling a defined element of institutional accountability and counselor outcomes. Counselors' work extends beyond guiding students to include ongoing collaboration with parents, teachers, administrators, and service providers, especially when coordinating support for students with disabilities. At the same time, they must balance administrative, instructional, and mental health responsibilities, all of which have intensified in scope and complexity in recent years (Behl et al., 2024; Lancaster & Brasfield, 2023). They also play a critical role in safeguarding student welfare by identifying and responding to issues that impact learning, often serving as the first point of contact for families in crisis. In addition to these relational and crisis-management duties, growing administrative demands—including meetings, documentation, and participation in school-wide initiatives—have placed a substantial strain on counselors' time and capacity.

In the United States, persistent inequities in access to professional guidance continue to limit students' educational and postsecondary opportunities. According to the American School Counselor Association, although the average school counselor serves 376 students per year, several are still deprived of the individualized attention they need (ASCA, 2025). Among the 35 states that report student-to-counselor ratios in high schools, the range spans from 178:1 to 326:1 (ASCA, 2023). These figures underscore a systemic issue, with nearly one in five students in the United States—about eight million children—having no access to a school counselor (ASCA, 2019). Studies have shown that such high caseloads assigned to counselors negatively impact students' college and career trajectories, as they are significantly less likely to discuss their future plans with overburdened counselors (Woods & Domina, 2014). Further compounding the problem, high school counselors devote only about 6% of their time to career advising (National Association for College Admission Counseling, n.d.).

While there is no definitive number of hours each student requires for postsecondary guidance, experts agree that students benefit from a multi-year, scaffolded approach involving a structured sequence of postsecondary exploration and preparation (Karp et al., 2021). However, the limited time allocated by current counseling systems to postsecondary advising suggests that they are not equipped to provide equitable, comprehensive, and sustained college and career guidance for all students. This gap is particularly pronounced among marginalized populations—especially multilingual learners—who often face additional linguistic, cultural, and systemic barriers that limit their access to consistent and personalized postsecondary planning support.

Addressing the Unique Needs of Multilingual Learners in Postsecondary Success

Multilingual learners often have layered academic, linguistic, and social-emotional needs. When these needs go unaddressed, progress toward postsecondary readiness can stall despite strong motivation and potential. Many multilingual learners are adapting to new languages and cultures while coping with poverty, family separation, and/or housing instability. These intersecting challenges require coordinated and sustained guidance that extends beyond language instruction. Instead of allowing these challenges to slow down their academic trajectories, educators and counselors should use tools and strategies that improve access, efficiency, and personalized support for both students and staff. Postsecondary success depends on systems that integrate academic advising, language and identity development, career exploration, financial and digital literacy, and social-emotional supports throughout the K-12 to college pipeline.

Systemic barriers often restrict student access to social-emotional support. High student-to-counselor ratios and pressure to graduate students on time reduce counselors' opportunities for individualized advising. In many schools, limited access to psychoeducational, neuropsychological, or health evaluations—especially in upper grades—means a multilingual learner may advance without the identification of underlying learning or sensory issues. When difficulties are attributed solely to limited English proficiency, other needs remain unrecognized, perpetuating inequities in access and readiness. Adding to these challenges, many school counselors lack specialized training or institutional support for working effectively with multilingual learners. A *School Counselor* newsletter article points out that counselors frequently lack preparation in cultural competence and in serving multilingual students and their families (Bell, 2019).

Multilingual learners are often excluded from advanced or college-preparatory courses because of restrictive placement policies and misconceptions about their abilities (Kanno & Kangas, 2014). Some counselors carry a stigma that advanced or honors classes are inappropriate for multilingual learners, steering them away from challenging coursework. Even after accounting for differences in language, background, socioeconomic status, and academic factors, significant gaps persist in the course enrollment patterns of high school students, with English learners having access to fewer rigorous academic opportunities (Callahan & Shifrer, 2016). As Kanno (2021) notes, once students are identified as English learners, their opportunity to learn rigorous academic content is often greatly compromised. These beliefs and practices collectively limit multilingual learners' engagement in challenging academic learning and undermine their preparation for higher education and careers.

Addressing these challenges requires a multi-year, scaffolded approach to postsecondary guidance that sequences advising, exploration, and planning across grade levels. Integrating academic, linguistic, and culturally responsive support with technology such as translation tools, multilingual chatbots, and predictive analytics can extend counselors' reach and ensure timely, equitable guidance. True postsecondary equity will emerge when schools view linguistic and cultural diversity not as obstacles but as assets that strengthen multilingual learners' college and career pathways.

Empowering School Counselors to Support Multilingual Learners' Postsecondary Readiness

School counselors play a vital role in promoting access and equity for multilingual learners by creating inclusive, linguistically responsive systems of support (de Oliveira & Wachter Morris, 2015). As the first point of contact for many families navigating unfamiliar educational systems, counselors help bridge communication gaps and build trust. Bell (2019) emphasizes that effective support begins with strengthening family engagement through interpreters, translated materials, and community partnerships that honor students' languages and cultures. Counselors must also ensure that multilingual learners are placed in courses that reflect their true potential rather than perceived language limitations, while actively advocating for their inclusion in advanced and college-preparatory pathways. In addition, colleges must arrange support programs, particularly for students who migrated during their adolescence and spent only a limited amount of time in high school before transitioning to their postsecondary education.

To sustain this level of advocacy and responsiveness, counselors must be equipped with specialized preparation and ongoing professional learning (de Oliveira & Wachter Morris, 2015). The complex responsibility of supporting multilingual learners requires empathy, advocacy, cultural competence, data literacy, and systems-level awareness. As schools continue to diversify, counselors increasingly serve as cultural brokers, interpreters of policy, and instructional partners. These responsibilities require targeted training and institutional support that extend beyond traditional counseling preparation graduate programs.

Building on this, Watkinson et al. (2022) highlight the importance of counselor preparation programs that develop cultural competence through experiential and multicultural training. Such preparation enables counselors to interpret the needs of multilingual learners more accurately, provide tailored academic and social-emotional guidance, and connect families to essential resources. Ultimately, school counselors serve as advocates who help multilingual learners overcome systemic barriers and chart meaningful postsecondary pathways. They also play a critical role in fostering belonging and school adjustment through accurate course placement, peer mentoring, small-group supports, and family engagement, all of which build confidence and readiness for postsecondary education and career (Colorado Department of Education, 2023).

As the educational landscape evolves, school counselors also need to develop the capacity to use AI tools ethically and effectively. Professional learning should include ongoing coaching, peer collaboration, and the integration of technology within established counseling frameworks such as the ASCA Mindsets and Behaviors. These efforts would ensure that counselors are equipped to use AI to enhance—rather than replace—the human relationships that are central to effective guidance.

At the systems level, successful implementation of AI tools requires coordination beyond individual schools. In large states and districts, cross-office collaboration is essential. Ensuring multilingual access requires alignment among translation units, technology offices, and counseling departments; the integration of AI tools follows the same principle. District-level leadership must drive this initiative by addressing equitable procurement, compliance, training, and community trust. The COVID-19 pandemic highlighted the criticality of technology access for student success and exposed the disparities in device availability and connectivity. Many districts continue to grapple with sustaining these systems and managing repairs, replacements, and upgrades so that all students, including multilingual learners, can fully benefit from emerging AI tools designed to support students' college and career readiness.

AI as an Enhancement, Not a Replacement

Emerging applications of AI demonstrate the potential for expanding the capacity of school counselors and postsecondary professionals to deliver more personalized and equitable support to students. As Jarudi and Sinha (2024) note, AI tools can enable counselors to reach more students by automating routine communication and analysis tasks, allowing them to focus on direct, meaningful student support. Further, tools such as AI-powered translation systems and adaptive advising platforms can help identify student strengths, monitor progress, and connect learners with academic and/or mental health resources. Yet, even the most advanced technologies cannot replicate the professional judgment, empathy, and relational trust that define effective school counseling. Therefore, AI should be used responsibly to enhance rather than replace human expertise, offering additional layers of insight and access. Its success, however, depends on digital literacy, ethical use, and ongoing human supervision to ensure that technology remains a tool for empowerment rather than substitution.

Case Study: AI-Enhanced Postsecondary Advising for Multilingual Learners

Composite scenario developed for educational purposes; identifying details have been altered to protect confidentiality.

Mamadou was an 18-year-old student from West Africa who arrived in the United States midway through secondary school. Motivated to continue his education, he had to decide whether to complete his high school diploma or pursue a GED while learning English and navigating a complex new system of college and career pathways.

Although Mamadou demonstrated strong motivation, analytical ability, and curiosity, his progress was limited by information gaps and unfamiliar terminology. Concepts such as *associate degree, Free Application for Federal Student Aid (FAFSA), dual enrollment,* and *credit accumulation* had no direct equivalents in his home language. To address these challenges, Mamadou's counselor adopted a multilayered AI-assisted advising approach that combined translation, tutoring, writing support, adaptive planning, and predictive insight within a human-centered counseling framework.

During the initial sessions, the counselor used AI translation and summarization systems to clarify key terms and generate simplified explanations of financial aid documents, graduation requirements, and local college options. A summarization feature converted district-approved materials into concise, multilingual overviews, allowing Mamadou to digest at his own pace and return with questions. These tools deepened his comprehension and strengthened his ownership of the planning process. A complementary AI knowledge base for families, built from district-vetted materials, enabled his parents to access accurate, translated information about graduation requirements and college pathways. This system facilitated the family's fuller participation in Mamadou's decision-making and reduced confusion caused by language barriers.

As Mamadou's understanding grew, the counselor introduced AI tutoring platforms to reinforce academic and language development. These systems provided adaptive feedback on reading and writing assignments, guided practice for college entrance exams, and helped build Mamadou's confidence in academic English. Mamadou also used AI writing assistants to strengthen his personal statements and scholarship essays. The writing tools provided structure, language feedback, and organization prompts that complemented the counselor's review, supporting the development of both writing skills and self-expression.

The counselor also integrated an AI-powered advising platform that offered daily prompts, reminders, and personalized check-ins in Mamadou's preferred language. The adaptive system generated customized recommendations aligned with his career interests and learning goals, translating complex college search information into culturally responsive guidance.

In the background, a predictive analytics dashboard supported the counselor in monitoring equity indicators such as course enrollment, GPA trends, and financial aid completion among multilingual learners. These insights guided timely interventions and helped identify potential barriers, ensuring that Mamadou remained on track academically and emotionally.

Throughout this process, the counselor supervised AI assistance and maintained ethical guardrails. Each AI-generated translation, summary, and recommendation was verified for accuracy, relevance, and cultural appropriateness. Sensitive data was protected in accordance with privacy regulations and local policy. When systems produced ambiguous or biased outputs, the counselor used these moments as opportunities to model digital literacy and critical thinking—helping Mamadou learn how to question, interpret, and verify digital information.

This approach produced tangible results: Mamadou successfully completed his diploma program, applied to two local community colleges, and was accepted into a healthcare certificate track. More importantly, he reported feeling "seen" and empowered, describing the technology not as a replacement for his counselor but as "a second advisor that speaks my language." Mamadou also felt empowered to enroll in a college program to advance his language development.

Reflection Questions

1 How did the counselor preserve the human relationship at the center of Mamadou's advising experience while integrating multiple AI tools?
2 What risks might arise from AI-generated translations or simplified summaries, and how should counselors mitigate them?
3 What safeguards must be in place to prevent over-reliance on algorithmic recommendations?

Translation and Communication Tools

Translation and communication barriers remain a persistent challenge in school counseling, particularly for multilingual learners and their families. These obstacles undermine equitable access to information and meaningful participation in educational decision-making. Between 2013 and 2023, nearly 4,000 federal complaints were filed regarding schools' failure to provide adequate translation or interpretation services for non-English-speaking families (Geduld, 2024). These lapses included excluding parents from special education meetings and limiting their access to counseling and college-and-career guidance, revealing a broader national pattern of inequitable language access in education.

This issue has become more acute following the recent policy changes that have reduced funding for language access services. Napolitano (2025) reports that translation and interpretation programs for multilingual learners faced significant funding reductions, weakening schools' capacity to communicate effectively with families in their home languages. As a result, many districts now struggle to meet even basic compliance requirements. These conditions make it essential for schools to adopt innovative, sustainable, and ethically grounded approaches, such as AI-assisted translation and communication platforms, to ensure that all families remain informed and engaged in their children's educational decision-making.

Traditional translation services at the school or district level are often inadequate to meet the scope and urgency of daily communication needs. External materials, including state and federal documents, are often not translated, placing additional strain on already overextended translation units. Consequently, essential information about academic programs, consent forms, and postsecondary opportunities may remain inaccessible to families whose primary language is not English, perpetuating inequities in educational participation and decision-making.

AI offers promising tools to expand schools' capacity for multilingual communication. Many critical educational and financial documents, such as the FAFSA, are currently available only in a limited number of languages, leaving families who speak less commonly represented languages without equitable access to essential information. With more than 350 languages spoken across the United States, and estimates reaching as high as 430 (Translators without Borders, n.d.), districts must use AI responsibly to bridge these gaps. The 1974 Supreme Court case *Lau v. Nichols* established that true equality in education requires meaningful language support, not just identical materials. This principle remains vital in the AI era. Districts must ensure that AI-driven translation systems are accurate, culturally responsive, and guided by human oversight. Language access is not a convenience; it is a civil right and a cornerstone of educational equity.

AI-based translation systems can help schools communicate across a broader range of languages and formats. When implemented with cultural and linguistic sensitivity, these tools make critical resources accessible, provide families with timely updates in their preferred language, and strengthen trust between schools and multilingual communities. For example, AI can support counselors and administrators by drafting communications, summarizing documents, or generating provisional translations when official resources are unavailable, while remaining transparent about the unofficial status of these translations (Sabella, 2025).

Emerging technologies such as NotebookLM enhance accessibility further by transforming complex documents into concise summaries or multimedia overviews in multiple languages. Schools can use these features to generate clear, understandable explanations of state or federal guidance in over 50 audio languages and 80 video formats (Google, 2025a, 2025b). Similarly, AI-powered design platforms allow schools to produce culturally responsive flyers, infographics, and social media posts that reflect the diversity of their communities. By combining linguistic inclusivity with visual representation, schools foster deeper trust and sustained engagement.

AI also enhances the inclusivity of live and virtual events. Schools and districts can now host financial aid workshops, college fairs, and family nights using real-time translation and captioning tools that allow attendees to follow along in their preferred language. They can also share clear instructions and platform guides in families' home languages before the event to help attendees learn how to access and navigate features such as breakout rooms or interpretation channels. Without this preparation, families may experience confusion or delays, which can discourage participation and lead some to rely solely on in-person meetings, despite many postsecondary events having moved online. In-person accessibility is also improving. Devices like Apple AirPods now support Live Translation, enabling real-time multilingual conversations without the need for a human interpreter (Apple, 2025).

Tools such as NotebookLM can be used to develop custom knowledge bases for multilingual families, drawing from district-approved resources such as handbooks and program guides. As these systems draw only from vetted local content, they reduce misinformation while providing families with on-demand answers in their home language. This creates a more inclusive and accessible communication ecosystem where human relationships remain central, and technology amplifies equity rather than replacing human connection (Table 12.1).

Table 12.1 Prospects for AI applications in translation and communication for postsecondary guidance

Application	*Description*
Translation of essential materials	AI translation tools can be used to provide college applications, financial aid forms, and program information in multilingual versions so families can access critical details in their home languages.
Summarization of complex information	AI-powered platforms such as NotebookLM can be used to generate concise, family-friendly summaries and video or audio versions of dense documents like FAFSA instructions or graduation requirements.
Enhancement of family communication	AI can be used to draft, translate, and distribute newsletters, reminders, and counseling updates so families receive timely and comprehensible messages.
Live interpretation	AI-powered captioning and real-time translation and interpretation tools can be integrated during counseling meetings, family nights, and college events to encourage full participation.
Development of culturally responsive materials	Multilingual flyers, infographics, and social media posts can be designed using AI design platforms to ensure materials reflect community diversity and inclusion.
Maintenance of information hubs	AI-driven knowledge bases can be built and trained on district-approved materials so families can ask questions and receive accurate, localized responses in multiple languages.
Monitoring of language access equity	AI analytics can be used to identify which languages, materials, or events remain underserved and adjust outreach efforts to ensure all families have equitable access to guidance and information.

Adaptive Advising and Personalized Guidance

An executive order titled *Advancing Artificial Intelligence Education for American Youth* was issued at the federal level in 2025, outlining national priorities for integrating AI across K-12 and postsecondary education. The initiative specifically highlights the role of AI in supporting "college and career pathway exploration, advising, and navigation" (The White House, 2025). Building on this vision, a growing number of AI platforms now provide multilingual, evidence-based college and career guidance at scale. Some feature interactive chat systems that help learners explore options, set goals, and track readiness in multiple languages (García Mathewson, 2025).

Recent national data show that nearly half of high school students use AI-powered assistants on college websites, with usage peaking among ninth and tenth graders (Levitz et al., 2025). One-third of them report using AI tools such as ChatGPT to explore careers, colleges, and scholarships, and/or for essay writing assistance (Levitz & TeenVoice, 2025). This early adoption suggests that AI has already become integral to how students envision and prepare for their postsecondary futures.

Predictive analytics and conversational AI technologies are increasingly being integrated into college and career counseling systems to help students and educators make more informed decisions. In addition to postsecondary advising, AI tools are now being used to help students select appropriate courses and educational pathways aligned with their long-term goals. These systems can analyze prior achievement, language proficiency, and student interests to recommend courses that balance challenge and support, ensuring learners remain on track for graduation and future opportunities. Some platforms also analyze historical application data to estimate a student's likelihood of admission, helping counselors and families build balanced college lists and make evidence-based choices regarding postsecondary education.

Other systems use algorithmic matching models to evaluate institutions against students' goals, academic interests, financial constraints, and preferred learning environments, generating personalized recommendations aligned with individual priorities (Greenberg, 2025). AI-powered chat platforms provide scalable and on-demand advising, making expert guidance more accessible to schools and districts facing counselor shortages (Legatt, 2024). These technologies can be particularly valuable for multilingual learners by reducing bias and guesswork, translating complex admissions data into accessible formats, and supporting equitable participation in postsecondary planning.

Some tools also employ behaviorally intelligent chat systems that deliver timely and empathetic reminders to guide students through financial aid, scholarship, and application processes. These innovations expand access to quality advising and make career development more inclusive and equitable for diverse global learners. Their adaptive design tailors guidance to each student's progress, interests, and goals, ensuring that support remains relevant over time. By offering personalized insights and actionable next steps, these systems empower students and families to make informed decisions about education and career pathways.

AI-Powered Advising for Multilingual Learners: Five Emerging Supports

1. **Language-Responsive Guidance**
   AI platforms now offer college and career advising in multiple languages, using translation and interpretation tools that help families access accurate information without delay.
2. **Culturally Relevant Recommendations**
   Adaptive systems can integrate student interests, language backgrounds, and prior experiences to suggest courses and pathways aligned with multilingual learners' strengths.
3. **Predictive Insights for Equitable Planning**
   Predictive analytics help counselors and families understand admission probabilities and financial aid options, reducing bias and supporting informed postsecondary decisions.
4. **Accessible, Always-On Advising**
   AI chat systems provide 24/7 multilingual support, answering questions about applications, scholarships, and deadlines in real time—bridging gaps where counselor access is limited.
5. **Empathetic and Inclusive Communication**
   Behaviorally intelligent chat tools deliver reminders and encouragement in students' home languages, ensuring that guidance remains personal, culturally sensitive, and sustained over time.

Addressing Admission Barriers Using AI

Standardized exam scores pose a significant challenge for many marginalized students, restricting their access to scholarships, selective programs, and college admissions. While affluent students often benefit from private tutoring, early test preparation, and individualized counseling; those from under-resourced communities face inequities that compound over time. Factors such as trauma, learning disabilities, limited English proficiency, and financial resources further hinder readiness and performance. For multilingual learners, language barriers can delay appropriate interventions and limit access to enrichment opportunities, especially in schools without bilingual or culturally competent staff.

To help mitigate these disparities, schools and districts can integrate equitable, AI-supported tutoring and preparation tools that personalize learning and extend academic support beyond the traditional classroom. Initiatives such as Khan Academy's Khanmigo, which leverages AI to guide SAT preparation, demonstrate how adaptive technology can scaffold instruction and provide individualized feedback to meet diverse learning needs (Thaler, 2024). Similarly, AI writing coaches are emerging as valuable tools that can help students strengthen their college admission essays as well as other academic writing. These platforms can guide students through idea generation, structure, and draft revisions while providing language feedback essential for multilingual learners.

Human-Centered Guardrails and Ethical Integration

While AI can expand access to postsecondary guidance, it also poses significant risks if implemented without ethical guardrails. When schools adopt AI systems without a clear commitment to accuracy, equity, and cultural sensitivity, the very tools intended to expand access may deepen existing inequities. Translation and advising technologies may improve communication for multilingual learners and families; yet errors in translation or interpretation can distort meaning, overlook cultural nuances, and lead to misunderstanding or misinformation. Therefore, continuous human oversight is essential to verify accuracy, ensure contextual and cultural appropriateness, and prevent overreliance on automation. Regular monitoring is also essential to detect and correct bias, as algorithms may unintentionally generate unequal recommendations, such as offering fewer STEM pathways or advanced coursework options to multilingual learners. Consistent bias audits are the cornerstone of equitable and culturally responsive decision-making.

Protecting sensitive student information is equally critical. AI systems process extensive personal and academic data, including language proficiency performance results, grades, and demographic details, all of which require strict safeguards against misuse or unauthorized access. Without strong privacy protections, multilingual learners may be particularly vulnerable to data misuse or profiling that perpetuates systemic inequities. To ensure compliance and accountability, schools and districts should require vendors to adhere to privacy regulations such as Family Educational Rights and Privacy Act (FERPA), local language access laws, and accessibility mandates. Clear policies emphasizing transparency, bias auditing, and human oversight, supported by sustained funding for equitable technology integration are essential for strengthening trust and ensuring implementation fidelity. Educators and counselors also need training not only to understand how AI tools collect and analyze information but also to interpret results through a lens of cultural competence and linguistic diversity.

For multilingual learners, the introduction of AI into the college admission process highlights how these technologies can unintentionally reinforce linguistic and cultural bias. As many systems rely on historical data sets that often fail to represent diverse linguistic and cultural experiences, learners from multilingual backgrounds may be underrepresented or misjudged. Although AI tools can assist with applications such as essay drafting, they may also introduce new forms of inequity by penalizing variations in expression, tone, or narrative style (Evaristo,

2023). Recent findings from Stanford University: Human-Centered Artificial Intelligence (2023) underscore this risk, showing that AI detectors are significantly more likely to misclassify writing by non-native English speakers as AI-generated, reinforcing linguistic bias and inequitable evaluation. These patterns reveal that even well-intentioned AI tools can harm multilingual learners by reproducing narrow assumptions about what counts as "good" English, "authentic" writing, or "college-ready" communication. Ensuring culturally sensitive human review within these processes is therefore vital to maintain fairness and inclusivity.

The need for equity audits and stronger data systems remains pressing. AI-assisted dashboards can help identify disparities in course enrollment, financial aid application, and scholarship access; yet many remain underdeveloped or underused. When designed without cultural and linguistic awareness, these systems risk normalizing biased patterns in data and decision-making. Conversely, when built with an equity and inclusion framework, such systems can transform data into actionable insights, helping schools close opportunity gaps instead of exacerbating them.

Five Key Steps to Ensure Human-Centered, Ethical AI Integration

1. **Establish Clear Ethical Guardrails**
   Adopt district-wide principles that prioritize accuracy, equity, and cultural sensitivity in all AI tools. Evaluate technologies for how they handle multilingual data, translation, and advising functions before implementation.
2. **Maintain Continuous Human Oversight**
   Never delegate final judgment to automation. Conduct regular human reviews to verify translation accuracy, contextual meaning, and cultural appropriateness. Audit algorithms for bias that may restrict course or program options for multilingual learners.
3. **Protect Student Data and Privacy**
   Audit all AI systems for compliance with FERPA, local language access laws, and accessibility mandates. Safeguard sensitive information such as language proficiency, demographic details, and academic records from misuse or profiling.
4. **Build Capacity Through Professional Learning**
   Train educators, counselors, and administrators to interpret AI outputs through a lens of cultural competence and linguistic diversity. Equip staff to recognize both the potential and the limitations of AI-generated insights when guiding multilingual learners.
5. **Conduct Ongoing Equity and Bias Audits**
   Use AI-assisted dashboards paired with human analysis to identify disparities in enrollment, FAFSA completion, and scholarship access. Conduct regular equity audits to ensure AI systems close opportunity gaps rather than reinforce them.

Artificial intelligence (AI) has the potential to enhance postsecondary guidance, but only when designed and used responsibly. For multilingual learners who have long faced systemic barriers, AI can amplify inequity or expand opportunity, depending on how cultural sensitivity and human oversight are embedded in its design. As Barnard (2024) cautions, the emerging "AI revolution" in college admissions must incorporate transparency, bias safeguards, and ethical review to ensure that innovation truly democratizes opportunity rather than codifies exclusion.

Ultimately, AI's role in education must be guided by a shared moral compass grounded in empathy, trust, and cultural responsiveness. Technology should complement, not replace, human care, preserving the relationships and cultural understanding that anchor meaningful guidance. By embedding fairness, inclusion, and dignity into every layer of innovation, schools can ensure that multilingual learners are not only accessing postsecondary pathways but also being understood, valued, and supported within them.

References

American School Counselor Association (2019, February). *School counselors matter.* https://www.schoolcounselor.org/getmedia/b079d17d-6265-4166-a120-3b1f56077649/School-Counselors-Matter.pdf

American School Counselor Association (2023). *ASCA research report: School and district administrators and the school counselor role.* https://www.schoolcounselor.org/getmedia/22407831-42f9-46da-8fe9-f5ffb64ee285/asca-research-report-admin.pdf

American School Counselor Association (2025). *School counselor roles & ratios.* https://www.schoolcounselor.org/about-school-counseling/school-counselor-roles-ratios

Apple. (2025, September 15). *New Apple Intelligence features are available today.* https://www.apple.com/newsroom/2025/09/new-apple-intelligence-features-are-available-today/

Barnard, B. (2024, September 17). College admission: An AI revolution. *Forbes.* https://www.forbes.com/sites/brennanbarnard/2024/09/17/college-admission-an-ai-revolution/

Behl, M., Green, L., Garcia, E., & Laux, J. (2024). Learning from the pandemic: School counsellor experience during the pandemic in the United States. *Journal of Psychologists and Counsellors in Schools, 34*(3), 319–333. https://doi.org/10.1177/20556365241268897

Bell, H. (2019, October). *How school counselors can support English learners.* ASCA School Counselor Magazine. https://www.schoolcounselor.org/Newsletters/November-2019/How-School-Counselors-Can-Support-English-Learners

Callahan, R. M., & Shifrer, D. (2016). Equitable access for secondary English learner students: Course taking as evidence of EL program effectiveness. *Educational Administration Quarterly, 52*(3), 463–496. https://doi.org/10.1177/0013161X16648190

Colorado Department of Education. (2023). *English language development guidebook: Designing, delivering, and evaluating instruction and services for multilingual learners (Chapter 9: Understanding secondary multilingual learners).* https://www.cde.state.co.us/cde_english/eldguidebook

de Oliveira, L. C., & Wachter Morris, C. (2015). *Preparing school counselors for English language learners*. TESOL Press.

Evaristo, E. (2023, December 4). Balancing the potentials and pitfalls of AI in college admissions. *USC Rossier School of Education*. https://rossier.usc.edu/news-insights/news/balancing-potentials-and-pitfalls-ai-college-admissions

García Mathewson, T. (2025, March 4). AI chatbots can cushion the high school counselor shortage—but are they bad for students? *CalMatters*. https://calmatters.org/education/k-12-education/2025/03/school-counselors-ai-chatbots/

Geduld, A. (2024, September 19). Left powerless: Non-English–speaking parents denied vital translation services. *The 74*. https://www.the74million.org/article/left-powerless-non-english-speaking-parents-denied-vital-translation-services/

Google. (2025a, April 29). *NotebookLM audio overviews are now available in over 50 languages*. https://blog.google/technology/google-labs/notebooklm-audio-overviews-50-languages

Google. (2025b, August 25). *NotebookLM's video overviews are now available in 80 languages globally*. https://blog.google/technology/google-labs/notebook-lm-audio-video-overviews-more-languages-longer-content/

Greenberg, J. (2025, June 20). How AI is helping students find the right college. *WIRED*. https://www.wired.com/story/how-ai-is-helping-kids-find-the-right-college

Jarudi, I., & Sinha, P. (2024, July 9). Opinion: School counselors are scarce, but AI could play an important role in helping them reach more students. *The Hechinger Report*. https://hechingerreport.org/opinion-school-counselors-are-scarce-but-ai-could-play-an-important-role-in-helping-them-reach-more-students/

Kanno, Y. (2021). *English learners' access to postsecondary education: Neither college nor career ready*. Multilingual Matters.

Kanno, Y., & Kangas, S. E. N. (2014). "I'm not going to be, like, for the AP": English language learners. *American Educational Research Journal, 51*(5), 848–878. https://doi.org/10.3102/0002831214544716

Karp, M., Ackerson, S., Cheng, I., Cocatre-Zilgien, E., Costelloe, S., Freeman, B., Lemire, S., Linderman, D., McFarlane, B., Moulton, S., O'Shea, J., Porowski, A., & Richburg-Hayes, L. (2021). *Effective advising for postsecondary students. A practice guide for educators (WWC 2022003)*. National Center for Education Evaluation and Regional Assistance (NCEE), Institute of Education Sciences, U.S. Department of Education. https://ies.ed.gov/ncee/wwc/Docs/PracticeGuide/WWC-practice-guide-advising-full-text.pdf

Lancaster, C., & Brasfield, M. W. (2023). school counseling in the aftermath of COVID-19: Perspectives of school counselors in Tennessee. *The Professional Counselor (TPC), 13*(2), 60–76.

Legatt, A. (2024, May 7). Pioneering AI addresses school, college counseling gaps. *Forbes*. https://www.forbes.com/sites/avivalegatt/2024/05/07/pioneering-ai-addresses-school-college-counseling-gaps

Levitz, R. N. & TeenVoice (2025). *The AI divide in college planning: Student adoption, resistance, and impact*. RNL.

Levitz, R. N., Halda, & Modern Campus. (2025). *2025 E-Expectations® trend report: Exploring college-bound high school students' online experiences, expectations, and behaviors*. RNL.

Najarro, I. (2024, October 23). This counselor used AI to help students apply to college. Here's how. *Education Week*. https://www.edweek.org/technology/this-counselor-used-ai-to-help-students-apply-to-college-heres-how/2024/10

Napolitano, J. (2025, October 1). Trump targeting services for multilingual learners leaves gaps in schools. *The 74*. https://www.the74million.org/article/trump-targeting-services-for-multilingual-learners-leaves-gaps-in-schools/

National Association for College Admission Counseling (n.d.). *School Counseling: Caseloads and Responsibilities.* https://www.nacacnet.org/school-counseling/

Sabella, R. A. (2025, January). *Exploring AI for communicating and connecting.* American School Counselor Association. https://www.schoolcounselor.org/Newsletters/January-2025/Exploring-AI-for-Communicating-and-Connecting

Stanford University: Human-Centered Artificial Intelligence (2023, May 15). *AI-detectors biased against non-native English writers.* https://hai.stanford.edu/news/ai-detectors-biased-against-non-native-english-writers

Thaler, S. (2024, June 3). *Unlocking success: How AI teacher tools enhance SAT preparation.* Khan Academy Blog. https://blog.khanacademy.org/ai-sat-prep/

The White House (2025, April 23). *Advancing artificial intelligence education for American youth.* https://www.whitehouse.gov/presidential-actions/2025/04/advancing-artificial-intelligence-education-for-american-youth/

Translators without Borders (n.d.). *Language data for the United States of America.* https://translatorswithoutborders.org/language-data-for-the-united-states-of-america#:~:text=There%20are%20between%20350%20and,other%20indigenous%20languages%20as%20official

Watkinson, J. S., Shi, Q., Slezak, H., & Litvin, R. (2022). Preparing future school counselors to work with English language learners. *Journal of Counselor Preparation and Supervision, 16*(1). https://research.library.kutztown.edu/jcps/vol16/iss1/6

Woods, C. S., & Domina, T. (2014). The school counselor caseload and the high school-to-college pipeline. *Teachers College Record: The Voice of Scholarship in Education, 116*(10), 1–30. https://doi.org/10.1177/016146811411601006

Chapter 13

Training and Professional Development for School Counselors to Support Multilingual Learners

Chelsea Hilliard, Jennifer Scaturo Watkinson, and Qi Shi

Introduction

School counselors should work within a Multi-Tiered System of Support (MTSS) when providing services to their students (Goodman-Scott et al., 2023). Utilizing an MTSS framework, school counselors attend to prevention, intervention, and collaborative or wrap-around care to meet the unique needs of all students, particularly those who need more specialized support. Although described in more detail further into this chapter, for context, Tier 1 includes interventions for all students, Tier 2 includes interventions for some students, and Tier 3 includes interventions that are more detailed and tailored to individual student needs, all of which need to be implemented with the unique needs of specialized student populations in mind. One such population is multilingual learners (MLs).

School counselors lean on their masters-level preparation in multicultural counseling, prevention, intervention, and collaboration to positively impact how MLs experience school. Second, school counselors are members of a larger educational team that could be made up of members from the community and the school building. Specifically, when working to support ML students, school counselors share their expertise and rely on the expertise of other members of the educational team. Cultural competence and self-awareness are foundational to school counseling. Counselors must critically examine their own beliefs, values, and lived experiences to better understand how these factors influence their professional interactions (Holcomb-McCoy, 2021; Sue & Sue, 2016). Implicit biases can unconsciously shape expectations and decision-making, affecting students' academic and socio-emotional development (Chao, 2012). By engaging in reflective practice, school counselors can challenge biases, develop cultural humility, and build meaningful relationships with students (Constantine, 2002; Ratts et al., 2016).

School counselors play a key role in implementing interventions aligned with a MTSS to address students' social-emotional, academic, and career needs (ASCA, 2021). Tier 1 focuses on school-wide prevention strategies, such as classroom instruction and community partnerships, which can improve student outcomes, including attendance and emotional regulation (Villares et al., 2024).

DOI: 10.4324/9781003711124-16

Tier 2 involves targeted support through small group counseling and collaboration with teachers and families to enhance academic performance and social-emotional well-being (Shi et al., 2023; Steen et al., 2017). Tier 3 interventions provide individualized support for students with chronic or complex needs, often requiring collaboration with educators and specialists (Purgason et al., 2023).

As a member of a larger educational team, school counselors are not isolated in their efforts, rather, they work collaboratively to meet the needs of ML students. Given their extensive caseloads, school counselors must effectively collaborate with educators, families, and community stakeholders to support student success. However, research suggests that counselors' assumptions about their roles may hinder proactive collaboration (Watkinson et al., 2025). Structured collaborative models, such as those outlined by Tuttle et al. (2018) and Moore-Thomas & Day-Vines (2010), provide frameworks for goal setting, shared responsibilities, and overcoming barriers to collaboration. Additionally, training in role clarification can help school counselors integrate collaboration into their practice.

Our position on the role of school counselors in supporting ML students comes from the literature and our own experiences as counselor educators and school counselors. This position informs our professional development (PD) recommendations and guides the framework for this chapter, which we have categorized into three distinct pathways. To effectively support students, and more specifically MLs, school counselors must engage in continuous professional growth. This chapter will go further into detail exploring three pathways we have identified and outlined to ensure school counselors are fully trained and prepared to work with MLs: Knowledge of Self, Prevention and Intervention, and Professional Development Specific to Collaboration.

Pathway One: Knowledge of Self

Cultural competence and self-awareness are foundational elements in effective counseling, particularly in school settings where students come from diverse backgrounds. Sue and Sue (2016) emphasize that for counselors to provide meaningful support, they must first understand their own biases, values, and cultural identities. These personal elements influence how counselors interpret and respond to their clients, especially in cross-cultural contexts. By developing cultural competence, counselors can recognize and challenge these biases, thereby improving their ability to connect with students in an empathetic and culturally responsive way. For school counselors, engaging in continuous self-reflection is crucial to this process. Holcomb-McCoy (2021) highlighted the importance of recognizing how a counselor's personal experiences, such as their upbringing, race, ethnicity, or socioeconomic status, shape their perceptions of students from different backgrounds. This self-awareness allows counselors to approach each student with an open mind, avoiding assumptions and fostering a more inclusive, supportive environment. Ultimately, when counselors are aware of their cultural influences and remain reflective in their practice, they are better equipped to build trust, advocate for their students, and create interventions that are sensitive to the unique needs of each individual.

Implicit Bias and Counselor Self-Knowledge

Implicit bias plays a significant role in shaping how counselors perceive and interact with students, often without conscious awareness. Research by Chao (2012) suggested that these unconscious biases can affect a counselor's interpretations of students' behaviors, academic potential, and socio-emotional needs. For instance, a counselor might unknowingly hold stereotypes about a student's race, gender, or socioeconomic background, which influences their expectations or approach to interventions. Such biases limit the counselor's ability to provide equitable support, as they may unintentionally favor certain students over others or misinterpret behaviors that are culturally or contextually specific. Therefore, recognizing and addressing implicit bias is crucial to ensuring that counseling practices are fair and that all students have the opportunity to thrive. One effective way to address implicit bias is through self-awareness training, which helps counselors become more attuned to their biases and understand how these biases influence their professional practice. Ratts et al. (2016) highlighted that such training empowers counselors to engage in introspection and develop strategies to mitigate bias, ultimately fostering more equitable counseling relationships. By engaging in regular self-reflection and learning about the ways implicit bias operates, counselors become more conscious of their responses to students and make a concerted effort to create inclusive and supportive environments. School counselors who are reflective and proactively engage in self-knowledge exercises set themselves up to be more effective when offering culturally responsive services, ensuring that every student receives the attention and support they need to succeed.

Multicultural and Social Justice Counseling

The Multicultural and Social Justice Counseling Competencies (MSJCC) framework provides a comprehensive approach to counseling that emphasizes the importance of understanding the complex interplay of privilege, power, and social identities. According to Ratts et al. (2016), counselors should engage in a critical examination of their own privileges and power dynamics to better understand how these factors impact their interactions with clients, particularly those from historically marginalized backgrounds. By acknowledging their position in the social hierarchy, counselors are better equipped to recognize and challenge systemic inequalities that may affect their students. This self-examination is not only crucial for effective counseling but also for advocating for social change within the educational environment.

Self-awareness is the cornerstone of this process, as it allows counselors to recognize their own biases, assumptions, and blind spots. For counselors working with historically marginalized students, this level of self-awareness is essential for advocating on their behalf and promoting equity within the school system. When counselors take the time to reflect on how their own experiences and social identities shape their worldview, they are better able to empathize with students facing oppression and discrimination. This foundational awareness helps counselors become more effective advocates, ensuring that marginalized voices are heard and that students receive the support they need to overcome barriers and succeed. Through the lens of multicultural and social justice counseling, counselors can work toward creating an inclusive environment where all students feel valued and empowered.

Impact on Student Relationships and Outcomes

When school counselors engage in self-awareness practices, they are better equipped to build strong, trusting relationships with their students. Holcomb-McCoy (2005) emphasizes that self-awareness allows counselors to recognize their biases, assumptions, and emotional reactions, which in turn enables them to engage with students in a more genuine and empathetic way. This trust is foundational to creating a safe and supportive counseling environment, where students feel comfortable sharing their challenges and seeking guidance. When students sense that their counselor is attentive, reflective, and nonjudgmental, they are more likely to open up, resulting in a deeper, more effective counselor-student relationship. Additionally, research by Constantine (2002) highlighted that students from diverse backgrounds felt more supported and understood when their counselors demonstrated cultural humility and a willingness to learn from their experiences. Cultural humility involves recognizing that one's knowledge of another's culture is always limited and being open to learning from students themselves. When counselors show openness and curiosity about their students' unique cultural perspectives, students feel validated, respected, and valued for who they are. This approach not only enhances the counselor-student relationship but also has a positive impact on students' academic and socio-emotional outcomes. Students who feel seen and understood are more likely to engage in school, build resilience, and achieve success. Thus, self-awareness and cultural humility are essential for fostering inclusive and supportive environments where all students can thrive.

Knowledge of Self

For school counselors to effectively support diverse students, it is essential that they possess a deep knowledge of themselves, which includes awareness of their own beliefs, dispositions, intersectional identities, and cultural backgrounds. This awareness is critical because counselors' personal identities and experiences influence how they perceive and interact with students, especially those from backgrounds different from their own. As Khalifa et al. (2016) and Ratts and Greenleaf (2018) suggest, counselors must examine how their individual power dynamics, privileges, and biases may impact their work with students. For example, a counselor's race, gender, socioeconomic status, or upbringing may shape how they view a student's behavior or academic potential. Recognizing these factors allows counselors to approach each student with a more open, reflective, and equitable mindset, which is essential for fostering an inclusive environment where all students can succeed.

This process of self-awareness is not a one-time task, but rather an ongoing, iterative practice that requires continuous reflection and growth. As Shell (2021) explains, counselors must regularly engage in self-examination to understand how their personal identities intersect with their professional role. This reflection helps them identify any potential oppressive practices they may unknowingly engage in, such as microaggressions or assumptions based on stereotypes. By regularly assessing and reassessing their practices, counselors can make conscious efforts to mitigate these harmful tendencies and ensure that their interventions and support strategies are culturally responsive and equitable. This ongoing process of self-awareness enables counselors to refine their approaches, advocate for marginalized students, and create more just and supportive environments for all learners. In this way, critical self-awareness is a foundational skill that enhances both the counselor's effectiveness and the overall well-being of their students.

Recommendations for Professional Development

There are several PD ideas that can further enhance the effectiveness of school counselors in working with diverse student populations, including ML student populations.

1 **Self-Reflection Exercises:** PD programs for school counselors should include self-reflection exercises to enhance their ability to work effectively with ML students. These PDs that help school counselors explore implicit bias and microaggressions can be instrumental in fostering a more inclusive environment. Counselors can benefit from reflecting on their own cultural biases, assumptions, and language barriers. Encouraging school counselors to examine their own cultural identities and experiences with language diversity can help them become more empathetic and culturally competent. PDs could also include case studies, role-playing, and discussions that focus on real-world scenarios involving ML students, providing opportunities for school counselors to explore diverse perspectives and reflect on their own. These reflective practices can ultimately improve the quality of support school counselors offer to ML students, helping them feel understood and respected.
2 **Cultural Immersion and Experiential Learning:** School counselors can benefit from PD that offers opportunities for cultural immersion, such as community engagement projects or internships in schools serving diverse

populations. Training programs that incorporate role-playing and critical discussions on race, ethnicity, gender, and socioeconomic status improve school counselors' readiness to support diverse students (Hays, 2020). Training in how to address sociocultural differences through theoretically informed and culturally responsive practices is necessary to prepare graduate students and practitioners to deliver programs and interventions aimed at improving ML students' well-being and success (Villares et al., 2024).

3. **Trauma-Informed Care Training:** Many ML students may have experienced trauma. PD programs focused on trauma-informed care can equip school counselors with the tools and strategies to support ML students who may have experienced adversity or hardship. Understanding the impact of trauma on ML students' emotional, social, and academic development can help counselors provide more effective, compassionate support.
4. **Restorative Justice Practices:** Incorporating PD focused on restorative justice practices can help school counselors develop skills to mediate conflict within the school community. Restorative justice encourages understanding and healing over punishment, offering students an opportunity to repair harm and reintegrate into the school community. This approach is particularly effective in addressing disciplinary issues in a culturally responsive manner and building a sense of belonging for all students.
5. **Social Justice Advocacy and Community Partnerships:** PD that emphasizes the development of advocacy skills for social justice can empower counselors to take an active role in addressing systemic barriers within the school system. This could involve training on how to collaborate with community organizations, families, and other stakeholders to address issues like racism, classism, and access to resources. School counselors can learn how to advocate for policy changes, develop support systems, and ensure that all students have opportunities to succeed.

Pathway Two: Prevention and Intervention

School counselors implement interventions at different levels of MTSS and align their work to meet the needs of students in the social/emotional, career, and academic domains (ASCA, 2021). Research has demonstrated the usefulness of MTSS-aligned school counseling programs on MLs (Donohue et al., 2024). MTSS are ideal for providing preventative, intervention-based work. The following section will give an overview of interventions, organized by tier, which have been implemented with ML students.

Tier 1

Tier 1 interventions are described as direct and indirect prevention for *all* students which include: school counseling classroom instruction; school-wide activities and initiatives; community partnerships; staff and family training and workshops; and student appraisal and achievement (Goodman-Scott et al., 2023). For ML students, Tier 1 interventions are most effective when they incorporate culturally and linguistically responsive strategies that validate students' identities and promote inclusive learning environments.

Tier 1 interventions can be conducted in various ways and for various reasons with differing topics. For example, Villares et al. (2024) conducted a Student Success Skills Program with grade 5 classes composed of mostly ML student participants. The program emphasized emotional regulation, goal-setting, and metacognitive strategies. After the intervention, students demonstrated improved attendance rates, emotional regulation in the classroom, as well as increased classroom participation. Similarly, school counselors could develop classroom lessons on a variety of topics, such as communication skills or growth mindsets, while intentionally integrating students' home language, culturally relevant examples, and visual aids to ensure student accessibility and engagement.

An additional example of a Tier 1 intervention might be a school-wide initiative, such as a Multicultural Week, where students are encouraged to share their cultures through music, art, food, and storytelling. Events such as these can foster school connectedness for ML students, aid in cultural awareness and understanding from fellow school community members, and positions ML students to share their stories in ways which are meaningful to them.

Tier 2

Tier 2 interventions are described as direct and indirect services for *some* students, particularly those who require more in-depth support. These interventions can include individual and small group counseling; appraisal and advisement; and consultation and collaboration with teachers, staff, parents, and community providers (Goodman-Scott et al., 2023). For ML students, Tier 2 interventions can offer more specialized interventions which can support students in navigating school expectations, developing coping strategies, exploring acculturation stress, and making connections with other students who may have similar experiences.

Similar to Tier 1 interventions, Tier 2 interventions can be conducted in various ways, for various reasons, and with differing topics. Unlike Tier 1, Tier 2 interventions are to support students who may have more specific needs similar to other students, which makes group counseling ideal. For example, Shi et al. (2023) implemented a small group counseling intervention during a summer SEL program which focused on building emotional literacy and coping skills for ML students who were internalizing symptoms. The students in this group showed improved social/emotional knowledge on internalizing symptoms, including the ability to identify and express feelings as well as fewer reported school-related anxiety by the end of the intervention.

Within a middle school setting, Steen et al. (2017) conducted an Achieving Success Everyday (ASE) group counseling model with ML students. The group's focus was on setting goals, academic engagement, and self-advocacy. By the end of the group, students showed an increase in their GPAs, school attendance, and school adjustment score, demonstrating the potential for Tier 2 groups to improve student outcomes in multiple domains.

In order to deliver these interventions with fidelity, practitioners and scholars must ensure they are culturally and linguistically affirming. Donohue et al. (2024) emphasized the importance of using best practices, which include incorporating students' native languages, using materials in multiple languages when possible, and collaborating with ESL teachers. In a case study described by Donohue et al. (2024), they demonstrated how school counselors can collaborate with teachers to support ML students within classrooms, including using culturally relevant literature and cooperative learning strategies, which resulted in higher student engagement and fewer behavioral referrals for ML students.

Tier 3

Tier 3 interventions are described as direct and indirect services for *few* students with chronic or complex needs, which often involve intensive, wrap-around support. These interventions include: advanced or additional consultation and collaboration with teachers, families, ESL staff, and/or community mental health providers; and additional referrals to services (Goodman-Scott et al., 2023). Although not all ML students have immigrated or have negative immigration experiences, those who have may sustain trauma, family separation, navigating new systems within and outside of school, or different forms of grief. These experiences may require individualized support through Tier 3 interventions.

An example of one of these supports may involve a school counselor collaborating with an ESL teacher and a bilingual family liaison to create a support plan for an ML student who is experiencing signs of depression and is frequently absent from school. This coordinated team could schedule regular check-ins with the student, connect the family to community mental health resources with bilingual staff, and provide accommodations for the student to ensure their learning needs are being met and their emotional well-being is cared for. One such collaboration model is described by Purgason et al. (2023), where school counselors develop intervention plans *with* ESL teachers and classroom teachers that include scaffolding assignments, bilingual peer mentoring, and targeted academic coaching. By applying this model, they were able to see improvement in a student's academic achievement and classroom participation (Purgason et al., 2023).

Tier 3 supports can also involve family-centered practices where families are either met at their home or invited into the school to understand what services are available to their student, and to include their input on possible interventions.

By utilizing a tiered approach, school counselors can address the varying needs of ML students. At the core of all interventions, school counselors must use strengths-based, trauma-informed, and culturally relevant approaches to ensure ML students are supported. When aligned with best practices and grounded in cultural humility, the MTSS framework can play a transformative role in supporting the academic, social/emotional, and career needs of ML students.

Recommendations for Professional Development

Overall, we agree with researchers who suggest that school counselors include ML students in the creation of PD and to prioritize seeking PD. By doing so, school counselors can develop, deepen, or refine expertise to become confident in fostering safe learning spaces, developing relationships, scaffolding instruction, and sustaining ML students' cultural and linguistic assets (Heineke et al., 2023).

The previously outlined research demonstrates the importance and need for interventions to support the academic, social/emotional, and career needs of ML students. This section draws upon this research to provide recommendations for PD which could help support school counselors in their efforts to implement MTSS for ML students.

1. **Tier 1:** To address the needs of ML students from a Tier 1 perspective, school counselors can utilize social/emotional curriculum programs which are tailored to support ML students, such as the adapted Strong Kids curriculum (Shi et al., 2023). However, more research needs to be conducted to determine whether original or other adapted programs and curricula are cognizant of the cultural nuances of ML students and address their needs across the lifespan (Villares et al., 2024).
2. **Tier 2:** To address the needs of ML students from a Tier 2 perspective, school counselors can enhance their group counseling interventions. Utilizing journals as part of the group counseling process can have multiple benefits: by reading student journal entries, school counselors can better understand the students' experiences; and with back-and-forth communication, school counselors can share feedback with students on their growth and development beyond the group counseling and classroom settings (Steen et al., 2017). An additional way to address ML needs at this tier would be to consult with ELL teachers before delivering classroom lessons or group sessions to check whether they are linguistically accessible, if they are relevant to the student's experiences, inclusive of cultural backgrounds, and if classroom instruction can support the intervention (Shi et al., 2023; Purgason et al., 2024).
3. **Instruction Strategies:** Understanding how to deliver SEL programs fully online and in alternative schooling options can be advantageous considering the educational landscape we are in with the various educational settings, distance learning resulting from COVID-19, and more (Shi et al., 2023).

No matter the setting, school counselors must ensure interventions include instruction strategies that support ML learning, such as: delivering videos in home languages or with subtitles; incorporating visuals, and animations; creating graphics organizers; and representing multiple languages in content (Shi et al., 2023; Purgason et al., 2024).

Pathway Three: Professional Development Specific to Collaboration

If school counselors are going to support ML students and balance a large caseload, collaboration is essential. Bedwell et al. (2012) defined collaboration as a process where individuals work interdependently to accomplish an outcome. In school counseling, ASCA (2019) identified several activities where school counselors can collaborate with other individuals to benefit students. Further, there are numerous accounts within the literature highlighting school counselor collaborations (Challenger et al., 2024; Moore-Thomas & Day-Vines, 2018; Purgason et al., 2023; Tuttle et al., 2018; Yates et al., 2019). For instance, Yates et al. (2019) highlighted how school counselors could collaborate with speech pathologists to support students who stutter. Specifically, Yates et al. (2019) argued that school counselors and speech-language pathologists could analyze data to determine if any of the students who stutter needed academic support and to educate students within general education on the impact of stuttering. When assisting students with disabilities in post-secondary planning, Challenger et al. (2024) suggested that school counselors work with transition specialists within a multi-tier framework. Collaboration opportunities included co-leading postsecondary exploration lessons (Tier 1), providing student groups with the knowledge and skills to apply and seek post-secondary options (Tier 2), and analyzing data to inform individual advising sessions (Tier 3) (Challenger et al., 2024).

Purgason et al. (2023) conducted a qualitative content analysis to understand how ESOL teachers worked with emerging bilingual students to identify opportunities for collaboration between ESOL teachers and school counselors. Findings suggested that school counselors and ESOL teachers shared an interest in supporting ML students and identified opportunities to support ML students could occur in classroom instruction and small group work (Purgason et al., 2023). Yet, despite shared interests, participants perceived challenges to collaborating with school counselors were confusion over the role school counselors held and the lack of time school counselors could give to collaborating (Purgason et al., 2023). Purgason et al. (2023) argued that when engaging in collaboration, school counselors must acknowledge the barriers to working collaboratively and identify workarounds to those barriers.

If collaboration is a process and to address the barriers to being collaborative, school counselors can be trained in collaborative models that emphasize the interdependence of individuals working toward a set aim. Tuttle et al. (2018) identified a model that included four steps school counselors can use when working with school nurses. The four steps were 1. mutual understanding of professional roles, 2. respect for ethical considerations, 3. establishing guidelines for collaboration, and 4. ongoing communication and collaboration. These four steps emphasized the need to understand each professional's scope of practice and training that included parameters specific to confidentiality. Moore-Thomas and Day-Vines (2018) utilized Ferguson's developmental stage model of community engagement to illuminate critical steps in collaboration. As part of Ferguson's model, the authors highlighted that collaborative partners should understand the needs and interests of each partner, including the time commitment that each can provide to accomplish the shared goals. Furthermore, Moore-Thomas and Day-Vines (2018) stressed the need for partners to work through the challenges that may impact sustained commitment and address power differentials that could threaten mutually beneficial outcomes (Moore-Thomas & Day-Vines, 2018).

Understanding what holds these challenges in place (e.g., role confusion, not having time) is essential if we want school counselors to engage in collaboration. Collaboration, working within a team to drive forward new initiatives and ideas takes leadership skills, particularly transformational leadership skills. Goodman-Scott and Ziomek-Daigle's (2022) phenomenological study examined the leadership practices of 10 school counselors who identified themselves as leading MTSS teams at their school sites. As the lead, participants collaborated with other individuals and were integral to the planning and implementation of MTSS. Findings indicated that prioritizing relationships and shaping school climate was important to leading the MTSS team. Prioritizing relationships highlighted the intentional collaboration school counselors did to gain buy-in that would help them advocate for students. Shaping school climate highlighted the expertise of school counselors, providing their unique expertise, along with situating themselves as cheerleader for MTSS, which included doing whatever was needed even if outside of the role (Goodman-Scott & Ziomek-Daigle, 2022). In their discussion of the findings, Goodman-Scott et al. (2021) raised an interesting point: could school counselors' willingness to do whatever was needed to get the job done negatively impact transformative leadership practices? If school counselors normalize their role to do whatever is needed, might that keep them stuck in reactive and outdated practices? Might this be why school counselors have not always prioritized collaboration with other professionals (Purgason et al., 2023)?

To explore this more deeply, Watkinson's et al. (2024) phenomenological study examined the assumptions or mental models that school counselors had about their role. Drawing from Senge's organizational learning theory (2006), Watkinson et al. (2025) sought to identify hidden assumptions that school counselors hold about their role that sustain outdated practices that go against nationally identified best practices and training. Findings from the Watkinson et al. (2025) study highlighted three major themes that revealed assumptions school counselor participants held about the role. Those three themes were the belief that their role was to be reactive, help students navigate difficulties, and cultivate strong relationships. Elaborating on the theme of being reactive, Watkinson et al. (2025) noted that school counselor participants believed they had to attend to the immediate needs of others and help everywhere to fill in the gaps. Taking a reactive approach as a role requirement impacts school counselors' ability to be proactive, something that is important if you want to engage in a collaborative relationship.

Recommendations for Professional Development

There are several PD ideas that can further enhance the effectiveness of school counselors to work collaboratively with other professionals to support the unique needs of ML student populations.

1. **Professional Development in Collaboration Models**
   While collaborative models and potential opportunities for collaboration exist, school counselors need to have PD in how to generate true collaborative partnerships to move forward their counseling goals, especially those that benefit ML populations who benefit from a multi-disciplinary approach. Introducing collaborative models to school counselors gives them a framework for how to establish collaborative teams, highlighting the importance of identifying expertise, solidifying roles, setting time expectations, and agreeing on the scope of work or outcomes.
2. **Navigating Challenges to Prioritizing Collaboration**
   Tuttle et al. (2018) identified that school counselors' lack of time challenged their ability to work in true collaborative teams. Yet, collaborative partnerships, where individuals work together toward a common goal, could extend the reach of school counselors, thus saving time. School counselors believe their role is to be reactive, doing whatever is needed in the school, even if it is not their job (Goodman-Scott et al., 2021). This reactive approach to the job can limit school counselors' ability to be proactive, giving them less time to attend to collaborative frameworks when setting up a team. PD could center on identifying and navigating through potential challenges that would impact collaborative teaming. One way to navigate the challenge of time could be to identify the assumptions (mental models) school counselors hold about time, to examine the truth of those assumptions, and uncover hidden opportunities that would allow them to prioritize the collaboration. Since collaboration is a proactive approach to practice that takes time to cultivate, school counselors need to explore the mental models that may work against cultivating such alliances (Watkinson et al., 2025). Thus, any training in collaboration would need to include an assessment of time as a resource to help school counselors identify hidden assumptions they hold about their role that would prevent them from prioritizing collaboration.

Conclusion

We identified and described three pathways which we hope will help conceptualize and evolve PD as it relates to school counselors supporting ML students. First, in Knowledge of Self, we described how cultural competence and self-awareness serve as the bedrock of effective school counseling. Counselors must deeply understand their own biases and values, as these personal lenses directly impact how they interpret and support students from diverse backgrounds (Sue & Sue, 2016). These include challenging biases - by identifying internal prejudices, counselors can move toward more empathetic and culturally responsive connections; continuous reflection - counselors must evaluate how their own upbringing, race, and socioeconomic status shape their perceptions of others; creating inclusive environments - this ongoing self-work prevents harmful assumptions and fosters a space of trust and advocacy. Ultimately, staying reflective allows counselors to move beyond a "one-size-fits-all" approach, ensuring that interventions are as unique as the students they serve.

Second, in Prevention and Intervention, we described the crucial role school counselors have in supporting MLs by implementing interventions at different levels of a MTSS to address students' social/emotional, academic, and career needs (ASCA, 2021). Tier 1 interventions focus on school-wide prevention strategies, such as classroom instruction and community partnerships, which have been shown to improve student outcomes, including attendance and emotional regulation (Villares et al., 2024). Tier 2 interventions provide targeted support through small group counseling and collaboration with teachers and families, helping students with specific needs improve their academic performance and social-emotional well-being (Shi et al., 2023; Steen et al., 2017). At the Tier 3 level, school counselors work closely with educators and specialists to provide individualized interventions for students with chronic or complex needs, such as partnering with ESL teachers to develop tailored support strategies (Purgason et al., 2024).

To ensure these interventions are effective, PD should focus on culturally affirming practices, linguistic accessibility, and evidence-based strategies tailored for ML students. School counselors can benefit from training in adapting social-emotional learning (SEL) programs, such as the Strong Kids curriculum, and integrating student journaling to enhance group counseling interventions (Shi et al., 2023; Steen et al., 2017). Collaboration with ELL teachers is essential for ensuring that lessons and interventions align with students' linguistic and cultural backgrounds (Purgason et al., 2023). Additionally, training should address best practices for delivering interventions in various educational settings, including online and alternative learning environments, by incorporating multilingual content, visuals, and scaffolding strategies (Shi et al., 2023). Ultimately, school counselors should actively involve ML students in shaping PD initiatives and seek opportunities to refine their expertise in fostering inclusive and supportive learning spaces (Heineke et al., 2023).

Third, in Professional Development Specific to Collaboration, we described how essential collaboration is between school counselors and other professionals, particularly given the extensive caseloads school counselors have. Despite the existence of collaborative models (Tuttle et al., 2018; Moore-Thomas & Day-Vines, 2018), school counselors' assumptions about their roles may prevent them from prioritizing collaboration. Watkinson et al. (2025) found that school counselors often view their role as reactive, focusing on immediate student needs rather than proactive engagement in collaboration. This mindset can limit their ability to form and sustain meaningful partnerships. To address this, PD should help school counselors assess how they allocate time, uncover hidden role assumptions, and develop strategies for integrating collaboration into their practice. Training should include structured planning for collaboration, goal setting, and strategies for overcoming common barriers, ensuring that school counselors can engage effectively in interdisciplinary partnerships to support ML students.

Delineated by Heineke et al. (2023), all educational professionals must examine their school counseling programs and their impacts on ML students in six facets:

a relationships and interactions between MLs and educators,
b integration and interactions between ML and non-ML peers,
c quality of classroom curriculum and instruction for MLs,
d equity in access to supplemental services and school activities,
e prioritization of home language and cultural practices, and
f students' and families' sense of belonging at the school (Heineke et al., 2023).

When ML students are intentionally included in program planning, it reduces the risks of unintended harm caused by misunderstanding and lack of representation. With repetition and intentional equity, incorporating these six facets will become second nature and have a lasting impact on ML students.

In close, to further push for equitable support for ML students, we pose questions which we hope will help educational professionals ensure ML students are prioritized in their programs and in future training and PD.

Questions to Consider for Future Training and Professional Development

For school counselors:

1. Are my interventions (i.e., classroom lessons, group counseling, etc.) designed with the cultural and linguistic needs of my ML students in mind?
2. If I am delivering classroom lessons to all English classes, am I factoring ESL classes into my schedule?
3. How can counselors evaluate their own effectiveness in supporting ML students and adjust their strategies as needed?

For professional development hosts:

1. Are there sessions which explicitly state their inclusion of ML student perspectives or considerations?
2. How can school counselors stay up-to-date with research and best practices related to multilingual students and culturally responsive counseling?
3. What ongoing support and resources are necessary to ensure that school counselors have the confidence and skills to provide long-term support for ML students?

References

American School Counselor Association (2019). *The ASCA national model: A framework for school counseling programs* (4th ed.). ASCA.

American School Counselor Association (2021). The school counselor and multitiered system of supports. ASCA position statements. https://www.schoolcounselor.org/Standards-Positions/Position-Statements/ASCA-Position-Statements/The-School-Counselor-and-Multitiered-System-of-Sup

Bedwell, W. L., Wildman, J. L., DiazGranados, D., Salazar, M., Kramer, W. S., & Sala, E. (2012). Collaboration at work: An integrative multilevel conceptualization. *Human Resource Management Review*, *22*, 128–145. https//doi.org/10.1016/j.jrmr.2011.11.007

Challenger, C. D., Lombardi, A. R., Duquette, K., Espositio, C., & DeJesus, J. (2024). Strategies to increase collaboration between school counselors and transition specialists: A multi-tiered approach to college and career readiness. *Journal of Education*, *205*(2), 153–165. https://doi.org/10.1177/00220574241309103

Chao, R. C. L. (2012). The influence of culture on the counseling process: A review of research and applications. *Journal of Multicultural Counseling and Development*, *40*(3), 162–174. https://doi.org/10.1002/j.2161-1912.2012.00016.x

Constantine, M. G. (2002). Client preferences for cultural treatment interventions: The role of culture in psychotherapy and counseling. *Journal of Counseling & Development*, *80*(3), 347–356. https://doi.org/10.1002/j.1556-6678.2002.tb00200.x

Donohue, P., Smith Durkin, S., & Frank, A. (2024). Strategies to enhance implementation fidelity in school-counselor-led, culturally affirming tier 2 groups. *Professional School Counseling*, *28*(1a). https://doi.org/10.1177/2156759X241234912

Goodman-Scott, E., Betters-Bubon, J., Donohue, P., & Olsen, J. (Eds.). (2023). *The school counselor's guide to multi-tiered systems of support* (2nd ed). Routledge. https://doi.org/10.4324/9781003306412

Goodman-Scott, E., & Ziomek-Daigle, J. (2022). School counselors' leadership experiences in multi-tiered systems of support: Prioritizing relationships and shaping school climate. *Journal of Counseling & Development*, *100*(3), 266–277. https://doi.org/10.1002/jcad.12426

Goodman-Scott, E., Kalkbrenner, M. T., Olsen, J., & Betters-Bubon, J. (2021). School counselors' leadership experiences in multi-tiered systems of support: Prioritizing relationships and shaping school climate. *Journal of Counseling & Development*, *100*(3), 266–277. https://doi.org/10.1002/jcad.12426

Hays, D. G. (2020). Multicultural and social justice counseling competency research: Opportunities for innovation. *Journal of Counseling & Development*, *98*(3), 331–344. https://doi.org/10.1002/jcad.12327

Heineke, A. J., Vera, E. M., Guo, W., Kaye, J., & Elliott, J. (2023). Considering the social-emotional well-being of multilingual learners: A comparative case study across program models. *The Elementary School Journal*, *123*(4), 599–624. https://doi.org/10.1086/723028

Holcomb-McCoy, C. (Ed.). (2021). *Antiracist counseling in schools and communities*. John Wiley & Sons.

Holcomb-McCoy, C. C. (2005). Investigating school counselors' perceived multicultural competence. *Professional School Counseling*, *8*(5), 414–423. http://www.jstor.org/stable/42732483

Khalifa, M. A., Gooden, M. A., & Davis, J. E. (2016). Culturally responsive school leadership: A synthesis of the literature. *Review of Educational Research*, *86*(4), 1272–1311. https://doi.org/10.3102/0034654316630383

Moore-Thomas, C., & Day-Vines, N. L. (2010). Culturally competent collaboration: School counselor collaboration with African American families and communities. *Professional School Counseling*, *14*(1). https://doi.org/10.1177/2156759X1001400106

Purgason, L. L., Johnson, G., Vallecillo, O., Covington, C., Parker, R. H., & Airhart-Larraga, S. (2023). English as a second language teachers' perspectives on interprofessional collaboration with school counselors: Supporting emergent bilingual students. *Journal of Educational and Psychological Consultation*, *34*(2), 168–197. https://doi.org/10.1080/10474412.2023.2240304

Ratts, M. J., & Greenleaf, A. T. (2018). Multicultural and social justice counseling competencies: A leadership framework for professional school counselors. *Professional School Counseling*, *21*(1b). https://doi.org/10.1177/2156759X18773582

Ratts, M. J., Singh, A. A., Nassar-McMillan, S., Butler, S. K., & McCullough, J. R. (2016). Multicultural and social justice counseling competencies: Guidelines for the counseling profession. *Journal of Multicultural Counseling and Development*, *44*(1), 28–48. https://doi.org/10.1002/jmcd.12035

Senge, P. M. (2006). *The fifth discipline: The art and practice of the learning organization* (2nd ed.). Currency Doubleday.

Shell, E. M. (2021). School counselors as leaders for social justice and equity. *Taboo: The Journal of Culture and Education*, *20*(2). Retrieved from https://digitalscholarship.unlv.edu/taboo/vol20/iss2/4

Shi, Q., Phillips, K., Moody, D., & Cordova, T. (2023). Adapted strong kids curriculum for English language learners during COVID-19. *Professional School Counseling*, *27*(1a). https://doi.org/10.1177/2156759X231160752

Steen, S., Liu, X., Shi, Q., Rose, J., & Merino, G. (2017). Promoting school adjustment for English-language learners through group work. *Professional School Counseling*, *21*(1). https://doi.org/10.1177/2156759X18777096

Sue, D. W., & Sue, D. (2016). *Counseling the culturally diverse: Theory and practice* (7th ed.). Wiley.

Talleyrand, R. M., & Vojtech, J. T.-G. (2019). Potential stressors of undocumented Latinx youth: Implications and recommendations for school counselors. *Professional School Counseling, 22*(1), Article 2156759X19847168. https://doi.org/10.1177/2156759X19847168

Tuttle, M., Yordy, M., Appling, B., & Hanley, E. (2018). School counselor and school nurse collaboration: Partnering for k-12 student success. *Journal of School Counseling*, *16*(4), n4. https://eric.ed.gov/?id=EJ1181068

Villares, E., Bowers, H., Brigman, G., & Bottini, C. (2024). The effects of student success skills on attendance and emotion regulation. *Journal of Counseling & Development*, *102*(2), 163–174. https://doi.org/10.1002/jcad.12503

Watkinson, J. S., Grimes, T., Sowell, S., & Roosma, S. (2025). School counselors' mental models: Missing piece to role transformation. *Counseling Scholarship & Practice in Educational Communities*, *1*(1), 185–211. https://doi.org/10.7275/cspec.2294

Yates, C. M., Hudock, D., Astramovich, R., & Hill, J. (2019). Helping students who stutter: Interprofessional collaboration between speech-language pathologists and school counselors. *Professional School Counseling*, *22*(1). https://doi.org/10.1177/2156759X19844506

Index

For Product Safety Concerns and Information please contact our EU representative GPSR@taylorandfrancis.com Taylor & Francis Verlag GmbH, Kaufingerstraße 24, 80331 München, Germany

Batch number: 10830924

Printed by Printforce, the Netherlands